GUNNERS
ON TOUR

Maurice Court

Spike Press

First published in Great Britain in 2007 by Spike Press
This edition published 2007

Copyright © 2007 by Maurice Court

The moral right of this author has been asserted

Spike Press
112 Broomfield Road
Coventry
CV5 6JZ

ISBN: 9781872916408

Cover photographs

From top:

Myself, in 1945, clearly proud of my sergeant's stripes

Under cover: Sgt Gerry Young, Bdr George Waterall and Gunner
Dalgety, all of A troop 206 Anti-tank Battery in Iran, 1942

Archers at rest: Bdr Levett and the B troop 206 Anti-tank Battery
17-pounder Archers in laager at St Andreasberg in summer 1945

Big guns: my father and other members of the 17 Medium Battery
between two 60-pounder guns at Ambala in the Punjab in 1932

Acknowledgements

———————◯———————

A number of people have helped me to turn my memories and thoughts into this published work, and I would like to thank:

- Sally McKeown, for having faith in the enterprise, and for being a supportive (and challenging) daughter
- Carolyn Gifford, for having helped me to find the right words and cutting out the wrong ones
- Diane James, for her great patience in trying to teach me to use a computer
- Tom Gifford, for his professional design
- Joe McKeown, for keeping up my spirits
- Monty Court, for keeping me on my toes
- The rest of the Court family, for being there

My thanks to you all.

Maurice Court
Coventry, June 2007

CONTENTS

Gunners on Tour is a title that reflects a father and son's joint service in the Royal Regiment of Artillery, overlapping the two World Wars.

In 1909, my father Maurice, a London-born boy now aged 18, ran away from home and joined the Royal Artillery at Woolwich. His father, a Yorkshireman, had had other plans for his eldest son, but Maurice was determined and served in several stations in the UK until, in 1911, he found his unit hustled out to the Far East. With the outbreak of the revolution that resulted in the formation of the Chinese Republic, the RA was sent to China to protect British interests. There Maurice remained for three years, for which he received the North China Campaign medal.

He returned home with his unit early in February 1915 to find northern Europe consumed by war. By now a sergeant, he went to France with the 34th Siege Battery of the Royal Garrison Artillery. In 1916 he returned from France to attend an officers' course and was offered a wartime commission. As a regular soldier, this held no attraction for him and he declined. It was the following year, 1917, that he met my mother, Ethel, while on leave from the Front. They married shortly after Christmas and the result of the union – six children, three girls and three boys – were all born during his 25 years of army service.

MY FATHER,
AGED ABOUT 28

All of us could be called 'Barrack Rats', an expression common in the Raj for children raised within the barracks when – such as during the Indian Mutiny – it was unsafe to live outside them.

Barracks were divided between the single troops section, and that for married troops – the dividing line being draped blankets hanging from the rafters. Wives and children were considered part of the army establishment, whether it was in Germany or hill stations in India, and my mother took each move calmly.

My father's life in the ranks was more rewarding to the army, for he served on every artillery piece, from medium artillery guns to mountain artillery, and he was a troop sergeant on siege guns when he was blinded by mustard gas in 1918. It took him two years to recover, during which her served as a gunnery instructor. As a fine horseman, he later did a spell as a rough rider, breaking in young horses and riding for the army at gymkhanas.

From 1926 until 1933, we served in India – I say 'we' since at the age of nine and a half I was sent to military boarding school at Sanawar in the foothills of the Himalayas. On our return to England, my father retired as sergeant major. Although called up in 1938, he was too ill to take up the officer's appointment he was offered. Our retirement from army life was brief, however – in March 1939 I joined a Territorial Royal Artillery Anti-Tank Regiment in Brixton. Anti-tank guns were the latest addition to the artillery's armaments, two-pounders that required the gun troops to be forward with the infantry. The fact that I had joined the Royal Regiment pleased my father immensely.

Along with my fellow recruits, I didn't realise the journey we were about to undertake. My unit joined the outstanding Fifth Infantry Division, with its 'Y' insignia for Yorkshire. During the Second World War the division served in 26 different countries and was the most travelled division in the British Army – it was no surprise that it became known as 'Cook's Tours' and the Globetrotters.

Action started in earnest in November 1939 when my unit went to France to join the BEF. My regiment, the 52nd Anti-Tank Regiment, joined field regiments to become part of the newly assembled British Fifth Infantry, a mix of regular and territorial units. This combination served Britain well.

Much in this book is based on my own experiences and observations; every battlefield I mention involved me in a minor role. During my six and a half years in the war, my division served under British and American army commanders of varying standards. The most telling, in my opinion, was General Gort, who made a number of major decisions just before Dunkirk, while the Cabinet was dithering in London. In so doing, he saved the bulk of the BEF and kept Britain in the war.

MYSELF, AROUND TWO

My recollections are taken from rough notes made from time to time, helped by George Aris's *The Fifth British Division 1939 to 1945*. Certain incidents have remained indelibly etched on my mind – and now that I am 88, it's time to record them or lose them.·

I was born in Hove on 24th September 1918, the year in which my father had been blinded by mustard gas. My mother had been sent away from London for fear of Zeppelin raids – and I promptly fell victim to the Influenza outbreak that was raging across Europe and beyond. Fortunately, I recovered, as did my father's damaged eyesight, and by the summer of 1920 he was able to take up a posting as the regular instructor to a Royal Artillery Territorial battery in Shrewsbury. Some four years later, my father was posted to Germany with the 17th Medium Battery Royal Artillery, which became part of the British Occupation of the Rhine forces. We returned to England in January 1926 to the military barracks compound in Christchurch, Hampshire. It was only a temporary posting, however, and the next seven years were to be spent in India.

It seemed I was destined to spend all my life in the army, and at the age of 15 I took an examination to enter the Army myself. In the event, I turned it down – by then, I was in London in the 1930s, and it had too many attractions. However, Adolf Hitler had other plans for me. If I wasn't drawn towards an Army career, I could be pushed towards it – and if nothing else, the 'training' of my childhood made a good beginning to going to war.

So this story starts with that early training, aged nine and about to set foot in the Jewel of the Crown, the Indian Raj of 1927.

CHAPTER 1

─○─

INDIA – THE PUNJAB

The *Neuralia* docked in Karachi in late January 1927. The trooper had taken just three weeks from Southampton – enough time for family friendships to have been made, which was usually the way with Army families in transit – so there was some sadness because passengers were parting company and going to different Army stations in India. For now, the overriding concern was ensuring the children wore their topees as a protection against the heat – not easy, for many were not used to wearing hats.

My father's battery was posted to Ambala, which was a three-day trip on the train, sitting on wooden seats. We bought food from the numerous stations along the line, and tried to take precautionary measures to avoid stomach upsets – the British stomach had to adapt slowly to some of the Indian food.

Ambala was a military cantonment in the Punjab, on the Plains north of Delhi. It was conveniently adjacent to the foothills of the Himalayas where a variety of hill stations provided the alternative accommodation for married families during the hot summer months. In this season the heat reached well over 100° on the Plains.

In earlier times Ambala had been a large cavalry station, but after the Great War it had become an RAF airfield. Strategically, it was in an ideal position to tackle Indian troubles, but the pilots of the Bristol fighters needed nerves of steel to coax their planes over the Hindu Kush and avoid being brought down by Afghan tribesmen firing black powdered rifles from their rooftops. It was also the home of the Fifth Medium Brigade RA, my father's unit, which consisted of the 17th and 21st batteries who fired 60-pounder guns when needed. In support of these potent British arms was a number of British and Indian Army infantry regiments which made Ambala a military stronghold.

Our bungalow was part of the married quarters within the cantonment with standard army issue furniture for married families in the Other Ranks. The beds were metal and the tables and other furniture was wooden and well scrubbed. The wash-house at the back of the bungalow was equipped with a large galvanised metal bath which was moveable within a cemented area. There was a water butt in the corner of the wash-house and this was replenished each day by a *bhistee* who carried the water in a hide carrier on his shoulder. He would only enter the bungalow if the sweeper was not present, because he was of a higher caste. The sweeper swept the stone floor of the bungalow and the wooden veranda each day with a long-handled brush made from rushes. Both these workers were employed by the Brigade to service a number of bungalows. Each house had strong electric fans which draped from the ceiling and helped to keep the whole area cool.

THE BARRACKS AT CHRISTCHURCH; MY FATHER IS FOURTH FROM THE LEFT

The bearer, who cooked for us, was a higher class Hindu than the sweeper and the *bhistee* and usually stayed in the cookhouse, which was adjacent to the bungalow, unless he was carrying out duties in the house. He was the servant of the family and only employed by our family.

Our bearer was Kippa Ram, who was a good cook and loved children. Other attributes were absent from his references, particularly his love of 'Billy Stink' – the local brew. We placed more emphasis on his good qualities, although he was 'fired' on a number of occasions but re-employed to please the younger children. He pleased my parents with his curry dishes and the kids with his splendid rock cakes. Every day after tiffin, Ivy, Betty and I sat on our haunches around him as he polished up the dixies (*dekshis*) with ashes and earth (*mutti*), until they glittered. He also had a great relationship with 'Spot' our dog, particularly when encouraging a local tradesman to see our point of view. In response to a sound the bearer made in his throat, the dog would suddenly appear and look menacing until negotiations were settled.

One day we had a problem with the large soak-away in the bath-house. The water would not drain away and came surging back up. My mother rammed the end of the broom into the drainage hole with some force – and suddenly there was a wild animal scream as a lynx leapt out of the hole, with Spot instantly on its tail. We waited an hour for Spot to return and, concerned for his safety, I went out on my bicycle to find him with Kippa running at my side. Eventually we found Spot, under a tree bleeding from wounds around his ears and eyes. He had claw marks around his body and his fur was matted with blood. He started to whimper when he saw us and I was stroking him when Kippa said gently, 'Baba' and pointed up into the tree. There the lynx lay across a branch, obviously dead.

We managed to get Spot across the bicycle frame and took him home. My father was at the house and rode his horse to the barrack lines for the vet, who followed him back to the bungalow in a Ford 'T' truck. He stitched the dog's wounds and said to my father, 'A close call, Casey – he nearly lost an eye.' The dog remained in the bungalow for about a month, pampered by the children until his growling and barking were back to form.

Mother got great enjoyment from two things in particular: doing the Charleston in the sergeants' mess and haggling in the bazaar

– where her element of Jewish blood stirred and made her a match in negotiations with the *babus* which sometimes lasted half an hour as she made trips to other stalls before returning to the fray. Occasionally we went with her in Busty's tonga – he was a large very cheerful Mohammedan who spoke broken English with great authority and had us all in stitches. The showpiece was the big, handsome stallion who wore a red plume at his forelock and drew everyone's attention by tossing his head. The tonga moved up and down in the shafts and swayed from side to side when it turned corners. We sang a rhyme composed by mother to the tune of Barley Mow and Busty moved his head in time with the tune:

> *Busty's ghora eats his corn,*
> *Busty's ghora drinks his chai,*
> *Then he neighs 'Bye Bye, Ta Ta',*
> *and gallops off to the Burra Bazaar.*

In those days getting shoes for us children was a problem and some of our shoes were made by a *moochie* (shoemaker) who came to the bungalow and drew a pattern of our feet on a strip of leather, completing the job at his workshop in the bazaar. The shoes were adequate at the time, but ultimately all of us suffered with bunions.

My sister Isobel and I attended the Garrison school, run by a formidable lady, Miss Adams. She did not seem to qualify as a 'Maid of the Fishing Fleet' – a term for schoolmistresses abroad who were hopeful of landing a husband. However, her intrepid qualities showed in emergencies, notably in Dagshai when, testing the piano keys, two cobras rose from the back when she lifted the cover. She calmly ushered out the children and locked up the school. She believed in discipline, which sometimes resulted in caning across the hand or being hit across the knuckles with a ruler. This was my fifth school, but for Isobel it was her first. I seemed to attract trouble – possibly because I grinned at the wrong time. My sister, a neat attractive child, sailed through the school day completely unruffled – and approved of by Miss Adams.

It took a year for us to settle as a family having returned to Ambala from our first hill station, Dagshai. I was nine and a half, Isobel was seven and Betty was five and about to join the garrison school.

Father, after consulting the education sergeant (who probably consulted Miss Adams) decided that I should be sent to a military school. This was not necessarily to fit me for a military career, but because the school in question, Sanawar, provided better education and discipline, a prized requirement in the late 1920s. It was the leading military school in the sub-continent and could only be compared with its sister school, The Duke of York School, Kent, England.

The only unanswered questions were whether I would be accepted at my age and whether my parents could afford the fees. They made the decision and in March 1928 I was accepted, at the age of nine and a half. As I parted from my family, my worried mother asked my father, 'Are you sure he is not too young, Maurice?' My father reassured her, 'He will be alright, Ethel!'

Not quite able to share their confidence, I left Kalka station with my father on a swaying train which climbed perilously for six thousand feet up the foothills of the Himalayas, to become a pupil at Sanawar – my home for the next four years.

CHAPTER 2

SCHOOL FOR SOLDIERS

Sanawar

The school was founded by John Laird Mair Lawrence in the 1860s when he became governor-general of India – and named The Lawrence Royal Military School, Sanawar. It was for children of British Military personnel and civil servants of the Raj.

AT SCHOOL
AT SANAWAR

The girls' compound was remote from the main boys' school, and was contained in its own area by huge steel stanchions with tall fences attached. The only creatures to get a sight of the female Sanawarians were the monkeys who hung from the trees showing off their red backsides. The pupils only shared the same area at the daily and Sunday church parades – the latter being a ceremonial affair, marching behind the school band wearing our 'blues'. In church the girls sat down one side of the aisle and the boys down the other, watched from the rear seats and a balcony at the back by their respective housemasters and house matrons. The various houses sat opposite each other on either side of the aisle. After I had been there a year or two and became an old hand, it was possible for me to ogle Hilda Baker, a little plump flaxen-haired girl, also in Nicholson House. The only occasion I talked to her in the years that followed, was on Founders' Day in October with our parents present. This was not enough for me, and I was savagely caned on two occasions for passing her notes in church; I don't know if Hilda was also chastised.

Sanawar was a military school in all senses of the word. We were fully kitted in uniform from pyjamas right through to our blues, our Sunday best. In the week we wore khaki drill with corduroy shorts – which left quite a mark on our posteriors when we were caned. The headgear was bush hats turned up at the side, with blue forage caps for Sunday best. The girls wore pinafores with gymslips for Sunday best and their headgear was bonnets. Each of the five houses had a colour, Nicholson's being Cambridge Blue, and our jackets had a flash on the side to indicate the house of each boy; the girls were similarly identified on their pinafores. Pupils ranged from ten to sixteen and the five houses in 1928 comprised boys and girls in each age group.

The houses were named after generals of the Indian Mutiny, four of them in the boys' school – Roberts, Hodgson, Herbert Edwards and Nicholson were the foot soldiers. Boys coming to the school to study music were placed in Lawrence House which provided the school band. Because they were specialists, the pupils in Lawrence House had a cushier time and were rarely caned whereas the pupils in the other houses were considered a hardier breed and dealt with accordingly.

Each house had a housemaster who was a sergeant or warrant officer seconded from the Army. These were generally quite benevolent types who rarely used the cane, having the man-handling experience and know-how of imposing discipline – which seemed to be absent in most of the school masters. The day started at 6.00 am with Reveille and ended with Last Post at 22.15. The whole of our day was governed by bugle calls – all we had to do was obey them. A good housemaster would ensure the barrack room was immaculate, his boys were clean and our marching and shooting were up to standard. Each year, standards as young soldiers were competed for by the four 'foot soldier' houses in front of a panel of army officers from Simla. The reward for the winning house was the Cook Cup. Marks were awarded for general discipline on the parade ground which involved full turnout – including weaponry – arms drill and marching. Every effort was made in each house to produce a squad of 24 boys representing all age groups to win this fêted chalice, and in so doing bring pride to the house and plaudits to the housemaster. We in Nicholson House had a fine record in this competition, mainly due to our housemaster Sergeant Wheeler, who was well liked by 'his boys'. I was proud to be in his winning squad twice …in my third and fourth years at the school.

Education was of a high standard, taught by masters from Oxford and Cambridge and a *Munshi Je* who taught the reluctant classes Urdu. They were permitted to cane unruly students, which if administered in the classroom was across the hand but occasionally the student was taken to another room and caned vigorously across the backside. The Munshi was permitted to hit non-attentive students across the knuckles with a ruler. Most of the pupils were very stoic, but the timid ones became ill and some were removed from the school by their parents. I didn't have that option, for if I had run away my father would have sent me straight back. The younger fraternity in the houses became quite clannish and this fostered little gangs as a protection against bullying and sexual harassment. If you were good at hockey, cricket, soccer, boxing, swimming or athletics you were favoured and your misdemeanours treated leniently. But to carry a candle for such as Hilda Baker was seen as an early sign of latent depravity that had to be remedied before it was too late.

On joining the school in March 1928, my protector Young Ben Riding had plans for me. However, he was 15 and I was not 10 until September. My parents thought he would treat me like a younger brother. He was already the welterweight boxing champion in the school and so anyone following from Ambala should be able to live up to his standards. Therefore, in a matey sort of way, he fixed me up to have a fight with another young intake and we were taken to a small room at the end of the dormitory to assess our fighting potential. Fortunately for me I made Pickering's nose bleed; but for the four years I was at the school with Pickering, we would never be friends, for much as I liked him, his pride had been hurt too much.

In the early summer of 1928 Young Ben Riding left the school to go to the technical college at Chepstow. His departure made me feel lonely, for my last contact with Ambala was gone; on the other hand it was unlikely that I would be dragged out of bed again to test my fighting skills. On my own I found the routine of Sanawar very testing – every day was a trial. Reveille sounded at six o'clock except Sunday, when it sounded at seven. At the last note of the bugle, the stampede started for the five washbasins or two cold showers with the older boys muscling in. *Chota Hazri* (early breakfast) was a rush but a mug of tea and two slices of bread was savaged in order to follow the bugle and be on parade for PT at 6.45. The bugle for breakfast followed at 8.00 am where the normal diet was *burgoo* and two slices of bread with *ghee* and a portion of

IN MY SUNDAY 'BLUES'

jam. If you were the fag taking around the tea urn, you had to watch your breakfast in case it was nicked. Beds had to be made and kit laid out for inspection before assembling for church parade at 9.15. This was followed in the first half hour in the classroom with a bible class. Classes went on until one o'clock. Dinner was usually some sort of stew, with a pudding twice a week on Wednesdays and Sundays. There was an air of relief usually at this time of day – it seemed everyone was talking and there was time to cuff a fag's ear. Back to the classroom at 2.15 to 4.30 then one and a half hour's exercise, either sports or marching drill. Supper at 6.30 with the inevitable two slices of bread and *ghee* with soup. Prep from 7.30 until 9.00 and then a mug of cocoa before First Post was sounded at 9.45; half an hour later the bugler sounded Last Post, when the housemaster wandered through the dormitory and turned out the lights, except the night light at the wash-house and toilet. Sleep when it came was always a wonderful salvation – particularly when you were a new boy!

My first term ended in December 1928 and surprisingly my father collected me from the school and gave me a hug. 'Your mother is looking after your new baby brother Monty,' he explained. On the way down the *khuds* in the army truck the thought of having a brother wasn't such a bad idea after having three sisters. I enjoyed that Christmas leave, for I had been away from the family for nine months. I was spoiled rotten but had to share the limelight with my new brother who was quite quiet for a baby.

I returned to Sanawar in early March and was more prepared for the fray now I was ten. There was an intake of new boys and some of the old hands had left the school, which meant I had moved up the pecking order.

In my second year, I had a few close friends and inevitably we had formed ourselves into a gang, with passwords and sharing our tuck which meant we starved together unless we supplemented our rations. We went out of bounds together and raided the farmers' fields to add to the scraps such as cold potatoes that we brought back from the kitchen, for at 6,000 feet above sea level we were always hungry. On our raids we brought back *bhuttas* (Indian corn), apples, mangoes, pomegranates and anything else that looked edible.

The leader of our gang was Bryant, a tough 14-year-old who could stand up to the prefects and the older boys in the school in physical combat. His father had been killed at Passchendaele and he was at the school on a state scholarship. My two close friends were called 'Old' and 'Young' Mahoney, two brothers who were given these weird titles, one being 12 and the other 11. Together with me, the youngest at ten, were the core of the gang, which occasionally had other fringe members. Young Mahoney was taller than his brother and was the daredevil of the gang. He was hyperactive, in keeping with his Irish temperament and inclined to take unnecessary risks. Their parents lived in Lucknow. Bryant's mother lived somewhere in the Central Provinces.

We cooked Indian corn over a candle, sometimes after 'Lights out', and added unappetising boiled potatoes and cabbage leftover in the tureens from dinner, making a form of Bubble and Squeak. My mother, when she came to the hill stations at Dagshai and Sabathu, sent me Kippa Ram's rock cakes which we shared. Each of us got four annas a week pocket money to spend but the Saturday cinema show cost two annas. Eight annas a week between us was what was left to spend in the tuck shop and we went scrumping frequently, often in inclement weather and invariably out of bounds.

Our world was suddenly shattered whilst on an outing in the monsoon season. We were hit by a torrential downpour whilst on the wrong side of a *nullah*. We were considering how to cross when Young Mahoney, the daredevil, stepped into the water on some slippery stones and a sudden cloud burst hurled him into the water and he was swept over a rocky incline beyond our sight. His body was not found for three days – down near the plains.

Bryant, the eldest boy and considered to be the leader who ought to have known better, was flogged and the younger ones in the gang (including me) were seriously chastised with religious fervour, as apparently God had punished us for taking the food of the poor farmers. Mahoney's parents took their other son away from the school and Sanawar was never the same again. Bryant became very morose and the following year he left the school. I became very subdued for a long time – being the only 'guilty one' left – and I missed the happy company of my friends.

After Bryant left the school I concentrated on sport and became good enough to get into the Colts team at hockey, playing at left inner and I represented the school against Bishop Cotton School in Simla – our arch rivals at senior and colt level. My athletic prowess at this time helped me out and in retrospect it seemed that Sergeant Wheeler, my housemaster, was also showing tolerance towards me, because he raised no objections when I bought a pair of parrots from a hillman. Unfortunately, the parrots did not last long – perhaps the fact that I too was half starved and would eat anything in sight, deprived them of vital titbits. They stayed with me long enough to contribute to my nickname – a fad at the time – Von Parrot Court, the Von because I had my first schooling in Germany.

The demise of my parrots made me turn my attention to collecting butterflies of which there were many rare specimens in the Himalayas. The prized species seemed to fly low across the playing fields below the school. The clear atmosphere and the background of the snowcapped mountains made it possible to spot the incoming beauties from a distance. There was a rare comradeship among the collectors, so that the first sign of an uncommon fluttering beauty was hailed with such cries as "Oakleaf coming!" which was acknowledged by a standard of etiquette such as keeping your position and not infringing on others' territory. It was never boring waiting for something to happen, for the great mountains of the Himalayas could be clearly seen on a bright day and looking down, the plains were stretched before us, with signs of smoke identifying aspects of the modern world. I became spoiled for beauty at the time – and since those days, all other scenery is pallid by comparison.

My butterfly net, made by my mother, was large and unique in the school and gave me a decent chance to catch the best species. In the summer of 1930, I caught a few rare specimens, including a unique crossbreed of two species, the Tiger, so called because of its stripes, and the Egg, with its huge egg-shaped blue spots. The specimens were pinned to a board above my bed, so they could be generally admired by other collectors.

At this time the school routine was disturbed by two serious events. The first was a plague of locusts which swept across the foothills, obliterating the light. The density of the swarms covered everything in sight and the grasshoppers crawled up our faces and got into our mouths and ears when we ventured outside. All doors and windows had to be shut otherwise our class work would be a nightmare. At night they were in our blankets. It lasted for three days and stripped the hill farmers' fields. The second crisis was an outbreak of Scarlet Fever in the boys' school. Quarantine restrictions were imposed which prevented pupils assembling together in church, or being in classrooms together and prevented some senior boys at camp returning to the school for a month. There were some casualties from this highly infectious disease, for it was before the advent of antibiotics, but at the same time, it allowed those of us catching butterflies an unhindered bonanza.

My butterfly net came to an unfortunate end, but its destruction brought me some fame. A flying fox became entrapped in the Nicholson House dormitory late at night, and its screeches and the heavy beating of its wings as it floundered around the dormitory beds was quite alarming. In desperation I stood on my bed and tried to ensnare it with my butterfly net, but it flew straight through it. After the flying fox had escaped, the lights were turned on by the housemaster, to reveal the tattered remains of the net and its twisted frame. This was viewed with some awe. The respect I got from this incident encouraged me to leave it in its torn state for future adulation. The housemaster, Sergeant Wheeler, was a kind man and allowed me a short period of glory but one day he said, 'Boy Court, I want that wreck moved out of the dormitory – do you hear me, boy?' I moved it with alacrity, because it had started to get boring and Sgt Wheeler was one of the masters I liked and respected. I think he quite liked me too – looking back at one of my school reports, his comment in the report for 1930 read, 'A cheerful boy and a good little sportsman.'

Our main sporting competitors in the Simla Hills were the teams of the Bishop Cotton School about twenty miles away in Simla. The two representative teams from our school were the Seniors and the Colts and I was in the colts team at hockey and soccer. The colts sharpened up their competitive skills by playing against our Senior Girls team at hockey – a difficult task, for our opponents towered over us. In one such match in 1930, I charged at a robust girl with such endeavour that she screamed as she hit the ball which came high from the stick and struck me on the point of the chin. I lay prostrate on the ground while my pleasant assailant fussed over me and then helped me to my feet. My jaw was sore for a while, while the memory of being cuddled by a comely female lasted much longer. From that time I realised that the creatures on the other side of the aisle in church had other features that were hidden by their shapeless dresses and pinafores. As I gazed at Hilda Baker in church, I realised there was more to her than a pretty well-scrubbed face.

About this time my mother moved from the Plains to a hill station which was nearer to Sanawar and it could be seen on a bright day from the top of Nicholson House. Having reached the age of 12, I was permitted to go there one Sunday a month on condition that I returned to the barracks before lights out. I had made the journey a few times successfully by climbing across the *khuds* instead of using the road, which was much longer. Sergeant Wheeler asked me if I would take a new boy with me as his mother had just moved there. I was not keen, but I wanted to please my housemaster. On the way, we had to cross a river, where an old man with a crook would carry each of us across the ford on his back for one anna. The boy took some persuading to climb onto the hillman's back. Our progress started to improve until we came across a cobra and a mongoose shaping up for battle. I dragged the boy down beside me, but his obvious distress disturbed them and we were then able to continue the climb until we reached the plateau on which Sabathu sprawled, by which time the boy was very distraught. During the final climb to Sabathu, the boy slipped and in grabbing hold of him I got some thorns in my right hand. We eventually reached the married quarters in the afternoon – too late for me to return to Sanawar that day. My mother dressed my hand and took me to the MO the next day. I returned to Sanawar on Tuesday by a Ford 'T' truck, with a note explaining my absence, but my companion never returned to the school.

PHYLLIS AND MONTY

In the spring of 1932 my father was posted to Bombay with the rank of Quartermaster. The family left the Punjab and were placed in quarters near to the barracks in Bombay. This was a difficult time for the family, particularly my mother who was nursing my young brother David. It was a disturbing period, for there were many riots in the area and in one of these mother was thrown through a shop window and sustained cuts and bruises to her hands and face. On a happier note, my young brother Monty was run over by a Rolls-Royce and miraculously crawled out unhurt. I was unhappy too that my family were so far away. After a few months I was relieved to learn that father was promoted to sergeant-major of the 12th Light Battery RA, which was a mountain artillery unit in Ambala and also the Simla Hills. Bombay had suddenly become a dangerous place for families, so mother came back to the Simla Hills early.

At the age of 13 I was too old for the Colts teams and too young for the Seniors so I focused on athletics where I was an average runner, but won prizes on sports days at long jump and high jump. In the classroom, I was having an unhappy time with my form master Sammy Cowell, who was unable to inspire me to produce better results. He disliked me and I hated him, and this resulted in me becoming the most severely caned pupil in my year. This did not bother me because it was the only achievement that marked my existence. The tight corduroy shorts enhanced the imprints on my backside and registered the terms of our relationship. I paid very little attention in the subjects he taught, but did better with other teachers. On one occasion whilst home on leave, my mother was examining my body while topping up the bathtub with hot water, and asked me about the bruises. I told her I had fallen down the *Khud*. She did not believe me but could do nothing because my father was still in Bombay. However, realising that other boys in the brigade had left the school, she was in no doubt about the harshness of the regime at Sanawar. This was apparently altered in the late Thirties, following an enquiry into the behaviour of the teachers towards the boys and girls in the school. I stayed at the school until December 1932, achieving better results when I was placed in a different class.

In the winter of 1932 I became critically ill with Peritonitis during my Christmas leave. The stomach pains became acute whilst I was at the Delhi Horse Show where my father was competing. The Army MO in Delhi decided I needed an enema, which he performed and declared I would feel a lot better in a few days. We returned the hundred miles to Ambala after the show in a Ford 'T', with me wrapped in a blanket, suffering from the jolts as the vehicle hurried back along the ill-made road. On arriving at our bungalow I was rushed to the Ambala Military Hospital and operated on the same night by an RAF surgeon. I was on the danger list for over a week and once I was able to appreciate my surroundings, I realised I was in the soldiers' ward because I was 14. My wretched appendix was put in a bottle for the hospital staff to view. The biggest problem for the nurses was how to keep my hands away from my wounded area – which had started to itch.

These were the pre-antibiotics days of draining the poison from the wound, and the matron Miss Reynolds decided it was necessary to adopt extreme measures to keep my hands otherwise occupied, so she brought me a mouth-organ. It drove the soldiers mad. In despair they got hold of a supply of old school magazines sent to them from Blighty. *The Magnet, Gem* and *Sports Budget* then became essential reading for the next four years.

I was in hospital for three months and regarded it as one of the happiest periods of my life. On the maidan outside, a cinema screen was erected in the hospital grounds where they showed the first talkies – Al Jolson's *Jazz Singer* and Eddie Cantor's *Whoopee*.

I could not return to Sanawar because I was in convalescence for some months afterwards. My education was continued under my father's battery 'Schooly' at Jutogh but I missed the competitive sport at the school, my housemaster Sergeant Wheeler and one or two friends in Nicholson House.

Jutogh

In the spring of 1933 we became a complete family for the first time since 1928 apart from the Christmas holidays. The 12th Light was a mountain battery and so my father was in the Hills with us – a family of eight in a lovely bungalow on the edge of the woods in Jutogh. Father had arranged for me to work in the 'Waxies Shop' in addition to studying with 'Schooly'. This involved me repairing saddlery and the sergeant Waxie was a very kind man who was in love with his trade and produced saddles of some distinction. On the education side I took the Tradesman's examination as an entry to the Army Tradesmen College at Chepstow, although I showed no artisan skills. I began to recover from my operation and started to kick a football about on the battery football pitch, which was close to the Waxies shop – occasionally with some of the troops in my father's battery.

Waxie was determined to turn me into a tradesman if just to please my father. I started to repair leather straps and do other minor leather repair work but didn't advance much further, for I lacked the necessary patience and technical potential to be a successful journeyman like my grandfather. It was whilst sitting astride a stool stitching a broken belt that I felt a sharp pain in my shoulder. An Indian tradesman working behind me knocked a scorpion off the back of my shoulder and killed it. I was taken to the MO with what was left of the offending species. The sting was at the top of my left shoulder which showed a large white patch. When I had been treated, the Waxie sent me home but later in the day I was allowed to go the battery football pitch and kick a ball about with no ill-effects.

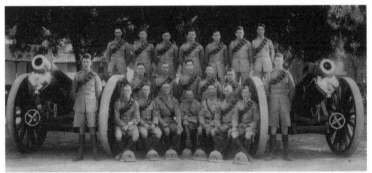

THE WINNING TROOP AND 60-POUNDER GUNS, RETURNING FROM FIRING CAMP IN PATIALA. MY FATHER IS THIRD FROM LEFT IN THE FRONT ROW.

I was able to go to Simla with soldiers from the battery to watch the 'Durand Cup', the premier football competition in India at that time, which involved civilian and regimental army teams. The team to beat was an Indian team called the Sandemonians. Whilst there I met some Sanawarians who thought I had deserted the school for the Bishop Cotton School in Simla. Returning to Sanawar was in the balance, mainly because my father's service in India would terminate before the end of 1933.

Jutogh held very pleasant memories as it had the casual aura of a the hill station. Our bungalow was on the very outskirts of Jutogh, about two miles from the 12th Light's Barracks. The only sounds that one could hear were the parrots and monkeys squawking and chattering. My mother loved it there. My father, being the sergeant-major was often away, either in his office or the sergeants' mess and he was still a robust man of 43 with no sign that his health would seriously deteriorate within five years. One day I was sitting outside the bungalow with my mother enjoying the cool of the evening – we had become quite close since my operation – when the sound of a military voice in the distance could be heard. Before I could ask the question, my mother said proudly, 'Your father is mounting the guard – he still has the loudest voice in the battery.'

FIRING CAMP AT PATIALA

I knew my father was a crack shot, the best billiard player in the battery and an outstanding horseman, but the sound of his voice from two miles away somehow added a new dimension to his persona. He still had the weakness of being unable to resist a challenge. Only the year before in Delhi, whilst under the influence of drink, he had walked across the parapets of Delhi Fort for a bet of fifty chips (Rupees), holding a glass of whisky in one hand. He nearly reached the other side of the fort when he fell 30 feet into the quadrangle, breaking the glass but miraculously unscathed. In my eyes his presence was immense.

Another night at home with my mother, I had the opportunity to appreciate her qualities. She had gone outside the bungalow with some rubbish and had not returned. After a while I went looking for her. She was standing still by the waste-bin, which was at the edge of the tree-line. The light from the bungalow showed her holding up her hand. Closer to the bungalow there was a huge pair of eyes glinting in the dark. We all stood motionless for a long time, until the creature moved across the line of the bungalow light – to reveal a black panther which then turned slowly away into the forest. We walked slowly back to the bungalow door. Mother didn't drink, but she made her way to the drinks cabinet and poured herself a large glass of whisky.

After this my father brought home a rifle from the battery armoury which he or I could use. Despite the risk of carnivores, of which the panther imposed the greatest threat, my mother had no wish to move closer to the barracks for we were living in the nicest house we had ever had in India.

Just before the autumn in 1933 we said goodbye to our friends in the 12th Light Battery and the wonderful scenery of Jutogh and returned to Ambala en route to the UK. We travelled by train to Bombay, with two more in the family than had made the trip seven years before. We were going back to a home that some of us could barely remember and my two brothers had never seen. At the age of 43 my father was coming to the end of 25 years' service in the Royal Artillery and indeed the British Army, so the future presented a challenge to us all – including my parents.

Sanawar School song

Never give in, Sanawar
Strive to the set of the sun
And we learn its truth
Through the days of youth
On the long Hodgson run
Oh, though your heart seems bursting
Up Sergeant Tilly's Hill
You may not win
You will yet come in
If you stick it still.
It's the way we have in Sanawar
The best school of all
And we live in its motto's power
Till the last bugle call.

Chapter 3

'Home' Again

The *City of Paris* trooper entered Plymouth Harbour just before Christmas 1933, with much damage to its upper rigging. A violent storm in the Bay of Biscay had smashed the windlass, and three Lascars had been swept overboard, never to be recovered.

The passengers had boarded at Bombay and Karachi. They were mainly military families returning to the UK after finishing service abroad but a few had come home for Christmas leave. All were thankful to get ashore and many of the adults had suffered badly from seasickness. The children were mostly in good fettle, however, having been put in the lower saloon at the height of the storm – they came ashore wondering what all the fuss was about.

After the necessary clearances and goodbyes, we boarded a train to Paddington. Our ultimate destination was the Union Jack Club, near Waterloo station. We had two rooms booked for a short stay, while my parents found accommodation in London. My father had to report to Woolwich but his discharge date – after 25 years in the Army – was not due until March so he still had two months' service to complete. The Royal Artillery was liberal, helping him on such matters as employment, for he was still only 43 years old.

Although jobs were difficult to get in 1934, my father did not ask his family for help. In fact, he hadn't informed them we were returning to England. My grandfather was by this time head cooper at Courage's brewery, and was a wealthy man with servants; Tim, the youngest son, also held sway in the brewery. My father had been a talented young man, but had never conformed to his family's wishes, so an early reconciliation was not on the cards. However, my grandmother was persistent, for she was meeting three of her grandchildren for the first time, and in a few months a closer association was formed.

Meanwhile, I was awaiting the results of an army examination I had taken in India. If I passed, I would be going to Chepstow to train as an artificer, presumably in the Ordinance Corps. But my heart was not in it. Meanwhile, I too would have to find a job to help things along, or start schooling again from scratch, which would be a costly business for the family.

Camberwell Green

After three days in the Union Jack Club, we found a flat on the top floor of the Modern Shoe Shop in the centre of Camberwell Green, adjacent to a noisy pub, The Father Red Cap. It was inadequate accommodation and we were very cramped for the three months we lived there. My three sisters went to the Greencoat School nearby, where they suffered much derision from their Cockney classmates who found their colonial accents strange. Betty at least was unconcerned: at the age of eleven, she was not averse to a decent punch-up and even looked for trouble. After a month, all the toughies in the school sought her company …and so peace reigned.

We were also getting to know our relations. Cousin Dennis, an only child, lived in Tulse Hill with his father Ernest Bartle, a kindly man and an indulgent Dulwich Hamlet supporter, and my Aunt Ivy. The ruling body in the household, she was thrilled with the sudden invasion of the six Court children to keep her son company. They were a God-fearing couple who worked assiduously for the church. Dennis played the piano with great enthusiasm, notably *There is a tavern in the town* to gain our approval – particularly that of my sister Ivy, who at thirteen was developing into a beautiful blonde.

A FORMIDABLE FORCE: (LEFT TO RIGHT) GREAT AUNT PHOEBE, AUNT ENA, AUNT IVY AND GRANDMA

My grandmother felt the need to dress me in the style befitting an up-and-coming youth in the 1930s, so I was taken to Jones and Higgins in Peckham Rye, where I was measured and fitted with a new suit, trilby hat, gloves, shoes and a raincoat. I felt distinctly overdressed when I first appeared before the locals, who greeted me with, 'Oh gawd, look at 'im! 'E don't 'arf fink 'e's somefing!'

It was going to be particularly difficult to get a job as a 15-year-old as naive as I was. My mother attempted to alleviate my fears by saying, 'Maurice, when you go for an interview, just say 'I have just come home from India'. Venturing forth for my first interview, which was in Walworth, I arrived at the pawnbroker's shop completely dressed as a young dude. The pawnbroker thought I was there on business until I explained I was applying for the vacancy. To break the ice I said that I had just come home from India, to which he replied, 'Really, lad!'. Evidently I was not cut out to be a three-balls assistant, so I departed with some relief to seek my fortune elsewhere.

I go up in the world

My great aunt Ena had a friend who was manager at the Snowhill Labour Exchange in the City – a Mr Tatham. Ena rarely took no for an answer and so Mr Tatham was under orders to find me a job. It was not easy because I had lost the last year's schooling through illness. Eventually I had an interview with White Drummond and Co. at Cloak Lane, adjacent to Cannon Street station. Mr East, the administration manager, interviewed me for the job of lift boy with prospects of being elevated to a position on the third floor, possibly as a filing clerk. I was engaged for a salary of 12s 6d per week – 8 hours a day Monday to Friday and 4 hours on Saturday – with the prospect of doing overtime for a small reward for work with the fledgling subsidiary companies.

My immediate boss was Mr Hudson, an old soldier bedecked with Great War medal ribbons, who wore a brown uniform and was a member of the Corps of Commissioners. He called me 'BOY' and I called him 'Sir'. He always had a cheese sandwich and a peeled apple for lunch. The peeling of the apple was a work of art and used to fascinate me so much that often I drooled as I watched. I sat in a corner seat by the window in the Waiting Room looking up Cloak Lane towards Cannon Street station, so that I could observe the managers and directors approaching. 'Mr Fairburn's coming, Mr Hudson!' 'Thank you, boy.' Hudson would then straighten his uniform, elongate his neck, mark Mr Fairburn into his record and say, 'Good morning Mr Fairburn! Take Mr Fairburn to the first floor, boy!'

I waited every morning with great anticipation for Miss Bradbury. She was management staff and came into the office at the same time as the directors, just before ten o'clock. She was in her late twenties, a buxom blonde lady with a nice smile. She invariably wore a tweed suit, the fashion for business women at that time, and to establish her standing, carried a smart briefcase, usually bulging with papers. As soon as she neared the office door, I leapt off my seat and Hudson would dryly remark, 'I suppose it's Miss Bradbury, boy?' 'Er yes, sir.' 'Well, take Miss Bradbury to the second floor, then!' As she got out of the lift, she gave her wonderful smile, and wished me 'Nice day, Maurice'. Even if it had been raining cats and dogs, the whole premises lit up when she arrived.

White Drummond had a cricket team of sorts, and the batting order followed the seniority of staff. The big annual match was against Bradbury Wilkinson, the bank note people, who printed many of our fixed trust prospectuses. This game was played in New Maiden, the home ground of Bradbury Wilkinson. In 1936, after I had been with the firm for over a year, our team was two men short. A youth named Wallace in the accounts department and I both had cricket experience, so we were drafted into the side at ten and eleven. Bradbury Wilkinson, batting first, compiled a score of nearly two hundred. Our firm was struggling to reach one hundred with nine wickets down, when Wallace and I came together. We put on over fifty between us and batted out time. On the strength of this performance, senior management decided I was better than lift boy material and promoted me to the third floor as a filing clerk. I was particularly proud that Miss Bradbury had been watching the game and said, 'Well done, Maurice!'

My promotion to the filing department placed me directly under the General Office manager Mr East, who was general secretary of Leytonstone Football club. On hearing that I had started playing for a local football team in Walworth, he suggested that I might like to come to Leytonstone for a trial. At the time their first team were doing well in the Isthmian league – the premier amateur league in London. I played a few games for their second team, but sadly the journey and the expense of playing was too much.

Much to my surprise Hudson was quite upset by my promotion to the third floor. I too had become very fond of the dapper little man, because he had always been kind to me. Standards in the thirties were based on having respect for your elders, even when you knew they were in the wrong. Later when serving in the Army during the War, I always made a point of visiting Hudson when on leave, which he appreciated.

Apart from the hustle and bustle of London, which was overwhelming, we Court children were bedazzled by the cinemas and music halls. Talkies had apparently been commonplace in London since 1929 but when we left India, we had seen but two talkies in an open-air setting, on the *maidan* in Ambala, Eddie Cantor's *Whoopee*, and Al Jolson's *The Jazz Singer*. Camberwell Green had a new plush cinema, The Golden Domes, showing the latest talkies and the New Grand Hall, which delighted in children's matinées at half price (2d per child), notably cowboy films on a Saturday morning. Tom Mix, Buck Jones and Ken Maynard were particular attractions and either my sister Ivy or I took our brother, the boisterous Monty, every week.

The Camberwell Empire was a top-class music hall with such attractions as the Two Leslies, Stanelli, and Norman Long. Within reach too was the Brixton Empire, probably the best music hall in South London. It was drawing in the crowds, with such new artists as the Henderson Twins. And only a short tram trip away was the Elephant and Castle and the latest in cinema design, the Trocadero. A huge cinema with a wonderful stage, it presented nightly a four and a half hour programme. This included Quentin McClean at the organ, two talkies and the news, and a stage show – usually a big-band concert such as Ambrose and his orchestra, with vocalists such as the blossoming Vera Lynn. Children's admission fee with an adult was 8d.

I was greatly surprised at this time to find that I had passed my army exam. This would enable me to go to Chepstow for an apprenticeship as an Army artificer, but I realised then that whatever future I might have, it certainly was not in engineering. In any case, I was enjoying life in London and the idea of going back to stringent army discipline did not appeal. I still had bad memories of the restrictions of Sanawar, so I rejected the offer. Had I known how things were to turn out, I might have accepted it.

We move to Walworth

Meanwhile, the cramped conditions above the Modern Shoe Shop made it imperative that we move. My parents managed to rent an unfurnished house, 38 Lorrimore Road, in Walworth. Although in a bad state of repair, it was quite large and seemed like heaven. There was no bathroom but we went to Manor Place Baths once a week for a bath. There was a sink and a kitchen, which was a vast step forward from cooking on the landing. My three sisters and brother Monty went to the John Ruskin School in a nearby street where they soon made new friends, and I started night school at the John Ruskin, taking six basic subjects. This was necessary because of two years' limited education in India. Nearby was the Nelson Institute in Trafalgar Street, where boxing, gymnastics and various indoor sports such as handball attracted me for four years, right up to the outbreak of war.

The Nelson was only half a mile away and they had a top rate gymnastics teacher named Peters. The boxing class was taken by Matt Wells, the former Lightweight Champion. Matt gave most of us a bloody nose each week and then sent us home with a bunch of football coupons with his name at the top to drop through letter boxes en route.

Peters not only produced an outstanding gymnastics team, but encouraged us to form a sports club for cricket and football.

Occasionally I lent a hand with the administration and eventually, in the late thirties, I took it over. Surprisingly, we developed some very good sportsmen in the four years before the war. Our football home ground was at Clapham Common, booked through the LCC, and our cricket ground was the ABC Sports ground at New Eltham. Expenses for the cricket team were mostly travel for away matches and equipment: a bat was two guineas, and a match ball was 3s 6d so every time one of our balls cleared the boundary fence, the members groaned; in a sense fours were more popular than sixes at home matches – even when we were batting! To finance our activities our subscription rate was 6d per week and we sold Pontoon Football tickets at 2d each. We also held dances in the largest hall of the Nelson Institute. At that time, the girls sat down one side of the hall and the boys on the other. When a boy invited a girl to dance, it inevitably made everyone giggle.

Our cricket side didn't look much when we took the field, but we shocked a few classy sides. We ultimately reached the standing of 'strong medium' as listed in the Challenger, the London medium for arranging fixtures. We in the club were very good friends and two years in succession we managed to go away for a week's holiday down on the Medway at Yalding. We hired a camping site by the river and lived in tents and the girls cooked meals on primus stoves. We fished and hired rowing boats and just lazed in beautiful summer weather. Some of the lads had brought their girlfriends or sisters and they had separate accommodation. We were far from promiscuous in those days – some smooching between committed couples was as hot as it got. In fact, most of us who went into the Forces in September 1939 were cock virgins – and a number still were when they were killed.

My father was by now working for the Government of South Africa and was located at South Africa House in Trafalgar Square. He worked in the reception area dealing with visitors and he always looked immaculate in his special uniform as he walked along Lorrimore Road to get to Kennington tube station. Although only in his mid-forties, he was by this time having breathing problems, possibly the aftermath of the mustard gas attack that hospitalised him in 1918.

He had always shown a great interest in wildlife and started keeping pigeons – not the healthiest pastime for someone with breathing problems. He was a great researcher and the origins of the homing species – Barker, Logan, Gurney and other popular lines in vogue in the 1930s – received his full attention. Within two years he was regarded in the Walworth and Kennington areas as being an expert on pigeon racing. He was often asked to speak on the subject and *The Racing Pigeon* and *Homing World* weekly journals often had articles and letters by him. My mother and I viewed this development with mixed feelings, because she knew she would be helping to scrape out the loft and clear the pigeons' droppings, and I knew I would be the carrier of the panniers wherever they were required. However, my father was a winner when it came to racing and breeding pigeons so he reduced his costs with his winnings and betting money and selling squeakers that he had bred at 10s a pair.

In due course we had the opportunity to rent a house in Kennington at 5 Methley Street, a three-storey Victorian terraced house which we ultimately bought. Methley Street was in a sense very select, being at the back of the Waifs and Strays building and heading an alleyway where Charlie Chaplin was born. The move was about three quarters of a mile and did not interfere with any of our recreational arrangements and it allowed my parents to entertain our relatives, mainly from my mother's side of the family. It was a great delight to see Aunt Fran, my mother's red-headed younger sister, come bouncing into our new domain, for she always appeared to be happy despite an unsuccessful retinue of husbands and boyfriends. We also saw our cousins Joyce, Maurice and Derrick, who were in the age group of my younger brothers and sisters.

It was around this time that we also got to know a tall, well-built young man named Johnny Ward, who had set up a rag and bone business and used to drive his horse and cart up Methley Street. He was an orphan, bringing up a younger brother, and took an interest in my father's pigeons. I liked Johnny, who was already in the Territorial unit of the Royal Fusiliers at Flodden Road and was the 'Terriers' light heavyweight boxing champion. No one was a greater patriot than Johnny, who was interested in all sports at a time when the country was top of the heap at football and cricket. My father admired Johnny's endeavour to improve himself, so he took an interest in his pigeons, boosting his loft with some pedigree stock, and occasionally examined the old carthorse. In the summer months in the late thirties, I too was occupied on Saturdays and sometimes mid-week helping my father with his pigeon chores.

In winter, I supported Charlton Athletic who were in the First Division of the league. To get to the Valley took 45 minutes in a no. 40 tram, jam-packed with supporters. On big match days, the 70,000-strong crowd scrambled up the slope into Charlton Church Lane to turn into Floyd Road, where the real crush started. Managing to obtain a suitable position on the steep slopes of the Valley was an achievement. On Sundays I played football for Trafalgar and so returning to the office on Mondays, often aching, was a relaxing experience.

In the early part of 1938, unit trusts lost a lot of their appeal in the financial market. The possibility of a war with Germany had affected the financial market and the future of Municipal and General Securities (M&G), one of our subsidiaries, became uncertain. Unfortunately, together with other junior staff, I was made redundant. This was a great blow, because I was the only regular earner in the family apart from my father's sick pay from South Africa House and his Army Pension. He was ill with gastric ulcers, a killer at that time – a condition that was to plague him throughout the Second World War.

Fortunately, I found a position in the General office of Stephenson, Harwood and Tatham in Old Broad Street, as the senior boy under the General Office chief clerk, a Mr Bond. About this time, Ivy, now aged 16, got a job with a stockbroker in the City, so the finances of the Court household started to improve.

In the late summer of 1938 I went with Percy Cope, a friend from my previous job, to the Isle of Wight and stayed in a house in St Helens named 'Smugglers', where I had stayed as a one-year-old. Although no athlete, Percy was an inveterate hiker and we walked everywhere. Photographs show us plodding along wearing open-

necked white shirts and sports jackets, the casual wear of the time. We practically covered the whole Island in a week, some days walking along the railway lines to cut the distance. The landlady was not too pleased when we returned to 'Smugglers' at midnight but we made a little bit of money go a long way. We returned home to London beautifully tanned.

In the autumn, Percy invited me to his home in Ilford for Sunday lunch. I did not know until I arrived that his father had died in the 1920s as the result of war injuries. The lunch was with his mother and three unattached sisters, who were all talented musicians. After a sumptuous meal, I was sat on the sofa and was entertained by the five of them playing piano, cello, two violins and Percy on flute. It's the only time an ensemble has ever entertained me alone – with the added bonus of being ogled at by more than one female. It was a lovely day that I have always remembered with great fondness. For some reason I never accepted an invitation to go again – Ilford seemed a long way from Kennington then.

Stephenson, Harwood and Tatham, together with Linklater and Payne, were arguably the biggest solicitors in the City at this time. Some of our largest clients were the Churchill family, the Jewish Board of Guardians and a great number of prestigious names of the 1930s. My job was general office duties with a special task on Saturday mornings of taking care of old briefs and conveying them in a wooden trolley along Old Broad Street to the strong room, which was in a small turning near Liverpool Street. The rattle of this contraption elicited a chorus of horn blowing from the cabs, which seemed to dominate that street in those days. The strong room had a large colony of rats which required frequent attention from the pest control people. On approaching the strong room I always made a deal of noise and reassured a worried junior clerk who often accompanied me.

The eight partners in the firm were dominated in those days by the Witt and Lousada families. Sir Robert Witt was the senior partner of the firm and tended to be rather eccentric – particularly in crossing Old Broad Street. From the pavement he took over by opening his umbrella, even on a dry day, and walking straight across the road usually heading towards Throgmorton Street. He totally ignored the sound of grinding brakes and prolonged horn blowing as cabbies showed their displeasure. We on the ground floor watched this performance with bated breath expecting the worst, but up to the time I was called up, in late August 1939, he was still hale and hearty.

Into the Territorials

I was interviewed by his son John Witt when I applied for the job. The fact that I got it owed as much to my father's military background as any outstanding merit I possessed. John Witt was a Territorial, as were many partners in City firms and he encouraged me to join my local unit which was an anti-tank regiment in the Royal Artillery at Brixton; they were a collection of all sorts, including entertainers and jockeys. John Witt was an officer in the Rifle Brigade who was not called up until 1941, because he was on various committees which had some wartime importance. But in 1941, serving in the Rifle Brigade in the Middle East and Italy, he was in some rather sticky spots. Throughout the war he used his influence to ensure that Stephenson Harwood paid my mother and the dependents of other Territorials in the firm our salaries every week. In my case it was a generous payment considering I had been with the firm less than two years. It did not surprise me to learn later that he was knighted for his charity work.

In the late summer of 1939, the public in general were aware that war was imminent and we in the Territorials were sent to hone our pathetic skills on the firing ranges at Okehampton and then taking part in manoeuvres on Salisbury Plain. Our two-pounder anti-tank gun was a fine piece of ordinance machinery but we had to remove the wheels to fire it. In our ignorance we thought it was great and firmly believed it would knock out any German tank that was unfortunate enough to get into our sights. It was a very accurate gun, and spun like a top to take on other intruders. In theory we always demolished the first target, but in reality it was a peashooter – as time would confirm.

We returned from the West Country full of zeal and enthusiasm and were then despatched to Lydd, on the Romney Marshes, for further firing practice. We had four anti-tank guns and a meagre allowance of small arms comprising four Bren light machine guns, a Lee Enfield rifle (one between five men) and an unpopular back-up weapon, the Boyes 505 anti-tank rifle. This had a huge rubber pad on the butt – indicative that the recoil was pretty fierce, as a number of bruised shoulders testified, but unfortunately it had no real penetrative power.

BOYES ANTI-TANK RIFLE

In all innocence, we thought we were well armed and could take on anyone. Our support vehicles carrying stores, cooking utensils and HQ equipment were still in the livery of the wholesaler from whom they had been requisitioned. In particular the three-ton vehicle carrying the kitchen equipment (fondly referred to as 'Kitchen Katy') had bold lemon and red stripes and proclaimed we were 'W. Brown & Co. Meat Wholesalers, Smithfield Market'. This garish decor was ultimately covered up with a dark grey paint, the colour of our gun towers, a more appropriate camouflage colour for the French and Belgian countryside. This old Foden, that never broke down, was eventually destroyed together with our other remaining vehicles and equipment, just before reaching the La Panne beaches to prevent them falling into German hands.

At the end of August we returned to our TA hall in East Brixton and went home. But the stay was short-lived, for on September 1st we received orders to report back to our unit. We were given 24 hours to settle our affairs – not long, considering that a number of Territorials ran their own businesses.

I spent my last day at Stephenson Harwood. A few of the old soldiers in the office gave copious advice on how to deal with the Bosch, and if I had followed some of their suggestions I would never have survived. The firm were true to their word and paid my mother for the next six and a half years and additionally paid her a Christmas bonus every year of £1. The fact that I did not return to their employ in 1946 was amiably accepted, for apparently five clerks had filled my post by the time war ended.

I returned home, collected my gear and reported to Brixton accompanied by my mother and sisters Ivy and Betty. I got the impression that my friends would have preferred me to go home and leave my sisters behind. The following day, my sister Phyllis and brothers Monty and David were evacuated to Devon – Kennington was regarded as being unsafe. My father was still in hospital on the Isle of Wight, and was too ill to return to London.

At Brixton we were billeted in a local church hall and remained there for over a week. We were not allowed out because being mobilised meant that we should be readily available. The church hall was surrounded by iron railings and the main entrance was manned by military police. The fact that we were Territorials, and as such were volunteers, did not detract from the fact that in the changed climate of events, some might do a bunk. My mother and two sisters fed me and my mates rock cakes between the church hall railings each night. As far as my sisters were concerned, it was giggling time, whereas my mother looked serious and worried, obviously concerned that my father was not available and four of her six children had left home in the space of a week.

War is declared

On our second day in the church hall, war was declared. The fact that Chamberlain had made an announcement became evident when for the first time we heard the air raid warning and a warden appeared at his front door wearing his new helmet which indicated his standing. He galloped up the road blowing a whistle and returned still puffing as he went to the other end of the road. Returning to the front of his house he then collapsed, either through exhaustion or excitement. We watched through the iron railings and rewarded his efforts with a cheer. For the next few days, we were marched to Ruskin Park which was about half a mile away and we dug the first air raid trenches and were suitably rewarded by dogs jumping excitedly in with us for a pee. We took the five Lee Enfields with us and on the third day the sirens wailed continuously, for what was regarded as a serious alarm. We deployed along the tree line with our five loaded Lee Enfield rifles pointed towards the sky, whilst old gentlemen smoking pipes walked slowly by with their dogs. It seemed in that first week that the imminence of war hadn't sunk in and the possibility of another politician hopping over to Berlin had not been ruled out. Many thought that as we'd only been at war with the buggers twenty years before, it didn't seem likely they would want to have another go yet.

We were at the church hall for about ten days, being marched out each morning for our exercise and digging routine and then locked up each night with a guard posted. Orders came through for us to be transported to Potters Bar with our guns and trucks and auxiliary transport to help us move into billets in that area. The day we moved out the local residents waved, for they probably wondered (as we did) why their Army had been locked up each night. My mother, who came to see me off, cried, and my two sisters blew kisses to all and sundry.

Our battery was billeted at Potters Bar, in an area of houses around a small recreation ground which became our B Echelon. The erection of large marquees with a cookhouse and stores alongside, met all our functional requirements. The Robin Hood, a coaching house close at hand, would ultimately be our watering hole on pay day.

My billet mate was Crabbe, an apprentice jockey. Our new landlady was a well proportioned woman in her thirties, who on our arrival greeted us in a friendly manner and gave the impression that we had added to her security. She led us to our room in the attic, which was to be our home for about six weeks. She had a young family including a boy of five who referred to me as 'My towdger'. On the nights I was guarding the Battery's few possessions, the boy brought a few of his young friends to gaze at me. I attempted to look the part of guarding the domain. This was difficult with him looking up at me as he tugged away at my trousers hoping to get a response.

The whole nation at this time was looking for inspiration and had their spirits uplifted by the radio with such renderings as *Run Rabbit Run* and *We're going to hang out the washing on the Siegfried Line*, and programmes with Tommy Handley, the nation's favourite radio comedian.

At our billet, the man of the house worked in an engineering factory on war work mainly at nights ... so we had plenty of company from his wife, who brought us cups of tea at the most unlikely times. Crabbe on more than one occasion said, 'I think she fancies you' to which I responded with the stock answer of the time, 'Get away with you!'. Later on, with more experience of the female mind, I reflected that Crabbe could have been right. She quite often put her head around the door to say, 'Your cooks are burning the stew – I can smell it!

We were given notice to move and started packing our equipment about two days before we left. On the last night we took our final drink at the Robin Hood. The locals were interested to know where we were going, to which we replied, 'No idea, mate'. Troops under arms in September 1939 were very sparse and we were the only unit in the Potters Bar area, so at the time of leaving, we were still a novelty. Security posters, such as 'Careless talk costs lives', were new and the locals just couldn't understand that we did not know our destination.

We stood outside our billet on the morning of leaving, feeling rather sad and realising that this emergency billeting was going to be the last good time we would have for some months. The boy was in tears and cried out 'Mummy, our towdgers are going!'. His mother too was quite upset, and gave us both a hug and kiss. Later I said to Crabbe, 'There you are Crabby, she liked both of us'. As we climbed into our vehicles we were given instructions that we were headed for Kempton Park race course. As the vehicles started up, we left to cheers and blown kisses and calls of 'Drop us a line, won't you?'.

CHAPTER 4

○

TO FRANCE AND BACK – THE HARD WAY

The unit left Potters Bar and moved to Kempton Park racecourse. The officers' quarters were in the offices in and around the Tote while those of us in The Other Ranks slept in the stands. I was lucky. With my jockey friend Crabbe, I shared the Royal Box, which was the area for Battery HQ. Our officer was Lt Berry, a handsome man in his thirties who, like many of us, was employed in the City. He was also an amateur actor and wore an immaculate black moustache which he stroked for effect. He was totally in love with himself.

Crabbe was bemused by his change in fortune, 'Yer know, Maury,' he said, as we moved in, 'I always wanted to ride 'ere, mate but I never fought I'd be sleepin 'ere. Maybe this is as good as it gets!'

I never got to know whether it did get better for Crabbe or not, for suddenly all Territorials under 19 were transferred out of the unit into a second line regiment, the 62nd Anti-Tank Regiment. This meant they would not experience action until they were older. The gaps in our ranks were filled with RA reservists, 'Old Sweats' – most of whom were in their thirties and had seen service in foreign parts, mainly India. The majority of this intake were put on the guns, but one or two came into the HQ Troop.

I join the babes and old men

The anti-tank regiments were the latest arm of the Royal Artillery establishment. All branches of the Army were coming to terms with the new role of Anti-tank Artillery, which involved fighting alongside frontline infantry battalions. Most of the reservists had served in the Field or Medium Artillery where guns were sited a mile or so behind the infantry regiments, so they found this new artillery role intimidating. Moreover, they joined our unit with the army rank they had held when they were placed into the reserve. This caused anomalies because the lower Territorial rankers were helping to train this new, rather stale intake of NCOs. However, most of the reservists hated Anti-tank Artillery work and, within a year, those who returned from France managed to get transferred to other Field and Medium Artillery units. The gaps in the ranks were filled, in due course, by young men from the first and second draft of the Militia. But we started our war in 1939 with a batch of inadequate NCOs and a sergeant-major from the distant past.

The reservist sergeant-major was called 'Soapy Joe' because he looked dilapidated and untidy, particularly on parade, when standing at the side of the immaculate Territorial officers. It was a creed in the 'Terriers' to emulate the 'regulars' in their dress, and it was apparent that the officers found it distasteful to stand at the side of their scruffy sergeant-major. Among the SM's string of ancient orders, was 'Pick up your parrots and monkeys' as a command to move our kit when we were in transit. His one redeeming feature was that he liked football and was keen to give special privileges to those who were representing either the battery or regimental sides, which pleased me at least. However, the structure of the battery had completely changed in the course of two months. It had become a unit of babes and old men.

I was saddened by the departure of Crabbe, who although rather foul-mouthed was good company. I never heard from him again. For a while, the 'Terriers' tended to stick together and so my particular friends included Jacobs, an aggressive Jew who worked in insurance, Norman Williamson who was in stockbroking, Harrry Woodhams, who was in the GPO, and Ronnie Lodge, an actor whose parents were still 'on the Boards', working with Ronnie's godfather, Bud Flanagan. Bud corresponded with Ronnie throughout the war, sending him scripts, memorably one about a milkman which had Ronnie in fits as he read it in his dugout on Anzio. I was also close to George Cordery, a shy handsome blonde lad who was a toolmaker, Gerry Young, nicknamed 'Kongy,' a strong muscular lad who was an NCO and worked on the Southern Railways, Bob Cracknell, who worked in insurance in the City and had a manic sense of humour, Tubby Dolan, a mechanical engineer, and Nobby Clark, a storeman. This variety of experience was typical of the Territorial Army at this time. Later, Hughie Robertson, a sturdy Scottish Territorial, was transferred to us from the 51st Highland Division and became part of our clan. We did not always call our friends by their first name – I was generally referred to as 'Langley', my middle name. Why, I don't know, but this name stuck with me throughout the war.

Kempton Park was a noisy place, where sound vibrated throughout the stands. It reached a peak in early morning. It seemed that most mothers (including mine) and wives had given their sons and husbands a going-away present of a Rolls razor. The whole kit was a contraption resembling an enlarged flat sardine tin. One stropped the razor on one side and honed it on the other. The explosion of noise before breakfast as these two processes were inflicted on the ear, helped to harden the senses of many a young soldier to the sound, heard later, of the deadly German Spandau machine gun.

I become a water expert

The Army at this time had a peculiar way of choosing men from the establishment for particular courses. It was therefore quite in keeping that I, an ex-solicitor's clerk, should be sent to Chelsea Barracks to attend a water course. I would learn how to obtain, clarify, test and sterilise water from rivers, streams and lakes, so that the troops in my unit could safely drink liquid or eat food prepared from water put in the Battery water cart. After a week on this course, I came away with a full knowledge of the 'Horrocks Test', which ensured that although water could be smelly it would be safe to drink. I had passed as a Driver I/C earlier as part of my basic Territorial training, so I was regarded as a specialist and accordingly allocated a 200-gallon Morris Water Cart which set me apart from the ordinary squaddie – but I wanted to get back on the guns.

We were stationed in Kempton Park until the end of October. During this period the Battery received from the Ministry of Supply 12 new two-pounder anti-tank guns, and new Bedford 15cwt gun towers as part of the updated standard equipment for an anti-tank battery. This enabled the gun teams in D, E and F troops to be able to train simultaneously on their own guns instead of having access to the four two-pounders every third day. However, in the course of the war years, the anti-tank equipment was changed very regularly, whereas the Field Artillery equipment, headed by the ubiquitous 25-pounder field piece, started and finished the war with the same weapon. At the same time our allocation of light machine guns (Bren guns) was increased to one per gun detachment. Every vehicle had a Lee Enfield No. 4 rifle, the standard British Army rifle, an updated version of the model used in the Great War. Although it was a very reliable firearm, it was but a single shot weapon with a magazine holding only ten rounds. In 1942 it was replaced by the Sten Carbine, a light automatic firearm which had a box magazine that held 32 9mm bullets. This weapon was similar in action to the superior American Tommy gun in that it could be fired from the hip but it was a crude weapon which was sometimes activated when the gun butt was hit on the ground. These carbines, when first supplied to our unit, caused casualties amongst our own troops but there is no doubt when properly handled, it was an effective weapon.

Also among our new weaponry in 1939 was the treacherous Boyes anti-tank rifle, which fired a 505 cartridge. It was a beautifully designed piece of weaponry but the average soldier could not fire it whilst standing up. As we soon discovered, it inflicted more damage on the troops of the British Army than ever it did to the enemy. Apart from decimating the firer, it had very little penetrative power against even the smallest tank. It was replaced in 1942 by the Bazooka.

The fact that we did not have a proper establishment of support vehicles and were reliant on lorries seconded from traders, still bearing their trading names for when they were handed back, did not seem to ring alarm bells in us. We were very optimistic, because all the popular songs on the wireless told us we had nothing to fear and it was 'a piece of cake'. The tolerant attitude of the establishment too, which allowed us to have weekend passes from Kempton Park, led us to believe that the Germans were having second thoughts and had probably learned something about our superior weaponry.

The visits home to Kennington enabled me to keep abreast of the rest of the family's activities. My father was still in hospital on the Isle of Wight, so my mother was fairly busy travelling there and visiting my young brothers and sister evacuated to south Devon. My brother Monty was a bustling kid, hyperactive, who could hold his own but he was no longer under the influence of my father. Phyllis was very responsible and David was very young and suffered from breathing problems. He had become an inveterate reader, which stood him in good stead later when he took his Matriculation exam. Isobel Ivy was working in the Bermondsey labour exchange, and doing fire watching at night whilst waiting for a call-up to the ATS. She was a beautiful girl and had many admirers. Sister Betty, also attractive, was working in the West End and later endured the Blitz with my parents.

After the initial shock of the Declaration of War and mobilisation, there was a lull in proceedings. Chamberlain resigned as prime minister and Winston Churchill took over with his new War Cabinet – it was as if a whistle had been blown for halftime. Calmness prevailed and everyone went about their business in the normal way. Customers in the pub bars discussed the 'Phoney War' as they drank their mild and bitter. The general opinion was that the Germans had nothing to gain by fighting us ...it was a lot of fuss about nothing!

Off to France

Regardless of the future intentions of Mr Hitler, we enjoyed our last weekend pass and prepared to sail for France as part of the BEF with our new guns and towing vehicles. The three-ton Foden, which carried our cookhouse equipment, still informed the world that we were 'W. Brown & Co., Meat Wholesalers, Smithfield Market' and was a constant reminder to us of our origins. Seeing us pass, anyone might have thought that we had picked up the Foden on the way to war as we made our way to Southampton Water, en route for Cherbourg.

It was a beautiful day in early November, and we had a smooth crossing. Upon arrival in Cherbourg, we were billeted with French troops for two days, while our vehicles and guns were unloaded from the ship and cleared from the docks. In the barracks there was a mixture of Foreign Legionnaires, French soldiers in transit and camp staff. All seemed to smell of French tobacco and cognac, and appeared unkempt and grizzled, but mature to our inexperienced eyes.

We left Cherbourg and travelled in convoy with our new guns and swanky Bedford gun towers, along the main road towards the city of Bayeux, occasionally running alongside the River Aure. We gradually adapted to driving on the right-hand side of the road. My new water-cart had been filled up at Cherbourg in case water was required en route and it gave Batchelor, my driver, a chance to get used to the sway of a full vehicle as well as driving on the right. The 200-gallon tank was compartmentalised by baffle plates, which helped to reduce the swish of the water. Later, we found the vehicle more difficult to drive when half full of water, particularly in mid-winter when driving on icy roads. We had some scary moments when on the move around St André, near Lille. We stopped overnight in Amiens totally unaware of our ultimate destination. The advance party had left a day early from Cherbourg and without the guns and heavier vehicles in convoy, they would reach our new billets in one day. We continued the following day passing by Arras – which was an important British Army garrison town – and ultimately reached our destination, the village of Penin.

The central feature of Penin was a war memorial showing pictures of each of the villagers who had been killed in the Great War. The sombre aspect of the village tended to belie its true perspective. This was quickly revealed when we met the chief citizen, Oscar. He was a farrier and also a barber, an *estaminet* owner, the mayor and local comedian. Oscar could fix anything, after a fashion. Being in his company at night listening to his theories, rattled out in broken English and French, was a delight. Penin was primarily a farming village with haycarts lumbering in and out in a very languid manner. They seemed to appear from any one of four roads which met in the centre. Most of us were billeted in stables, but the village managed to house the whole of our battery. Once settled in, we started training, which included learning other skills, such as drivers learning how to fire the anti-tank guns, and gunners being taught to drive.

THE MORRIS QUAD

I try to become a despatch rider

I had been on the guns in my earlier Territorial days and had also passed as a driver so it was thought I would benefit by being taught to ride a motor cycle and become a stand-in despatch rider. Our consignment of motor cycles included Nortons, BSAs and Matchless. My instructor was Tubby Dolan, an ample lad with large blue eyes, a freckled face and a mop of red hair. He was a totally fearless rider who had won all the regimental trials. It was generally accepted that he was the best despatch rider in the regiment – but he was no instructor! He assumed that anyone should be able to climb onto a bike and ride first time. I had been his friend for over three years and he assumed it would be a piece of cake for me. And so he gave the brief instructions: 'Get on Langley, and let's see what you can do. There's the throttle, there's the clutch, you know how to brake and you have the best Norton, so we'll have you riding a motor bike in no time at all!'

I rode out of the village and after a mile I turned the Norton creditably well. As I returned to the outskirts of Penin I accelerated, confident I had become a DR in less than an hour. Suddenly a farm horse, pulling a haycart, emerged from a side road ahead of me. As I veered to the other side of the road, a troop of soldiers doing marching drill came into view. Seeing me in full flight they scattered. I chose what seemed to be my only safe course, but I had forgotten the war memorial. The Norton hit the protective fence around it at speed and the front wheel became enmeshed with a spar. As I hurtled through the air, I saw the faces on the memorial following my progress as I cleared the obstacle and landed in a heap on a patch of grass. Apart from grazes to my shins, I was relatively unhurt but the Norton was extensively damaged. Dolan gazed down at me wide eyed and said in a shocked tone, 'What have you done, Langley? Now look at my bike!' I know I could easily have conquered the motor cycle, but the establishment were not taking any more chances.

It was apparent that our stay at Penin was to be short-lived, because the winter in the Nord area was expected to be severe and we required warmer accommodation. In any event, strategically we needed to be nearer the Belgian Border, preparing gun-pits in a defensive position on the Franco-Belgian frontier line. This defensive line would complement the Maginot Line, but this strategy would ultimately prove to be France's Achilles' heel when the German attacks started. The night before we left Penin, the local *estaminets* were overflowing with squaddies who were on double orders of eggs and chips with French bread. Any move towards the obvious front caused trepidation and the most curative measure, it seemed, was a feast of French *frites* washed down with the local brew.

On to Lille

We moved into accommodation on the outskirts of Lille. Our battery – 206, had to toss with 207 for the choice between a brick kiln and an empty cinema. We lost the toss and got the brick kiln, where we stayed the first part of the winter. The accommodation was so cold that very few of us ventured outside to use the toilet at night and as a consequence one corner of the kiln stank. Later in our service career, we adapted and were better able to pace ourselves so avoiding these unpleasant moments. But the dust and cold of this accommodation resulted in a long sick parade. The 207 battery were very happy in their cinema and refused any idea of a swap.

Our purgatory was relieved when we were moved from Lille to the Chateau La Cliquena in the St Andrea area which was spacious and relatively luxurious. The chateau was surrounded by a moat and screened by large elm trees. It was fairly remote so it required constant policing – frequent guard duties and regular patrols to protect our weaponry from inquisitive eyes. At the time, there were many informers in the area, which was close to Belgium and not far from the Rhineland. We also provided special guards for the Lille power station. This was regarded as a vulnerable target for Fifth Column Nazis and if sabotaged, it could cause disarray among the defensive forces. Our officers made surprise visits at night to test the vigilance of the guards. Our Captain, a Dutchman named Bunge, was particularly keen and used various ploys to catch out the sentries. The guards had to challenge but they were not permitted to fire, since a vigilant guard had nearly shot an officer who was prowling around.

The chateau had been unoccupied for months before we took it over, and was in dire need of repair. The water pipes were frozen up in mid-winter, so my water cart had to be refilled every day to supply the needs of the battery. These water duties, together with football training and playing in matches against French and British Army teams, meant that I did very few guard duties, which made me extra zealous when I did. And so one night I was posted at the end of the vehicle park on the midnight duty. It was a moonlit night and I had positioned myself in the shadow of a tree listening to a night owl, when I saw a figure move between the vehicles in the gun park. I waited for a long while wondering whether it was my imagination, until I heard a rustle at the back of one of the guns. I crept up behind the gun as the breech cover was being removed, and saw a figure fiddling with the breech of the gun. I raised my rifle and using the rifle butt hit the marauder in the back, at the same time yelling 'Halt! Who goes there?' as a warning to the guard commander, who came running out from the guardroom with one or two of the guard. My torch revealed a prostrate Bunge lying on the ground, gasping for breath. He was helped to the guardroom by the sergeant of the guard, but managed to say, 'Congratulate your sentry on his vigilance'.

Considering he was limping around for a week or more, he was quite amiable on the few occasions I saw him. I was sad to learn later in May that he was missing in the Battle of the Yypres Commines canal.

We join the Fifth Division

The 52nd Anti-Tank Regiment, which comprised four batteries, 205, 206, 207 and 208 and a headquarters, was the senior Territorial anti-tank regiment in the British Army because this was a relatively new branch of the Royal Artillery. In consequence we were allocated to a regular division – the Fifth British Infantry (Yorkshire) division. This division's nucleus was nine regular army infantry regiments and one regular army artillery regiment. This strong core of experience was complemented by senior frontline territorial formations of Royal Artillery, Royal Engineers, Royal Signals, a Heavy Machine Gun regiment (the 7th Cheshires) and the various support services which form part of an infantry division. In spite of everything, the 'phoney war' period had enabled us to blend into a respectable fighting division.

At an early stage the Fifth division was identified as a War Office Reserve division. This resulted in it ultimately having the sobriquet 'Cook's Tours' because in the following six years it became the most travelled division in the British Army – and probably the allied forces. It made its presence felt in 26 different countries and the 'Y' insignia became famous on many battle fronts. The division also had four pipe bands, three Scottish and one Irish. They were in great demand and were preferred as entertainment to both ENSA and the Army concert parties. The Yanks loved the bagpipes and asked for the 'Limey guys in skirts'. They obliged by playing even in the division's action areas such as Anzio and later in Rome and helped to keep up the morale of the active units.

The division's task in the early months of 1940 was to take over the Halluin Sector from the 51st French Division, to improve defences and train to defend this part of the line in the event of a German attack. During the appalling weather conditions of the 1939–40 winter, first wet and muddy and then cold and hard, the division worked strenuously to improve their positions. Field and anti-tank guns, machine guns and their support weapons were cunningly concealed and disguised as houses, haystacks and chicken sheds. This preparation involved the laying of much cable and constantly baling out water from the prepared gun-pits. It was not possible to reconnoitre neutral Belgium, an area that lay between the divisional front and any German attack through the Low Countries and so the prepared Divisional line was the best possible defensive line.

We sample local life

It was not all gloom, however. There was a lighter side, and along with football matches, ENSA was showing the *Two Lesleys* with their troupe in Arras. The local *estaminet* was a reasonable substitute for a pub, with the added bonus of better food. The old sweats in the battery wandered down the back streets of Lille into the brothel area and on one occasion they induced some of us younger TA boys to go with them. This outing was headed by a seasoned bombardier named Stanton – who had served many years in India – and ended in a brothel where the drinks were appallingly dear and were served by gyrating, lightly dressed tarts. One of their particular stunts was to pick the coins up from the edge of the table with their private parts. Stanton meanwhile heated a coin with his lighter and placed it on the edge of the table and as the prancing lady came to collect her money she let out a blood-curdling scream. We prepared ourselves for trouble, as a number of powerfully built Frenchmen made their way towards our table. Stanton yelled, 'Let's go, boys!' and we were bundled out into the street, slightly bruised. Stanton said, 'Put it down to experience lads – if you'd stayed in that dive, you'd have got pox, food poisoning or worse!'

In the years ahead, Stanton emerged as a father figure whose advice helped some of the more naive squaddies to avoid trouble when the battery was located in squalid places. Unfortunately he did not see the war through and died of dysentery at Ranchi in India.

The Fifth Division seemed to have good raw material in its Regular and Territorial units, but it was woefully short of training. New equipment had only reached some of the units in January 1940. It was obvious that the only way the Fifth Division could assimilate the new units into the infantry structure and become a dependable fighting force was with intensive training and combined exercises. Although each unit could be efficient in its own role, the great need was to blend with other branches of the division who were providing other skills. Moreover, the divisional staff officers, who had no experience of planning battles within the framework of a modern army, needed to hone their strategic skills and this made intensive training involving all branches of the division obligatory.

The opportunity was also taken to train the15th Brigade with part of a French Division. This Brigade managed to get this kind of intensive training during the snow period of January and February 1940. They controlled a small sector some 30 miles north-east of Metz on the Saar front. They carried out patrolling duties in front of the Maginot line and apart from the odd skirmish with German troops which resulted in casualties on both sides, it did not become a sustained battle, but it was good experience for the junior leaders. Apart from this short association with the French Army, there were no combined exercises with our allies, for at this stage the BEF was still forming and each division had to strive on its own to attain a degree of excellence for the battles ahead.

The French military thinking was focused on the defence of their homeland. In this regard, the Maginot Line was the pivot which governed military strategy. Every shop or café sold Maginot Line metal lapel badges. The impregnability of this defensive line was so ingrained in the public mind that it gave the average Frenchman a sense of optimism. He could happily drink his cognac thinking that the Germans would have to struggle to break down the French defences.

The British had no real contact with the Belgian Army, who stayed in their own country and were still unsure which side they would be on, for the devastation of parts of their country in the Great War still haunted them. And so the allied armies in 1940 were all thinking different thoughts, doing different things and remaining relatively remote from each other. This lack of unity would manifest itself in the struggle ahead.

Home leave

Meanwhile, in the early months of 1940 we were granted leave in the UK. I was lucky in getting a week's leave in March. I arrived back in Kennington and changed into my civvies but with the Maginot Line badge in my lapel, because I too believed this impregnable line would save the British Army if things got rough. This feeling enabled me to assure my friends at White Drummond and colleagues at Stephenson, Harwood and Tatham that there was nothing to worry about, because the French were well prepared and the British Army was in good fettle. My mother, who was now used to her eldest son being away, assured me that my employers were sending her my adjusted salary allowance every week.

HOME LEAVE, 1940,
COMPLETE WITH
MAGINOT LINE BADGE

My aunts and uncles in London decided to have a party to welcome me home. It would be a typical south London knees-up, but this time it would be a get-together in a Stockwell pub, where my aunt Fran thumped the piano every Friday night, after she had shut her florist's shop at the side of the Oval underground station. I took along two of my army friends and we were about a quarter of a mile away walking down the Stockwell Road when one of my friends said, 'Christ! Listen to that noise!' The sound reassured me that my family was in fine form. 'That's my Aunt Fran,' I said proudly. We entered the pub and there she was, a large and cheerful lady with greying red hair, hitting the piano keys so hard it caused dust to rise from under an ill-fitted carpet. My mates and I were pampered and fussed all evening.

I returned to the Army with a portable, battery-operated wireless set, bought by my mother on the 'never-never' and a pack of marked playing cards, presented to me by one of my aunt's dubious friends, who said in a grating voice, 'Maury, yer don't want to come aht of the Army broke, boy – do yer?'. The wireless was a great success, because we had few links with home, and any newspapers sent arrived a week late. Some time later, the wireless was left buried in the sand dunes of the La Panne beaches.

The phoney war is over

The Fifth Division was placed on alert in the early days of April to go to Finland to support the Finnish Army against the Russians. Part of the Division was also earmarked to be sent to Norway in support of 148 Brigade of the 49th (TA Division) who were already in action following the invasion of Norway by the German Army. In response to the growing crisis, the 15th Brigade was withdrawn at short notice from the Belgian front and sent to Norway via Scotland. The rest of the Division, who were on the move to the French coast, were hastily returned to the Senne River line south of Brussels, and it became evident that the phoney war was at an end. The German invasion of the Low Countries and France was imminent.

A continuous supply of water became vital to fill water bottles and containers and supply the cookhouse, particularly as a strong rumour abounded that German collaborators had poisoned water wells. This meant that water could only be obtained from either established Royal Army Service Corps water points, or drawn from lakes or rivers. Because the Fifth Division was constantly on the move, Batchelor and myself were away from our unit searching for suitable lakes to keep the battery well supplied. Drawing from lakes and rivers was our main source, so the Horrocks test was used frequently. Using my specialist skills, together with my new freelance role of finding water, was considered to be responsibility enough for me to be promoted to Lance Bombardier. The battery HQ only saw us when we were delivering the goods in the water cart.

Measures to conserve water now became obligatory. Living on the move became the norm, for never again would we return to the Chateau La Cliquena, or any other form of fixed accommodation in France. Operational conditions would apply from mid-April until the end of May, when the remnants of our division with its two brigades would be evacuated from the Continent.

To start with, a move to the Senne River Line by the 5th Division was made to protect the right rear flank of the BEF. The Division moved forward towards Belgium from as far back as the Amiens area. In order to get to their front line, our infantry did much of the mileage by marching through packed roads of refugees desperate to escape from Belgium.

On the march

Our infantry marched and our transport moved 25 miles to Barneville on 11th May, 12 miles to Ligny-sur-Cache on 12th May and a further 13 miles to Hernicourt on 15th May, eventually arriving in the Hal area on 16th May. The battalions had an exhausting final move against an overwhelming flood-tide of homeless Belgian refugees. These pitiable people, laden with their household goods on carts, pressed on westwards, persistently driven off the roads into the ditches by machine-gun attacks of the Luftwaffe or by the harassed drivers of the divisional vehicles. All roads were in the same state of chaos as people fleeing from Brussels joined those already on the move from Louvain and the villages in between. The move of the division to the Senne line was completed just in time. The position that the division finally took up was quite near the old battlefield of Waterloo. The 13th Infantry Brigade finally dug in around Hal and the 17th Infantry Brigade north of that area. The only direct contact with Germans at this stage was with the Luftwaffe, who constantly attacked the front and rear echelons with Stukas which caused casualties by dive bombing and machine-gunning – but they suffered losses too from Bren gun fire and the heavier machine-guns of the Cheshire regiment. Unfortunately, the infantry divisions did not have the rapid-firing Bofors gun, the Royal Artillery light anti-aircraft weapon. Later in the war, the division was much better protected from air attack when the 18th LAA Regiment RA joined the division. They proved very successful in inflicting casualties on the Luftwaffe and Italian air force in the invasions of Sicily and

Italy. The chances of bringing an aircraft down in 1940 with a machine gun were slim.

Under attack

My battery HQ was in and around a farmyard behind the 17th brigade front line, but receiving a lot of attention from Stukas, possibly because of the smoke rising from the battery cookhouse. In the climate of things, it was quite surprising therefore to see a group of people walking calmly along in the fields near the farmhouse and pausing as they picked things up from the ground while everyone else was diving for cover. The battery captain handed me his binoculars and asked me to climb the barnyard ladder and try to identify them. According to him, they were wearing a strange uniform. I perched myself on a corner of the roof and examined this slow moving group. I could hardly believe my eyes and reported, 'You are not going to believe this, sir... they're picking flowers!'

I was in the process of climbing down when a Stuka dived and dropped a bomb at the side of the farmhouse. I was thrown into the air and landed in a hayrick. My left leg became trapped as my body turned and there was quite a distinctive cracking sound from my knee and a dull throbbing pain. As I regained my feet and clambered gingerly down from the hayrick, the strange group came abreast of the farmhouse completely unscathed, holding bunches of flowers. It transpired that they had been inmates at the local lunatic asylum, which had been badly damaged.

After the more serious casualties around the farmhouse had been seen to by the medical orderly, he wrapped my rapidly swelling knee with a pressure bandage. 'That's going to ache like hell, Langley!' he said cheerfully, as he handed me a handful of aspirin tablets from a large bottle.

On 16th May, General Billotte, commanding the Northern Group of Armies, withdrew the Dyle divisions behind the British divisions manning the Senne Line. The first serious attack on the divisional front was easily withheld, partly due to accurate shooting by the division's artillery. A number of German cyclists were captured and some were killed. They were no doubt being used for reconnaissance purposes. In the meantime the French Army on the Southern front, under great pressure from the German Panzers, were forced back and in consequence the BEF had to withdraw to conform with the battle situation.

Tactical withdrawal

The Division was placed into reserve and moved to Seclin. This involved a lot of marching by the infantry to achieve a sound tactical withdrawal. A tricky operation, especially when under constant air attack, it was hindered by panic- stricken refugees, and with rumours of enemy parachute attacks. The final move in the tactical withdrawal was made by the Cameronians in 13 Brigade whose last company had to double for two miles and just managed to get over the bridge at Grammont before it was blown.

On 18th May, General Gort realised enough of the situation in the south to worry about the gap between the Allied Forces which was widening due to the German thrust to the French coast. Unless that gap could be closed quickly, the BEF would be left with but two alternatives: either move back to the Somme, or evacuate from the Channel Ports. The former course was becoming more remote hourly, for ten German divisions were making good headway in the space between the Allies just south of Arras. It was agreed in a meeting with the British Chief of the General Staff that the only option was to counter-attack towards Amiens and to persuade the French to attack from the south at the same time.

The 5th British Division commander Major-General Franklin's orders from Gort were to support the garrisons in Arras by occupying the line of the River Scarpe to the east of Arras and establish contact with the French by patrols and create road blocks to the south – in an effort to rupture the long lines of communication of the Germans. These orders were subsequently changed by orders from the British Cabinet which entailed the whole of the available army reserve being used to make a localised counter-attack to the south of Arras, cutting the German line of communication – which by this time had stretched to the coast by Abbeville.

This British force, code-named 'Frankforce' after the commanding general and consisting of the whole of the BEF reserve that was available, comprised the 5th Division (two brigades) the 50th Division (two brigades, mainly Durham Light Infantry battalions) and the First Army Tank Brigade. The Tank Brigade contained 73 Matilda tanks, but only 16 MkII were armed with two-pounder anti-tank guns. The bulk had only heavy machine guns.

Meanwhile, the garrison at Arras had been given an injection of other available units and came under the orders of the local commander, General Petrie, and were coded 'Petrieforce'. By now Arras was holding out against several German armoured divisions and should it capitulate, it would spell disaster for the BEF for it was the key communication centre with the French Army in the south.

Major-General Franklin had no specific orders as to how to carry out his role, but liaison with the French in the south would be a significant factor in making the counter-attack a success. He met Weygand once, shook him by the hand and that was as far as the planning went because there was a serious language difficulty. There was no time to establish a proper plan, for the Wehrmacht was upon them.

Franklin goes it alone

Unfortunately, the promised French assistance was withdrawn and moved to other areas, so Franklin had to go it alone. He consolidated his reserves in and around Vimy, and set up a line along the Scarpe to the east of Arras, placing one of his brigades in Arras, to strengthen the garrison's defences. He launched his attack around Arras with 151 Infantry Brigade heading towards the Cojeul river. This was followed by 13 Infantry Brigade crossing the Scarpe and moving west to join up with 151 Infantry Brigade to the south of Arras. The two brigades met a large concentration of the enemy in each of their areas and were unable to continue the joint advance south. Nevertheless, with the help of the divisional artillery, they inflicted many casualties on the enemy and prisoners were taken.

The tanks, led by Major-General Martel, went round the west of Arras in two mobile columns with the object of reaching the Cojeul River by nightfall. The right-hand column ran into opposition almost at once with Rommel's 7th Panzer in the village of Duissans. This village was taken after a stiff fight and two companies of infantry were detached to hold it. The rest of the column pushed on to capture Warlus and Berneville, advancing as far as the Arras-Doullens road. Here the infantry were pinned down by heavy mortar and machine-gun fire. The Luftwaffe's Stukas took a hand bombing the British positions unopposed. There was no Allied air cover.

Martel's tanks continued their advance and captured the village of Wailly. In the process they ran full tilt into the SS Totenkopf Motorised Infantry Division, which had just arrived at the front. The sudden appearance of the British tanks sowed panic among the German troops, who suffered heavy losses in the ensuing confusion. Soon afterwards, the British tanks were stopped by a battery of German 88mm guns, firing over open sights. This forced the Matildas to withdraw, leaving several of their number in flames. The left-hand column meanwhile enjoyed even better fortune, its armour virtually wiping out a motorised column at Dainville; the supporting infantry rounded up over 400 prisoners – the largest bag of enemy troops in a single engagement since the campaign began. The column pushed on rapidly and some of its advanced units actually reached the Cojeul, but the main body of the armour – the tanks of the 4th Royal Tank Regiment – became involved in a fierce fight with Rommel's forces and, without supporting infantry, had to relinquish the ground they had won.

By the end of the afternoon it was clear that the forces committed to the British counter-attack were in no position to hold the ground that had been gained. Unfortunately, neither the BEF nor the French were in a position to seriously breach the German Panzer's overlong lines of communication. However, Von Runstedt was so alarmed that he ordered a temporary halt to his advance, believing he was faced by five British infantry divisions. He redirected the movement of Von Kleist's armoured group, comprising the 6th and 8th Panzer, who were en route for Calais and made them swing back towards Arras. He later stated that this British counter-stroke on 21st May was the most serious threat to his advance towards the Channel – posing a danger that his Panzers would be cut off before the infantry divisions could come up to support them.

Major-General Franklin at that time had no way of knowing the psychological shock that Frankforce's relatively puny counter-attack had inflicted on the enemy. Both he and Gort thought it had been a failure, so he cancelled the offensive and decided to inflict the longest possible delay on the Germans, by holding onto the line of the Scarpe and the high ground north-west of Arras: Vimy Ridge.

At the time of this battle, in which my battery was involved, I was searching for water, which had become a serious need. I was heading towards the river Cojeul amid much turmoil close at hand. Batchelor became very alarmed and kept reminding me that he had a wife and kids at home. A retreating despatch rider stopped near our vehicle and told us that the Germans were building a bridge across the river and that their advance units were less than a mile away. And so we turned back and found a rather muddy lake along the way. In desperation I threw my floats in and managed to obtain nearly one hundred gallons of water after two hours pumping into the turgid morass. It had one redeeming feature: it was full of carp, so it ought to be safe to drink.

The increased racket of nearby fighting around us and the presence of Stukas machine-gunning the road behind us, made it clear that it was a good time to leave with partially filled tanks rather than not return at all. And so, with the filters of the water cart badly clogged, we detached the pump, draped the hoses across the tank and drove hastily away, hoping our paraphernalia would not fall off.

Vimy Ridge

I eventually found our battery headquarters, which had moved again and was near the Canadian War memorial on Vimy Ridge. In between attacks by Stukas I managed to sterilise my consignment of water, although my testing beakers were constantly blown over by blasts and I glimpsed the awful sight of a driver's head leaving a passing vehicle and rolling towards my vehicle after a diving Stuka had made its kill. Batchelor was by now suffering from shell shock and developed a hideous attack of the shakes. From then on I had to drive in spite of my throbbing left knee, which ached every time I pressed my foot down on the clutch. The amount of powder needed to adequately sterilise my latest consignment was immense but my reward came the following day, when one of the squaddies announced, 'The 'burgoo' was smashing!'

The next two days on Vimy Ridge were hectic, it being the front line for everyone. The siege of this high ground meant that all supporting troops with weaponry were firing at diving Stukas while the anti-tank guns, field artillery and infantry were holding German armoured and infantry divisions at bay. Looking down from the Ridge, the movement of German Panzers below us indicated we were probably cut off. Aircraft recognition was easy – everything in the sky was German – but tank recognition was more difficult, and so it was no surprise when a troop of 207 battery guns took on a squadron of French tanks, believing them to be Panzers. The puny two-pounders bounced off the armour and all four British guns were wiped out by our allies, with many casualties.

We in HQ took up positions in and around B echelon, firing at Stukas with rifles and Bren guns. There was an occasional lucky shot which received a ragged cheer as a plane hit the ground, but our casualties were fairly high even though we were dug in, for Vimy Ridge was very exposed. My friend George Cordery was crossing the field with one of our few Bren guns when he fell to the ground, obviously hurt. I dashed across to him and got to the ground with him as the machine-gun bullets from a passing Stuka zipped around us. Eventually I managed to help him to a ditch at the side of the field. Later it seemed that the large bruise on his back was from a stone which had probably catapulted from a nearby bomb explosion. He hobbled around for a few days and managed to keep out of trouble.

The area around Arras and Vimy Ridge were holding out against an onslaught by both German Panzer and infantry divisions. The divisional front was sorely pressed and being forced back behind the Canal line. The gallant defence by Frankforce and Petrieforce had gained valuable hours for the BEF. General Gort realised that he had no option but to withdraw Frankforce from the Arras Salient to ensure that he did not lose his Reserve Division. The delaying tactics were by now less important than the need to defend the vulnerable Ypres Commines canal, which was about to be assaulted by the German Sixth Army.

Retreat from Arras

The night of the 23rd to 24th May saw one of the miracles of the campaign as the remainder of the 5th and 50th Divisions made an orderly withdrawal from the Arras Salient along the one road through Henin Lietard, which was clear of German forces but cluttered with refugees and partly blocked by wrecked vehicles blasted by the Luftwaffe. This phantom column wound its way through these obstacles, using just sidelights but aided at various junctions by the Divisional Military Police, using torches and hurricane lamps.

I was driving because Batchelor was still suffering from shell shock. My experience was limited, so the orders to drive as close to the vehicle in front severely tested my night-driving ability. During the course of the night we lost the whole of 'F' troop who were at the rear. Indeed, 'lost' was the word: we did not see those friends in that troop who survived the war until a month after VE day, when they were released from Prisoner of War camps.

The defence of the Ypres Commines canal had become more vital following the collapse of the Belgian Army in this area. There was very little defence against the oncoming frontline units of the German Sixth Army – in fact only 143 Brigade of 48th Division was available and they would come under command of the 5th Division, still referred to as 'Frankforce'. Our battery moved as part of 17th Brigade and took up positions with the infantry on the forward slopes of the canal bank where we were in full view of the advancing German Sixth Army and vulnerable to shell and mortar fire. The canal itself was of no real use as an anti-tank obstacle, being completely dry; it had long been disused and contained only mud and weeds.

The advancing enemy also had excellent cover by way of a raised railway line embankment on the opposite side of the canal. Nevertheless the canal formed the only barrier in an otherwise featureless countryside, and Franklin had to make the best of it. The breaching of this canal line would close off the main withdrawal route to the Channel ports which were still available to the BEF. The battle that ensued on the 27th and 28th May fought by the remnants of Frankforce with other support units of infantry and artillery that General Brooke of Second Corps had obtained and placed under the leadership of Major-General Franklin. He had the advantage of being familiar with the area, having fought over the same ground as a young officer in 1916. The 13th and 17th Brigades took up positions in the vulnerable centre of the canal just as the advance units of the German Sixth Army opened fire with heavy mortars. A few hours later the two brigades of 50th Division, who had been seriously hampered by refugees, took up positions on either side of the 5th Division. The battle that raged over the next two days rates very highly in the annals of both the 5th and 50th divisions and is part of British military history, most notably recounted in *Dunkirk* by Robert Jackson.

The Second Corps Commander, Lt-General Brooke (Lord Allenbrooke) stated later in sending his congratulations and thanks to the 5th Division, 'It is my opinion that it was entirely due to our action that the whole Corps was able to effect a withdrawal and that unless we had held the Ypres-Commines canal so successfully, the safety of the whole BEF might have been put in serious danger. I am confident that this fact will be confirmed by history.'

It is also worth recording that the brigade commanders of the 13th and 17th Brigades in the Division were Brigadiers Dempsey and Stopford, who later in the war were commanding British Armies in Europe and Burma respectively. The 5th Division was indeed fortunate in having three outstanding commanders at the helm. In this battle, the six infantry battalions in the 13th and 17th Brigades of 5th Division were practically annihilated, totalling less than two battalions on the withdrawal to the Dunkirk perimeter. The 7th Cheshires (machine-gun regiment) and the 52 Anti-Tank Regiment were severely mauled. In my battery, which was supporting 17th Brigade, all the officers but one were killed, including our CO. Our two remaining troops 'D' and 'E' lost seven of their eight two-pounder anti-tank guns, some destroyed by gun crews before they were overrun by the enemy. In a strategic withdrawal from the Ypres Commines canal area, our battery left with one anti-tank gun, our small arms weaponry, the HQ transport including the water cart, and about 30 men. Although ultimately just over 50 got back to the UK, it was less than half the original battery, a tragic loss of men, and of friends.

We make it to the coast

On the route back to the Dunkirk beach-head my water cart was carrying about 100 gallons of water and some twenty soldiers draped over various parts of the tank. We stopped occasionally to fill up the water-bottles of troops walking towards the beach-head and once to relieve an overturned NAAFI van of some of its burden of whisky, brandy and gin. I stopped again near a Belgian bakery to persuade the shop manager to part with some of his bread for francs and one or two bottles of spirits. The fact that I carried a rifle may have helped. At the time the British troops felt that the rapid collapse of the Belgian Army was responsible for their predicament and we were peeved seeing them riding home on their bicycles without their weaponry. The Belgians, too, were antagonistic, knowing the British were about to leave the Continent. On the night of 29th May, our small convoy drove into Houtham and were halted by Military Police who informed us that all trucks and equipment were to be destroyed. The one two-pounder anti-tank gun we had with us was posted opposite a bridge that was being left open for troops involved in rearguard action on the line of the river Yser. The water cart still had some water, and was left intact for troops to top up their water bottles. We parted with some of our spirits to the military police. The other vehicles in our small convoy were blown up.

We believed our two-pounder could stall any Panzers approaching the bridge. The following morning we removed the breech cover only to discover the firing mechanism had been removed. This was probably done by one of the gun crew as a precaution when it was taken out of action. A search of the towing vehicle revealed nothing. The fact that we had been manning a useless gun all night shocked us, but it was just part of the turmoil of the withdrawal.

The water cart, which had served us well, was eventually blown up after we had topped up our water-bottles. We removed the rifle and spade to take with us. By then, the whole area was in chaos and smelling strongly of cordite. A number of French cavalry horses were running loose, obviously terrified by the noise and the low-flying German planes headed for the beaches. The final walk to the beaches in the La Panne area of the Dunkirk Perimeter set my knee throbbing. With the rest of my group I settled down around a small hillock in the sands and started to dig in. The wireless set was giving us the latest news from England and was spelling out details of the evacuation. This commentary drew the attention of a smartly dressed Military Landing Officer (MLO), one of many involved in the evacuation. 'Bombardier, I want you and your men to guard some very important people', he announced, adding 'I will come back and collect them later!'

So it was that for about three hours I and 'my men', who had probably tagged along because we had some food and drink and the wireless set, found ourselves guarding part of the Dutch Cabinet who were being evacuated to England. It was obvious that they were not keen to communicate, so we concentrated on their defence and fired at anything that moved in the sky, notably diving Stukas that had made life a misery in the previous three weeks.

The MLO returned and took our guests away to a rowing boat in a special landing area – presumably for VIPs. He mentioned we would be better off if we moved nearer Dunkirk ports. Most of the boats would be leaving from there on what had suddenly become a rapidly contracting beach-head. Near at hand, naval rowing boats were coming to our beach, to ferry the very seriously wounded to a British minesweeper lying at anchor about a mile from the La Panne section of the beachhead. Its ack-ack gun had joined in the general hubbub as it blasted away at the various Luftwaffe planes. There were occasional cheers from the squaddies as bits of the marauders hit the sea. There was also the occasional dogfight when Hurricanes and Spitfires became prominent for the first time in our campaign. It was tragic to see one or two smaller English craft manned by civilians being sunk.

Into the sea

A large boat from a minesweeper came ashore near us to collect the stretcher cases. They filled the boat and we could see that boats from other beaches were headed out towards this minesweeper, the *Gossamer*. One of the sailors said this was the last boatload from the La Panne beaches, because the Germans were getting quite close and so the next trip would be nearer Dunkirk. Despite a throbbing knee, I was confident I could swim the distance. I stripped to my singlet and underpants and wearing one adornment – my identification tag – I prepared to step into the sea. The others in my group started to walk towards the Dunkirk area, except Hughie Robertson, who was undecided. I buried my wireless set and other clothing and handed my rifle to one of the unarmed squaddies going towards Dunkirk. I slid into the water and Hughie Robertson suddenly made up his mind and stripped down to join me.

The sailors raised no objections but said they wanted us behind their boat. The water was quite warm and I felt confident I could make it. About halfway there, Hughie Robertson got into difficulties. I helped him to the back of the boat, which had stopped when they saw he was in trouble. A sailor grabbed hold of him and held him to the side of the boat which then moved off smartly towards the *Gossamer*. I followed as best I could, a rating threw a net over the side, I grabbed it and was fished out of the sea. On clambering aboard, I was wrapped in a blanket and taken to a drying room. Soon the rating came back, with a hot cup of cocoa and a pair of thick Navy socks. 'There you are, matey, that should keep you going!' I remember him saying.

The ship's wireless was tuned in to a German station, and Lord Haw-Haw was spelling out the British ships that had been sunk that morning ...which included the *Gossamer*. I was looking at *Gossamer* painted on the ship's lifebelt and asked, 'Any other *Gossamers* in the Navy, mate?' 'No,' the rating responded, adding 'That's the third time we've been sunk this week!'

I felt very content as I leaned back with the boat's engines throbbing into my back as she started to move. In later years I was sad to learn the *Gossamer* had been sunk doing escort duties for a convoy carrying supplies to Russia. Later in the war, I was asked to provide a statement confirming Hughie Robertson's claim that he had nearly drowned leaving Dunkirk. It helped to get him a war pension when he was invalided from the Army suffering from stomach ulcers – a very serious condition at that time. Hughie was taken to hospital when the *Gossamer* docked at Dover and I never saw him again.

Back on dry land

I was able to walk down the gangplank in vest, underpants and Navy socks as the *Gossamer* retrieved the blanket as it was returning to Dunkirk to continue the rescue operations until 3rd June. I was given an army shirt, trousers and gym shoes on the dock and then put on a train bound for a destination that could kit out a soldier who had landed half-dressed. I found a corner seat and fell asleep.

The train stopped at Reigate station, where I was woken by a knocking on the window. A friendly female voice was saying, 'Young man! Young man! Would you like a cup of tea?' It was a WVS lady holding a steaming cup of tea which she handed to me, adding, 'Would you like to send a postcard to your mother, telling her you have arrived home safely?' I nodded dumbly, overwhelmed by her kindness, as smilingly she handed me a postcard and a pencil. Looking back, I think my great love affair with British women started at that moment!

My mother died in 1982 and the postcard was among her possessions. In faint writing it reads, 'Dear Mum, Have arrived home safely in England. Love, Maurice'. The card is date stamped 31st May 1940, Reigate.

The train left Reigate and eventually we all disembarked at Salisbury. The Military Police and other army officials loaded us onto three-tonners, which took us to an army camp in Winterbourne Gunner. There we were greeted not as returning heroes but 'Bleedin' losers!'

CHAPTER 5

―○―

DEFENDING THE HOME FRONT

In the first week in June 1940, the bulk of the troops who had returned to the UK from Dunkirk, about 335,000 including French troops, were being shuffled to various parts of the country, preparatory to taking defensive roles against a probable invasion by the Germans. Britain was on its own, with the Achilles heel of Eire close at hand. The Channel Islands were also vulnerable to attack and this occurred three weeks later on 30th June. British troops were still engaged in battle at Calais and Boulogne but it was only a matter of time before all the remaining British Forces there – which included the 51st Highland Division – would become prisoners of war and France would call for a ceasefire with Germany.

After a short rest, the remnants of the various BEF divisions were allocated to different parts of the UK to add experience to the home-based troops. So the few 5th Division squaddies at Winterbourne Gunner were delighted to be posted to the assembly point of the Division in Scotland to strengthen the defences and protect the seaboard of the north-east Scottish coast.

It was not only manpower that was needed, but weaponry too. In the case of 5th Division, all heavy offensive equipment such as support artillery, heavy machine guns and mortars, Bren carriers of the 13th and 17th Infantry Brigades, together with all the division's support vehicles, had been destroyed before leaving Dunkirk. This lack of arms applied to all divisions evacuated from France.

The division's 15th Infantry Brigade – the Yorkshire Brigade – had been despatched in haste from France to Norway in April, in time to put in a classical withdrawal from Kwam to Andaalsnes, which enabled trapped British troops of the 49th Infantry Division – a territorial unit – to be saved by the Royal Navy. This battle was the first time in World War II that British Army regular troops fought the German Army. History records that this Brigade more than held their own against the Herman Goering Regiment, despite overwhelming German superiority in the air. The 15th Brigade, in this prolonged battle lost 32 officers and 552 other ranks. Despite these losses, the 15th were in better shape than their sister brigades the 13th and 17th, who had each lost over two thirds of their front-line infantry strength and also heavy casualties in the anti-tank regiment and the heavy machine-gun battalion.

Troops returning from Dunkirk and resting at most other locations were reluctant to leave their temporary watering holes, having spent a week living it up in luxurious surroundings such as holiday camps, where they were treated like heroes. We at Winterbourne Gunner had been bullied by a sod of a sergeant-major from the time we had been unlucky enough to arrive at this camp. His greeting to us on arrival was, 'You're not effing 'eroes ere, you're effing' losers!', as he relieved some of the infantry of weaponry and ammunition. It was strictly army routine at Winterbourne Gunner, each of us was identified by Army number and Division and held in divisional lots until we were moved to our part of Britain, which in our case was listed as Aberdeenshire. After a week at this base camp, we all left with the fervent hope that this particular SM would be posted away from a haven of peacetime spit and polish, to an active unit, for a taste of real soldiering. The fact that the British Press had welcomed 'Our returning heroes' was as much an expression of relief that over 300, 000 troops had returned to help defend the island against an imminent invasion.

I eventually found my battery under canvas in an area called Invermay Wood, near Turriff. I was greeted with, 'Where did you get to, Langley? Someone said you might have drowned...' I realised then, that because I was the only one from my unit at Winterbourne Gunner, they would not know what had happened to me or Hughie Robertson. This was the situation throughout the UK, with troops struggling back to their units in ones and twos – and of course a number who took the opportunity to desert or take prolonged leave until they felt able to rejoin their unit or be posted elsewhere.

I was shocked that only about fifty of us had returned and only one officer, Berry – but as expected, none of 'F' troop. My leg had been giving me pain since I climbed aboard the *Gossamer* but in the climate of things, it was of little consequence. The fact that no more than 50 out of 140 had made it to the camp, that was the real blow ... for some friendly faces were missing. However, two members of 'E' troop had been decorated for bravery: Troop Sergeant Hewitt with a DCM and Gerry Young with an MM.

The first arrivals at the camp were from depots of the Second Militia draft which showed that the planners had started to move reinforcements urgently to returning BEF frontline units on the basis of a 25 per cent casualty rate. It soon became obvious that some were missing for no apparent reason and there were many more reported shell shock cases than expected. However, whatever the numbers, invasion was regarded as imminent and already there had been one or two false alarms.

It was arranged for me to have my leg checked out at a local Army Field Ambulance unit. However, before this examination took place, my knee collapsed whilst doing early morning PT and it was serious enough for me to be taken by ambulance to Aberdeen Royal Infirmary. I was admitted for what turned out to be a fortnight's rest and physiotherapy to help ease the badly ruptured ligaments of my left knee. Suddenly, being a Dunkirk Veteran at the age of 21 seemed a passport to heaven. The injury, all in the cause of King and country, was something to be treasured, until I was returned to my unit where the glory would pass and others would be hobbling in. The medical staff of the Infirmary decided I deserved something better and for the time being I was placed in Crathes Castle, Deeside, a newly opened convalescent home for the forces. I arrived there under the pseudonym 'The soldier from Dunkirk' and for the next two months I received royal treatment.

Two sappers from the 9th Scottish Infantry Division – a home-based outfit – suffering from ingrowing toenails were the only incumbents when I arrived. Their wants were brushed aside as the matron, sister and three nurses fussed around me; even Sir James Burnett of Leys, the Laird and Colonel in Chief of the Gordon

Highlanders, poked his head around the door, to find out how I was doing. 'I hope you can play croquet, laddie – that is, when you start to get better?' he said as he left. Lady Burnett mentioned that she was going shopping in Aberdeen and enquired what records I would like because the gramophone had not been used since the war started when her two sons had left to join the Navy. The selection of the old 78s did not impress my two new friends, or me. She returned with two Bing Crosby records. 'There you are, Maurice, I managed to get *Tumbling Tumbleweeds*.' I felt quite choked being addressed by my Christian name by a lady for the first time since I had left home. She was one of the kindest people I have ever met.

The number of patients increased by the end of June, but my morning game of croquet with Sir James continued. An occasional visit by an MO to assess who was to return to their units did not seem to affect me. I learned one morning from Elsie, the gamekeeper's daughter, who was one of the nurses and my regular confidante, that the laird had told the MO that I was having trouble walking the stairs and would be quite useless back with my unit – and so the croquet mornings continued. In mid-August, I was ready to return to the army.

Back to health again

I returned to my unit, the 206 Anti-Tank Battery, who were in billets for the winter, in and around Huntingtower, a suburb of Perth. The defence of Scotland had been re-allocated with the original 9th (Scottish) Infantry Division, reconstituted as the 51st Highland Division, taking over the north-east coastline from our 5th Division. Our unit had swelled with a number of reinforcements, mainly conscripts from Scotland, but we were still well below establishment. British anti-tank guns were not available and we were temporarily equipped with French 75mm guns of ancient design, obtained from American stocks – but any weapon was better than none.

After my spell in hospital, I was temporarily classified A2. Any hope I had of attending OCTU for officer training was put in abeyance because I had to be A1 to attend the course. In my favour was the fact that I had attended a military school for four years. So the matter was on hold and I was put on light duties for six months, which meant I was expected to use my brain and not allowed to play football. I became a bombardier with HQ Troop, helping out the Quartermaster, a man called Edwards, who showed every sign that he was going to hang on to me as long as he could. After a month, I started to take the water cart out for the occasional spin. This was not a very good idea, for my left leg couldn't work the clutch properly. And one Saturday afternoon, with about 100 gallons on board, I chased a hare down a road heading towards Crieff. I was concentrating so hard on the hare that I forgot a hairpin bend ahead of me. As I applied the brakes, doing about 45mph, the swish of the water put the vehicle into a skid, but miraculously, as I left the road, I managed to miss all the huge pines and bring the water cart to a halt on top of a grassy bank. The gap between the trees was so narrow that it took the recovery vehicle four hours to get the cart back on the road. Luckily, because there was no damage to the vehicle, I managed to avoid being put on a charge.

On 7th September 1940, a national false alarm named 'Cromwell' was given when a number of fishing vessels in the West Country were mistaken for an invading force. All troops in the UK were turned out, expecting German paratroops to be landing simultaneously in their areas. This possibility had been rehearsed a number of times in Scotland, and so the 5th Infantry Division went into the alert around Perth and Dundee. It proved to be a very useful exercise for the real thing – should it occur.

The Division, it seemed, was reverting to its old role of Army Reserve and was moved to Lancashire and Cheshire to enable us to do some recruiting and training and bring us back to full strength. Our battery was based in Stockport, in commissioned accommodation in and around Mersey Square. Locally called-up troops came directly into our unit and obtained their training from us. This intake were in their late twenties and thirties and contained some professional types such as school teachers, clerks and a number from the surrounding farm areas. They were welcome reinforcements to a Territorial unit that had contained this sort of mixture of personnel at the outbreak of war. An army unit needs all skills and all types to give it the right balance. Now the 'Cor blimeys' were mixed with various Scottish elements and accents, and leavened with the 'Tha knows' from the Lancashire countryside. I had a role to play in taking classes on the anti-tank role in the British Army and also taking Bren gun classes. It was one of the most rewarding periods of my army career, for I really did like the new intakes. To those of us that had been in the unit from the outset, Stockport was a very restful place, despite the fact that we carried out many military exercises. Friday evenings, flush with pay, we were often to be found in the Beehive Pub in Mersey Square, playing darts on their smaller, rather strange dart board, which was devoid of trebles.

On the home front

About this time the air raids started in London. Those of us who had homes there were given special leave, particularly as our unit's Territorial area of Brixton, Camberwell, Kennington, Elephant and Castle and Walworth had been subjected to persistent, intensive bombing and some of our families had been bombed out. My parents' house in Kennington had been hit by incendiary bombs, and a paving stone from the explosion of a large bomb which had landed near The Horns, Kennington had hurtled over 200 yards and come through our roof, destroying a mantle shelf in the top bedroom, where it had come to rest. No one was hurt, but my parents had to move out and they took up residence in my Aunt Ivy's house in South Norwood. Before leaving Kennington, my mother – well behind on the instalments on my radio – told a persistent salesman the exact spot on the La Panne beaches he could repossess the radio.

My father had returned from the Isle of Wight, but he was still very much an invalid and my mother had her hands full with occasional trips to the west country to visit the three children. I did what I could in the week's compassionate leave I had been granted. I went round to the Kennington house to make sure it was secure. The pigeon loft was untouched and the pigeons were all in their nest boxes for the winter months. A friend, Jack Heavens, was looking after them. I visited one or two neighbours who were still living in Methley Street, and got the news of their loved ones who were in the forces or doing other war work, but the area was quite a mess.

On returning to Stockport, I started a concert party which was aided by the talents of Ronnie Lodge (Bud Flanagan's godson) which we put on for the local population. It wasn't very good, but the fact that we did it and made fools of ourselves went down quite well. I quite fancied a girl who was serving in a large baker's shop in Mersey Square. She was blonde, buxom and bouncy and good fun to be with. Just when things were going with a swing, the whole division – which stretched from Southport to Knutsford and inland – was put on notice to move to Northern Ireland. We were all quite concerned about leaving Stockport, because the air raids had started in and around Liverpool and Manchester and the army was able to support the fire brigade ...and we wanted to give something back to our friends. It seemed we were leaving Lancashire just when we were needed.

However, the six counties of Northern Ireland had suddenly become very vulnerable to attack by the Germans. U-boats had been seen to land in various parts of Ireland at the turn of 1941 and sectarian murders were commonplace in Northern Ireland. The War Office gave priority for us to carry out our role as an anti-invasion force, in preference to supporting the home services in the case of air attacks, so we were on the move again.

Keeping Hitler out of Ireland

The division left their friends in Lancashire and Cheshire in early April 1941 and headed up the East Lancashire Road and onto the main Carlisle road for the port of Stranraer in south-west Scotland. Most of the movement by large military convoys was carried out at night – driving with sidelights only and travelling slowly in close convoy. The movement was not taxing, for the snows in Cumbria had thawed and the Division's experience of night driving in France stood them in good stead.

The short crossing by steamer from Stranraer to Larne in Northern Ireland was always rough, but there were no major mishaps on this occasion. The vehicles and guns were driven onto ferry boats that before the war had plied between Dover and Dunkirk. On arrival in Ulster, the Division split up by brigades, mainly along the Eire borders. The threat of Hitler securing a footing in southern Ireland was very real and from there he would have a springboard to attack northern England, in an area less heavily defended than the redoubtable fortifications of the Channel ports.

The 13th Brigade was allocated an area in and around Armagh. The 15th Brigade took up positions in the Border county of Tyrone and near Omagh while the 17th Brigade was further south, on the border in and around Enniskillen. My regiment was spread over the three brigades – with my battery part of 17th Brigade and stationed on its own in Lisnaskea.

Our unit was lucky in having accommodation in an empty workhouse in the village. This was an imposing stone building with spacious rooms and a large courtyard for our vehicles and guns. We were about three miles from the border, with the 6th Seaforths, our closest neighbours, who were stationed in Crom Castle and guarding the Newtown Butler area of the border. This famous battalion had distinguished itself in the Ypres Comines battle just before Dunkirk and although it had suffered grievous losses, was now returned to full strength. Our battery was attached to them for rations and medical facilities. Their MO wore tartan trousers and had a brogue from that area in the Western Isles that had spawned his regiment. The whole of our battery was vaccinated by him in the summer of 1941, a clear indication that our stay in Ireland would be short. My scratch didn't take and after the third attempt had failed, he said 'Don't worry, laddie, you'll kill the bugs!' He was right: in my subsequent four years abroad in Africa, India, the Middle East, Sicily and Italy, I was lucky and suffered just two days of Sandfly Fever.

This period in Northern Ireland enabled us to play more inter-unit sporting events and become aware of how many top sportsmen there were in the division. Hedley Verity and Norman Yardley, the

Yorkshire and England cricketers, were serving in the Green Howards in 15th Brigade. Wilf Mannion, the England footballer, was also in the same battalion, and Ted Sagar, the Everton goalkeeper was in the Service Corps. A number of semi-professional Scottish footballers were serving in the three Scottish battalions of the Division. Our battery had lost its best known footballer, Geordie Gibson, who was killed in France before Dunkirk. Unfortunately, Verity did not survive the war, dying from wounds incurred in the battle for Catania.

Lisnaskea was a village dominated by a main street, with Protestant pubs down one side and Catholic pubs on the other. The 'Troubles' were in evidence despite the war and three sectarian murders occurred in the area while we were there. Our church parades in Enniskillen were to us strange affairs. The protestant preacher thundered about the battle of the Boyne and William of Orange, which none of us understood, and showed the religious hate that existed then in Northern Ireland. We wondered how the Inniskilling Fusiliers, in our division, coped with the situation.

From our quarters in the workhouse, which was on a small hillock, we overlooked the village and strategically were in a good position. The main road to the border ran past our main entrance and the village was self-contained, surrounded by farming country. Given the chance, we would have been happy to stay there for the rest of the war. I had a temporary girlfriend – a farmer's daughter called Maud Armstrong, whom I met at the Tennis Club. She was in her late teens, and she was beautiful, she was blonde and she was happy. When we left Ireland rather suddenly the following January, the first Americans started to pour in about two months after Pearl Harbour, showing that America was seriously at war with Germany and Japan. I reflected later that it would have not surprised me to have learned that Maud had ended up a GI bride. As for my future, serving in a mobile British Infantry Division, our destination was unknown, our postal services lousy, our security brilliant ... so the chances of me keeping in contact with Maud throughout the war were slim.

About two months after settling in Northern Ireland, and for the first time since Dunkirk, our division revealed its identity by painting our divisional insignia – a 'Y' representing 5th British Infantry (Yorkshire) Division. We added the unit number 46, on a red and blue background (RA) on all our guns and vehicles – and a huge sign outside our front entrance with unit information, mainly to show other military units where we were. It was also a psychological stroke, to demonstrate the pride of the division, which was now back to full strength. Moreover, it engendered confidence in the local population, who were pleased to have a front-line division on their doorstep. Everyone was aware that Northern Ireland was vulnerable to attack through Southern Ireland and it was also fairly common knowledge that German U-boats were receiving 48-hour refits in Cork, which as part of Eire was theoretically neutral.

I take charge of the petrol station

I took over a petrol pump in the village, on behalf of the Army, and reported to the quartermaster. This filling station was for all Army vehicles using the area up to the border. This was my prime responsibility and because I had a background of clerical experience, I had no problems with accountability and documentation. I worked closely with a tall, very talented graduate, called John Morse, who was responsible for unit supplies and the small NAAFI in the village. Johnny was unfortunately afflicted with a very severe stutter, which had precluded him joining the Navy, where his father was a serving captain. He joined the Army, but was restricted to administrative work, which depressed him somewhat. His hobby was shooting, mainly hares and rabbits, which abounded in County Fermanagh. Army personnel with shotguns were always made welcome by the local farmers, particularly if they shot rabbits. One Saturday Johnny went out with his shotgun, accompanied by a friend. Sometime in the afternoon, he tripped up with the breech closed and shot himself through the throat. At the inquest, a verdict of death by misadventure was brought in.

...and the NAAFI too

Suddenly, the NAAFI became my responsibility. It was adjacent to the petrol pump which was convenient for supervisory purposes. I also took on board unit supplies on a temporary basis but for the remainder of our stay in Northern Ireland, Army petrol was dyed red and needed close control so that it could be identified. By this time strict rationing was in force throughout the UK, but this did not prevent some of the locals using their powers of persuasion to do a deal. At the forefront of these approaches was the local Irish doctor, who promised to provide me with a suit and take me dog racing across the border, 'fer some of that red stuff!'. After many rejections, he got his own back by declaring in the main pub that his car had never run better since using the red stuff! This declaration put the ball in my court and caused me some embarrassment.

There was much traffic passing through Lisnaskea, including a surprising number of funeral cortèges from the border. I was standing chatting with the NAAFI girl one day when a particularly large funeral went by, and asked why so many people dying in Eire were being buried in Northern Ireland. She shrugged her shoulders and said, 'It may not always be bodies in the boxes – you know?' I was left in no doubt that a lot of smuggling was being carried out this way.

New equipment at last

The stay in Northern Ireland also gave our unit an opportunity to experiment with alternative anti-tank guns. The British Field and Anti-Aircraft Artillery units had excellent fieldpieces in the 25-pounder and the Bofors guns and apart from minor improvements, these guns were not changed throughout the war. As the senior TA anti-tank regiment in the British Army, we were experimenting and using other available guns in an anti-tank role, such as the French 75mm, which proved to be too cumbersome. In this process the existing standard two-pounder AT gun was withdrawn and transferred to the infantry. A new gun – the six-pounder – became the Artillery's standard anti-tank weapon until in 1943 a cumbersome 17-pounder gun – named Pheasant became part of our armament. The penetrative power of this gun was equal to the best German anti-tank gun but it only became a fiercesome weapon when mounted on a Crusader tank chassis called the Archer. Unfortunately it was not brought into commission until the latter part of 1944, when it made its mark during the last months of the war – too late for many.

An intensive period of training occurred in the summer and autumn of 1941 – the early signs that we were going somewhere in a hurry. In particular the Divisional Artillery shot their guns in a field role up in the Sperrin Mountains and in the anti-tank role at Hog Park Point on Loch Neagh. The Engineers practised bridging, as river crossings had again become prominent. Almost all exercises included long concentration marches. Wireless technique and procedure became more fluent and the supporting services started to function as part of the fighting machine, so all units became aware of each other's capabilities. Speeding up in and out of action was practised assiduously. Large-scale exercises including inter-divisional battles ranged over the six counties for nearly a week. There was even a concentrated 'gas week' where all exercises were done in gas respirators... these events were not without humour.

We enjoyed the best Christmas of the war in 1941, with a strong rumour that we would be leaving the Six Counties in the New Year. In McCaffrey's we drank poteen (with serious ill-effects) and held a farewell dance in the workhouse. Sure enough, we were under orders to move back to England in January 1942, preparatory to moving abroad in March. It was obvious that a number of new factors had entered into the war scenario since Pearl Harbour and the enlargement of the Japanese threat. A number of coastlines and islands in and around Africa had now become vulnerable. Our division would no doubt become involved in one of these hotspots, under code name 'Operation Ironclad'.

On the move again

The Division left Ireland during January. Because of bad weather and the state of the roads we had a hazardous journey, finally arriving in the Surrey and Kent outskirts of London. Once billeted, the units of the Division stretched from Oxted to Hayes Common, with the headquarters near Redhill. The whole of 52 Anti-Tank Regiment was billeted in Raynes Park, near Wimbledon. On 1st February, all units in the Infantry Division received mobilisation instructions which were put into immediate effect. Our guns were calibrated at Lydd in Kent in extremely cold weather – even though we had been issued with tropical khaki drill. The rumour was that we were going to Colombo, with the purpose of re-taking Rangoon from the Japanese and thus helping General Alexander's great battle in Burma.

Before embarkation, we were granted leave, so I travelled to my aunt's house in South Norwood, where my parents were staying. Night raids over south London meant that we spent most nights under the stairs or in the Anderson shelter in the garden. It was an unhappy time for my parents, as my father was still quite ill. My sister Ivy was serving in the ATS, based at Aldershot. Betty was working in London and the three younger children were still in the west country. Little did any of us know that I would not see them again until exactly three years later, on leave from Belgium in March 1945.

CHAPTER 6

○

MADAGASCAR, INDIA AND THE PERSIAN GULF

On 12th March, His Majesty spent all day visiting the units in the Division. He looked very tired but nonetheless impressed us all. Immediately following his visit, all our regimental offices closed and the division left south-east England, by road convoys or rail parties, for the port of embarkation – Gourock on the Clyde.

It was then that we learned from the War Office that 17th Infantry Brigade had been earmarked for Operation 'Ironclad' – the occupation of Madagascar by a mixed force known as Force 121 and commanded by Major-General Sturges of the Royal Marines. This was disconcerting news to the GOC 5th Division, as the ships were not tactically loaded, and 17th Brigade units were spread over a number of them. Our battery, 206, which was part of 17th Infantry Brigade, was aboard the *Nieuw Holland*, separated from our infantry battalions, although we had some Commandos on board. Some reloading took place in Gourock, including the 9th Field Regiment, which was also part of 17th Brigade. These last-minute changes meant the convoy remained on the Clyde for three days and finally sailed on 23rd March. For many it was to be their last view of the British Isles; as the blackout mass of Glasgow and the hills to the north slowly receded, a number of groups on board the ships sang sentimental wartime songs.

The convoy leaves

It was an impressive convoy, the largest long-haul battle group to leave the UK since the Second World War started. Amongst the protector ships was the aircraft carrier *Illustrious*, the battleship *Malaya*, the cruiser *Devonshire* and many destroyers and corvettes. Among the merchant ships carrying personnel – all of them great liners – were the *Nieuw Amsterdam*, the *Windsor Castle*, *Duchess of Atholl*, *Almanzora*, *Franconia* and the Polish *Sabieski*. The *Nieuw Holland* was one of the smaller vessels in the convoy – a mere 10,000 tons!

We didn't look like a cruise liner as we left Scotland, however: all ships flew barrage balloons and manned anti-aircraft guns in defence against enemy aircraft. The destroyer screen continually weaved in and out, ever alert for submarine attack. The whole convoy turned this way to port and then that way to starboard, at the command of the siren on the Commodore's ship. The weather was fine and calm for the time of year, although the Bay of Biscay as usual claimed many victims, which provided extra breakfasts for those made of sterner stuff.

The *Nieuw Holland* had over 2,000 troops on board, packed on three decks, with most of the troops sleeping in hammocks, though some were under the mess-deck tables. A few got up early to see the sun rise from the top deck. A company of Commandos were somnolent on the lower deck and did not seem to be involved in any training. One of their number, a gangling fair-haired youth, climbed decorously up the steps to our deck early each morning with hand on hip, and usually made his presence felt with, 'Good morning boys!'. A friend of his explained, 'He's as queer as a coot, but don't annoy him – he's a killer!'

Our time was occupied with lectures, lifeboat drill and practising with small arms. Leisure periods involved the very keen types in boxing, wrestling, and rehearsing concert parties. Card schools, Housey-Housey and Crown and Anchor were in play most of the time, while some loners passed the time away with a book. The pack of unused marked playing cards, given to me earlier in the war by a bookie friend of my aunt to boost my earnings, were in my holdall. When the cards in one of the schools had become worn, and quite innocently, I lent them my pack. They were handed back to me later, with one of the players a heavy winner. Equally innocently, I pointed out to them that the cards were marked and gave a demonstration – and then made myself scarce in order to allow the ensuing fracas to run its course.

After ten days at sea, it became too warm for battledress so we changed into khaki drill for the first time. Apart from the revealing of knobbly knees and unshapely legs, a lot of sewing work had to be done to some squaddies' gear, in order to turn them into respectable British soldiers. The persona of some of the guys seemed to change completely, whereas others – particularly when wearing the outdated Wolseley pith helmet – looked as if they had been performing on a Drury Lane stage.

On Easter Monday, 5th April, the great convoy steamed into the harbour of Freetown, the notorious 'white man's grave'. Nobody was permitted to go ashore, and the only movement between ships during this three-day fuelling stop, were those of the General and the Brigade Commanders, who were allowed to visit their units. Whatever plans for Madagascar that could be made were made and company commanders were informed accordingly.

The convoy was split into two parts before we left the bay. The first was to go on ahead and make for Durban. This included the 'Ironclad' ships carrying the 17th and 29th Infantry Brigades, and 5th Commando with supporting troops. The remainder, the slower part containing the rest of the Division, proceeded towards Cape Town. The two masses of ships sailed on 9th April and on the 13th crossed the Equator. The usual peacetime Crossing of the Line Ceremony was observed on our ship where a husky squaddie wearing a 'Y' on his chest was regaled as Father Neptune.

The Cape was rounded on 21st April and could be seen quite plainly from all ships. The famous Cape swell was in great form, so it was fortunate that most of the troops had found their sea legs. Our part of the convoy sailed into Cape Town, where we parted from our Commando unit. They had business elsewhere and went by overland transport to Durban. We flew the flag, by parading before the dignitaries of the Province, after which we were whisked away and allocated to various South African families for lunch and tea, before returning to our ship at night. We had been treated royally and this refreshing experience showed us how vulnerable the average South African felt since the attack on Pearl Harbour only three months before. More recent Japanese attacks on islands in the Indian Ocean were a further display of the strength of the Japanese Navy and their air power. The presence of part of the British Fleet and the landing of powerful land forces in Cape Town and Durban helped to allay their fears.

Madagascar – the plan

The assault on Madagascar by British Forces was planned before the attack on Pearl Harbour and the size of the invading force was based on intelligence that discounted Japanese interference. The plan had to be greatly modified to counter any possibility that the Vichy French Garrison had allowed their new allies, the Japanese, to use the island facilities. Being the third largest island in the world, with a deep water harbour at Diego Suarez, Madagascar would provide an ideal base to monopolise the East African coast. Should this area be dominated by the Japanese, then the main supply route to the Middle East and Burma, that lay around the Cape, would effectively be closed to Allied shipping. It was therefore essential that the enemy should have no suspicion of the intention to invade Madagascar, and that the force should be large enough to capture and secure the island quickly.

Warlike preparations gathered pace and to the list of warships present was added the battleship *Ramillies* and the aircraft carrier *Indomitable*. On 28th April the invasion convoy sailed from Durban, headed by the HQ ship *Windsor Castle*, which also carried the Commandos. It made an imposing sight as it passed out of harbour, particularly the carrier *Illustrious* with decks lined by ratings, her band playing and flags flying. The plan was to attack the northernmost peninsula of the island at Courier Bay, where there were a number of good beaches for landing. Here the Commandos would land with 29th Infantry Brigade and supporting tanks and guns – all part of the original Force 121 – while the 17th would wait offshore until it was possible to land, at which point they would pass through the 29th and exploit the Orangea Peninsula and east of it. The whole operation was to be supported by naval aircraft from the *Illustrious* and *Indomitable*. Before dropping bombs these aircraft were to drop leaflets proclaiming the anti-Japanese object of the expedition.

Madagascar – the reality

That had been the plan, at any rate. Unfortunately, General Alexander's fighting withdrawal from Burma was now getting near Assam and Bengal, so it was decided to limit the Madagascar operation to the capture of Diego Suarez and its dockyard of Antsirane, a mile across water. This would release the frontline troops to move on to their original destination and then secure the island of Madagascar with a garrison.

The action started on 5th May at 0530. The Commandos landed first in Courier Bay, after an extremely hazardous approach through a narrow entrance, covered by extensive minefields. These were efficiently cleared by the Royal Navy. The Coastal Defence gun crews were still in their beds and were unable to put up any resistance, so all the Commandos' objectives were taken by the late afternoon. Meanwhile the three main landings had taken place in Ambararata Bay. There was only minor beach opposition but a heavy swell caused considerable difficulty in getting tanks and guns ashore. One landing craft turned over completely and the vessels waiting outside with 17th Brigade troops on board dragged their anchors half a mile.

The bombing of the airfield six miles to the south of Antsirane was effective enough to prevent any significant interference by enemy aircraft, and bombardment of approach roads by the guns of the warships distracted the enemy's attention from the main landings. The assault gathered pace with the tanks destroying lorry-borne infantry. However, having marched 18 miles in extreme heat along a single road, the assault brigade were halted by an anti-tank ditch at a main position, and suddenly met by heavy fire from well concealed Vichy 75 mm guns. An assessment of the position showed it to consist of a mile and a quarter of trench system, stretching across the peninsula of Antsirane, with a formidable fort at either end. Each flank was edged by steep bushy slopes which descended into mangrove swamps which were curtailed by the sea. Gaps in between this defence line were well covered by pillboxes mounting field and machine guns ... a veritable minor 'Maginot Line'. This could not be tackled immediately after a long march in tropical heat – it required at least a full brigade attack with Howitzers which, in any case, had only just landed.

When it came, the attack was put in by three battalions of the 29th Infantry Brigade. Although several hundred prisoners were taken, the firepower was inadequate and what shooting was done only set fire to the bush and hindered progress. Moreover, the wireless sets behaved erratically, a frequent problem. Many casualties were suffered and so it was decided to call off the attack and wait for the 17th to arrive.

The 17th Brigade began their march from the coast at 0100 hrs on the morning of 6th May. After experiencing a rough landing, it was hardly the best preparation to go straight into battle. They reached the start line one hour before the time for the attack, scheduled at 2030 hrs. The 9th Field regiment had been unable to land in time to support them and so they were given artillery support by getting destroyers up in time to fire offshore as part of the attack and a diversionary raid by some fifty marines landing on the jetty in Antsirane Harbour.

The attack was put in by the 6th Seaforths on the left and 2nd Northamptons on the right with the 2nd Royal Scots Fusiliers in reserve. The Seaforths had the harder task of cleaning up the pill-box area bristling with machine guns and 75mm field guns. They had an extra company of the Royal Welsh Fusiliers from the 29th Brigade, who were not used in the earlier action. During the hour between finishing their march and crossing the forming-up line, they revived themselves with special 'pep' tablets and mugs of tea. There was little time to plan the attack without the aid of air photographs and the maps they had were inadequate. And so the platoon commanders of the Seaforths were briefed on the march – to the effect that they either took the 'effing town or they didn't effing well come back'. In the event of the former they were to put up a green light as a success signal; in the unlikely event of the latter, it would be considered that no known signal was necessary.

The Seaforths started their attack at 2030 hours in semi-darkness. They encountered a little sniping on the way up to a track junction, near a particularly memorable dead cow. Here the ground became open with long grass and a few bushes and the troops could not avoid making a crunching noise as they pushed through a crop of maize. The first objective, a railway line at the side of a native village, became discernable. To their right they heard much firing on the front where the Northamptons should be. Suddenly they came upon the anti-tank ditch, about which they had not been warned, and the enemy fire covering it opened up from no more than twenty yards away. In an instant, with the regimental cry of 'Cabar Feidh', they went into attack with the bayonet until the French resistance petered out. They went on to take a native village and then, becoming doubtful about their next objective, they took up a defensive position at 2300 hrs. Almost immediately success signals went up from the Northamptons and also to their left. They had some casualties, which included the Adjutant, Captain McCall, and the Intelligence Officer, Captain Black, who were both killed.

Meanwhile the Northamptons had fared well on the right. Their first objective was a radio station south of the village of Anatanambao, about a mile and a half beyond the start line, which they took over very rapidly. Major Houchin (C Company) put in a very lively attack on a pill-box and together with B Company they secured the village.

Further ahead, the group of 40 marines had successfully landed in Antsirane and the 2nd Royal Scots Fusiliers who were carrying out mopping-up operations were able to march into the town headed by their pipers. Antsirane was by now well on fire which helped the Fusiliers considerably in clearing the town. The final touch was the pipe bands of the 1st Battalion (29th) and 2nd Battalion (17th) of the Royal Scots Fusiliers, marching to the Governor's Residence to indicate that the main resistance in the town had ceased and the mission had been accomplished. Other pockets of resistance in the harbour were cleared by first light. Meanwhile, a battery of 75mm field guns, on the right of the main position, were surrounded by B Company of the Northamptons and surrendered. The two forts and the coast defence guns on the Orangea peninsula held out until midnight.

The resistance from a number of pill-boxes was snuffed out by individual attacks – one in particular was a brilliant personal attack, by Corporal Lyle of the 2nd Scots Fusiliers on a resisting pill-box, for which he was awarded the DCM.

Although the French and their Colonial troops fought at times with their traditional brilliance, the surprise element achieved by the battalions of the 17th Brigade coming up between the forts in their main attack was totally unexpected and threw them off their stride. The courageous leadership shown throughout by all three battalions never allowed their enemy to recover.

It was a great achievement for the 17th Brigade to march for so long and then successfully tackle such a formidable position with inadequate preparation. However, their visit to Madagascar was not without its consequences, for they were persistently bitten by insects which would later take its feverish toll with cases of malaria and Sandfly Fever and there were significant battle casualties, which infantry battalions suffer when they are forced to attack heavily defended fortifications from the front, without their normal field artillery back-up.

The 13th Brigade took no part in the battle. They landed as planned and did the 18-mile march and took up defensive positions until it was certain that they would have no fighting to do. They stayed a week in Madagascar before sailing to Bombay, but remained long enough to also contract malaria and Sandfly Fever from which they suffered considerably when they arrived in India. The 17th Brigade now with the addition of their 9th Field Regiment RA, took up defensive positions on the Orangea Peninsula for six weeks to protect the main military objective against Japanese landings, which were quite possible at this stage. In fact a Japanese two-man submarine got among the shipping in the harbour, causing a few casualties notably to HMS *Ramillies*, which was seen to be listing sharply as a result of this foray. Apparently the two men expected to be picked up by a Japanese seaplane in the harbour, but they were taken into custody by the Commandos instead. During this time a French officer tried to reach the mainland on a yacht, which a 25-pounder gun of the 9th Field Regiment sank with one shot.

There were some delicacies to be overcome in completing the French surrender. Apparently the Royal Navy had fired on the French when the Armistice was first put into force. An assurance that there would be no repeat of this incident and that their wives would remain unmolested, were two of the key issues. But quite a few small pockets of French die-hards nobly refused to recognise the Armistice and had to be 'mopped up' to satisfy their honour.

The 17th eventually left the island mid-June 1942 to catch up with 5th Division in India. They were relieved by a brigade of the King's African Rifles who would be part of the occupational force on Madagascar. It was a parting of the ways for the 5th Infantry Division, for they had to leave behind the 9th Field Regiment, the senior artillery regiment in the division, who were needed on the island to bolster up its defensive fire power. This excellent RA regiment never rejoined the 5th Infantry Division again, and ultimately ended its war in Burma. It is interesting to note that the occupation of Madagascar was not officially completed until November 1942 although, as Mr Churchill put it, the resistance after the 17th Brigade left the island was 'mainly symbolic'.

On to India

We in the convoy not involved in the Madagascar landings sailed on past the Mozambique Channel, after the Divisional Commander had been assured that the task of 17th had been well and truly done and it would be just a matter of a few weeks before the Division would be complete again in India. The main task for the Division was by now urgent, which was to join General Alexander's campaign either in Burma or as part of a defending force on the borders of India.

As we reached the Indian Ocean the sea became calmer, the weather hotter and the air charged with the possibility of attack by Japanese surface raiders. And so, for ten days the gunners manning the Bofors guns on the troopers were particularly vigilant, whilst the accompanying battle fleet zigzagged amongst the convoy until it steamed into Bombay on 16th May in impressive line formation, having not been molested. In fact, the only sign of aggression was the impolite exchange of signals between the Commodore of the convoy in the *Windsor Castle*, and the Commander of the naval escort in his flagship, concerning matters of precedence and professional etiquette, but it was quickly forgotten.

We disembarked the same night and marched through the streets of Bombay, picking our way through the recumbent beggars lying about the roads in white shrouds. We arrived at Victoria Station and boarded a train to Ahmednagar, one of three concentration areas for the Division, the other two being Kirkee and Poona. It was but a short journey in the smart new electric train which was completely devoid of windows. We moved into a large barrack room made familiar to us by the writings of Kipling, where the *punkahs* were rhythmically pulled by small boys to cool the stifling atmosphere at night, but the barrack room was surprisingly cool in the heat of the day.

This was the first time an English division mobilised for war had landed in India. The British residents did not take kindly to the invaders, for it was the first time in the war that their world had been disturbed. The core were regular battalions, flying the flag for the British Empire and in so doing avoiding Dunkirk and indeed rationing in the 'Old Country'. It seemed ironic that we, the 'invaders', were a regular division but boosted with Territorials and conscripts, and had been moulded into a trained fighting force while the regular British Army battalions in India were only suited to carrying out a peacetime role and virtually untrained to fight a war as part of a division or army.

At this time, the status quo was made clear by a north-country regular battalion stationed in Poona. They were calling the shots and regarded us as outsiders, because we wore khaki drill and had no 'whites' for evening wear. Their band, immaculately attired, played at the Saturday night ball in the Gymkhana club. Appropriate ranks in our Division who tried to gain admission got short shrift from the residents, who openly forbade their daughters to dance with our chaps. Officers from the Division were welcome at the Yacht Club in Bombay but had to eat behind screens in the dining room – to set them aside from the club members. Later, travelling on the road towards the Bengal front, many of the British establishments held the same attitude towards British convoys that were resting in their cantonments for the night. It was a bit different from the rapport we had with the South African families in Cape Town and Durban. Having distanced themselves from the war, it was no doubt an almighty shock to those who ultimately found themselves fighting in Burma. One of the unusual sights at this time was to witness one colonel on a large white horse inspecting an armoured unit. He was rather a short man, however, so possibly he got a better view of the tanks and their crews.

By road to Ranchi

The 15th Infantry Brigade group had been in the Ahmednagar and Poona area for a week when the Brigadier informed them they would have to go ahead to the eastern side of India to prepare for a possible Japanese invasion of Bengal. The rest of the infantry regiments on Madagascar duty would join the division at the new location in a place called Ranchi in the Native State of Bihar. The 13th Brigade arrived in Ahmednagar as the 15th Brigade started out on their journey.

The road parties, which consisted of the vehicles and their drivers, assembled in Colabar Camp Bombay, and set off with a day's gap between each party. The Division's Service Corps, who were responsible for the logistics of the trip, would lead off on a venture which would take fourteen days. The journey was to be quite an undertaking: never before had a division attempted to cross India by road in the heat of summer. The vehicles were not designed for tropical heat and where possible, many modifications had to be made. Each vehicle carried two *chaghals* (canvas water bottles) which were to be refilled regularly on the trip.

I was in a road party, having been allocated the Battery Major's 8 cwt Dodge, a vehicle better suited than the heavier vehicles to the sweltering conditions that were to be met on the route ahead. My amiable co-driver was a lad named Belcher. Our springy vehicle was capable of coping with the worst road conditions and was designed for hot climates, so we were to have a relatively easy passage.

The rail parties consisted of the infantry and most of the other troops not involved with transportation matters. They had a four-day journey to Barkakhana, the station for Ranchi, travelling in packed and poorly ventilated carriages in the heat of the Indian summer. Hence the troops were glad to reach Ranchi even though they had to build their own camps, on a bare stretch of semi-jungle and paddy fields. The first of the road convoys arrived in Ranchi on 11th June, after nearly a fortnight on the road. They found the camps quite well organised, but a lot of road building still had to be done.

The road journeys had been full of incident, and most of the troubles with the vehicles were caused by grit getting into the fuel pumps. The roads were often badly made and in some stretches were no more than tracks. Vehicles were down to snail's pace going through villages, where half-clad grinning children ran between the vehicles and the occasional snarling dog threatened the heels of the despatch riders. In one case, an old woman ran into the road and spat into the face of a motor cycle orderly of the RASC convoy. Wild water-hogs belted across our path and turtles and crocodiles scared a water cart driver when he stopped and threw his floats into a river in order to top up and sterilise his dwindling supply of water. A couple of monkeys leapt onto a truck, and then left in a hurry as it gathered speed. One night was spent surrounded by howling jackals, but the headlights of vehicles kept them at bay. In Jhansi we enjoyed comfortable barracks, but it was extremely hot and the plain outside was strewn with boulders and dead trees with vultures picking at the remains of water buffalo that had probably died through lack of water. Each vehicle had two drivers, because some fair-skinned ones tended to become heat casualties – a number of drivers in the convoys became ambulance cases.

Belcher and I arrived in Ranchi in an early convoy. On arrival I was told to report to a new battery major, who had been appointed to take over 206 Battery. He told me that I had been reclassified from A2 to A1 and that I was to be his driver whilst I was in India. According to my Army File, I spoke Urdu – which made me regret that I had not paid more attention to the *Munshi Je* in my school days at Sanawar.

My first job was to complete a Monsoon Trench around the camp. To do this, I had a gang of coolies from a local Dravidian tribe. They were magnificently tall natives who were not used to seeing white soldiers but they were remarkably friendly and willing to do any task given to them, once they understood what was wanted! They carried bows and arrows, which they fired with great accuracy and used for shooting the local game and for their own and their families' protection. On addressing them for the first time, I realised from the expressions on the faces of my gang, that my Urdu describing a monsoon trench, bounced off them. It was obvious that their local tongue was one of the dialects that even the *Munshi Je* would have problems with!

In desperation, I cut some long canes to varying lengths and gave each one his own area. The smallest cane for the start of the trench at the top of the slope and the largest one for the bottom, with one cane, about four feet long, for the universal width of the trenches. Each coolie had a 30-foot trench to dig and when the trenches were finished, all the resultant steps in between were sliced out leaving long smooth trenches around our camp ... approved of by the happy nods of my Dravidian gang. Our camp was at the top of the slope, so we had constructed the main horizontal trench at the top of the hill, which would protect all the camps. All that was needed was for the lower camps to join their side trenches to ours. However, the other units did not place the same priority on the need for monsoon trenches as our major, who was an experienced 'Indian Wallah'. And so the waters of the first monsoon rushed past our camp, a foot below the rim of the trenches, but unfortunately flooded the other camps, because their scanty scrapings had not been joined up to our trenches. I had to lend my gang to the other units to sort out their problems, which pleased my Dravidians immensely, for they earned a lot of 'buckshees'. My major was also quite pleased with our dry camp and totally unconcerned that the lower camps had been flooded out. 'Bugger them, Court!' he said cheerfully, 'They ought to get someone who speaks Urdu!'

The rapid journey the Division had made from the UK began to show its toll when our troops started to fall ill in Ranchi. The varying climatic conditions experienced by the men of three months on the move resulted in outbreaks of malaria, Sandfly Fever and dysentery and, in the case of the 13th Brigade Infantry who had rejoined the Division, some severe cases of Blackwater Fever, contracted from their stay in Madagascar. There were insufficient hospital facilities in the area and the local military hospital was soon full. The Division set up its own hospital, but it could not cope with the scale of the outbreaks. A number of men in each unit died and others were so ill they were temporarily invalided out of the area. Some only returned to their units months later. Desperate measures were required, including setting up small emergency centres in each unit, supervised by the Regimental Medical Officer, who visited the small isolation areas each day. By this time all the troops were paraded each day to take Mepacrin and salt tablets. At night an ointment was smothered on the arms and neck.

The troops were sleeping in their tents on groundsheets but the sick needed to be off the ground and under mosquito nets. I was instructed by the Major – who was suffering from dysentery – to go to the nearest bazaar and buy up as many charpoys as I could get. I set off in a three-tonner, with crew and a large sum in rupees, obtained from the battery funds. After much haggling we brought back as many as we could load onto our truck, and handed them over to the quartermaster. Some casualties benefited and recovered by sleeping on charpoys. Strangely, many of the seriously ill were old soldiers who had served in India before, which raised the possibility that infection had remained dormant in their systems from the earlier tour of duty in the sub-continent. Many who were too ill to be moved out of the area died in the camp, including my old friend Stanton. Those with malignant malaria had repeated attacks throughout the war, and after.

The evenings in Ranchi were the best times. The quaint chromatic Indian music from the local villages drifted into the camp on the cool evening breeze. Occasionally troops attended the village *ram-samis* (parties) which were fairly frequent, for the Dravidian

Indians loved music. The Divisional bagpipes had them grinning from ear to ear as the pipers paraded around their villages in full gear. To the list of soldiers' pastimes were added contests between centipedes and scorpions, which were easy to arrange and allayed boredom in the camp. These matches were more interesting than the arranged but more hackneyed contests between cobra and mongoose, introduced to the troops in the Bombay area.

My friend Cracknell, who had very fair skin and fair hair, was suffering severely from 'Doolally Tap' (sunstroke) and heat exhaustion. One morning a kite hawk swooped while he was in the breakfast queue, and took his bacon out of his mess tin. He screamed out, 'Why me, you bastard? Come back, you've forgotten my beans!' He raised his arms high in the air, suggesting that not only the kite hawk but the heavens too had had conspired against him. The turning point came when it was thought that he had vented his spite on an officer by blowing him up in the officers' latrine. This officer, a creature of habit, always went across the *maidan* at 6:00 am and perched himself on the latrine bar, lit a cigarette and threw the lighted match down into the pit. On this particular morning, someone went into this latrine first and poured a liberal amount of petrol into the pit. The officer carried out his chores according to plan, and the camp was shaken by an explosion which blew down the latrine screens, to reveal the unfortunate man galloping towards his tent with his backside black and obviously singed. No one could prove who was the perpetrator of this outrage, but Cracknell was sent away to recover from heat exhaustion and did not return to the unit for nearly a year, when the Division was preparing for the invasion of Sicily.

The immediate role of the 5th Division in the Bihar area was to repel any Japanese invasion of the north-east coast of India or through the Assam jungle. The 70th Division, part of the Indian Army establishment, was close at hand but at half-strength, and was to support the 5th Division in this defensive role. A special task for 5th Division was to defend the valuable Tata Steel Works at Jamshedpur. The Divisional Reconnoitre Regiment made many detailed and exhaustive surveys of all possible routes into Assam that might be used to halt the Japanese Army's impending advance into India. Meanwhile the two brigades of the Division and the Divisional support groups were training for what was thought to be an imminent confrontation with the Japanese. Fortunately, the early monsoons helped General Alexander in his withdrawal through Burma and lessened the threat of an immediate attack by the Japanese on India.

Just when it was considered safe to give leave in Calcutta to the Divisional troops, a more serious threat to the Middle East became evident with the German Army nearer to Iran, fighting in the Caucasus. It had always been Hitler's dream to take Persia – particularly the area around the rivers Tigris and Euphrates known as Iraq, for he needed the oil in the Persian Gulf to conquer the Middle East. Some years before the war, Hitler, with great foresight, prepared the groundwork by sending German engineers to improve and build new railways in Persia. He had also infiltrated engineers and scientists into other industries and had encouraged Raschid Au in Iraq to plan a revolt against the British when the time was ripe. It was all part of a grand strategy which started when he launched his armies against Stalingrad and the Caucasus. If successful, his armies would gain momentum, pour down into Persia and control the Middle East – a sweep then to India would be virtually unopposed.

In response to this, a mythical British Tenth Army consisting of ten divisions would be waiting for him – in fact only the Army Headquarters was in being at this time. In consequence, all leave was stopped in the British 5th Infantry Division and orders were given for us to be out of India in ten days en route for Persia. This sudden move was promulgated by uprisings occurring in Baghdad and Kermanshah (Iran) which had been temporarily quelled. A special force of two brigades, hastily assembled in Iraq, was placed under the command of General Slim and was on its way to Kermanshah.

The camps we were leaving in Ranchi would not be wasted, for the Second British Division had landed at Bombay and were on their way to take over our role before ultimately advancing into Burma, where they would serve for the rest of the war.

To Persia by Dodge

To get the Fifth Division into the heart of Persia in the shortest possible time would involve moving by road the infantry Bren carriers, artillery towing vehicles and guns, engineers' heavy plant vehicles, signals vehicles, field ambulances, various tracked vehicles together with unit and divisional administration vehicles – and water carts, which were a priority in all convoys. The road party journey would take the convoys across India to the North-West Frontier, over the river Jumna bridges at Quetta, and enter Iran by crossing the Baluchistan Desert. The route through this desert had not been attempted before by a large force with heavy vehicles and equipment because there was no system of roadways. The little-used trails had to be made as secure as possible and navigational centres linked by radio and set up at frequent intervals; a system of fuelling and feeding points was also needed. In this regard, much help in the planning was given by Indian military staff. The infantry and other troops not involved in the transportation of the Division's vehicles and guns were scheduled to reach Persia by a series of rail and road routes.

The road convoys set off in the first week in August in pouring rain that became heavy enough to delay the overall move by two days. The route retraced the previous journey for most of the way. At Benares there was civilian trouble led by the Vice Chancellor of the University. The convoys avoided these minor skirmishes, but were subjected to some brick throwing and mud slinging which was ignored. At Delhi, where the troubles became more serious, Divisional Carrier Parties were used to help the civil authorities quell the rioting. Further along the route at Allahabad the troops had small arms handy as a protective measure. Driving the major's Dodge with my assistant driver Belcher alongside, I had a Sten gun in the cab, but the trip for our convoy was relatively quiet – and the sight of the Taj Mahal and the river Jumna in the late afternoon was awesome. The next leg of the route to Quetta was cancelled because the Indus had burst its banks and carried away the crucial bridges at Quetta. This meant that the great desert epic could not take place, because there was not enough time to wait for the bridges to be rebuilt. The convoys were redirected to Bombay, where the organisation along the way had been tightened up and residents were less hostile. Staging arrangements had improved and Station Staff Officers – a peculiar breed of English *Babu* – had become alert and helpful: it seemed that someone had shaken them up.

We drove down to the western *ghats* into Brabourne Stadium, made available for us to prepare our vehicles for the desert. This included fitting desert tyres, so that all our units would be mobile once our vehicles reached the staging point at Shaiba Camp in Iraq. We should then be capable of tackling the Iraq desert to Baghdad without delay. Before that our vehicles had to be suitably sealed and prepared for hoisting onto creaky old tramp steamers, which had been chartered at short notice, and would be embarking either from Bombay or Karachi en route to the Gulf.

Once our unit's vehicles had been loaded, we awaited our embarkation to Basra in a Karachi rest camp. We had furloughs at night to go into Karachi and spend some of the rupees that had accumulated over a few months on the move. Karachi was full of all sorts of uniformed troops and the town was becoming very prosperous because of its importance as a military port at this stage of the war.

One evening in Karachi, while awaiting embarkation, about a dozen of us were in a restaurant for a meal and a few drinks. We were joined at our table unannounced, by a rather slovenly individual in army KD, who welcomed us like long lost brothers. After offering his view on the merits of Dennis Compton's batting as compared with Don Bradman, he slowly turned the conversation on why we were in Karachi. Where were we going? Some typically British lewd suggestions he did not understand confirmed him as a phoney. His un-British like voice aping a public-school manner of speech and his rather swarthy complexion had made us suspicious from the start for we were not seriously drunk, and so we played him along. I asked him where he came from in Britain. He responded, 'Crewe'. I looked suitably mystified and asked, 'Where?' He said, 'Crewe' again and was looking anxiously at us. We all played it dumb and looked puzzled. 'Y'know' he added, 'Crewe in Surrey?' At this stage, we all started to move away from our chairs. Realising he had made a mistake, he took off, with us in pursuit. Sadly, we did not catch him, but it was quite clear he was an informant, probably for the German cause because of Karachi's Moslem links with the Gulf and Persia.

We boarded our ship the following day and did not take the matter further. In any case, a bustling port like Karachi would have many such incidents which would be difficult to investigate.

By sea to Basra

The journey up to the Persian Gulf was a relatively restful period but with the climate getting hotter each day. The haste with which the personnel convoy had been assembled resulted in there being a scarcity of escort vessels. One of these, a destroyer, took on board a gunner suffering acute appendicitis and took him to Karachi for an operation before catching up with the slow moving convoy. The journey lasted for ten days, delayed by a dense fog, off the oil refinery at Abadan but it eventually proceeded up the Tigris to reach the port of Basra at Maghil. From here, the troops were taken over flat hot desert to Shaiba. It was the month of August, the hottest month of the year, with temperatures of 136°F and hot water coming out of the cold water taps. The troops were not acclimatised to take such heat; about thirty of the most serious heat exhaustion cases were placed in refrigeration units to recuperate and some were left in the local military hospital.

The trampers carrying the vehicles and guns arrived at Basra and had to be collected by the road parties, most of whom had travelled on the steamers to Maghil, because of lack of accommodation on the trampers. Because I was officially still the major's driver – though I was short on Arabic – I picked up the Dodge and brought it back in company with the other vehicles to Shaiba. A few days were spent in getting the vehicles roadworthy, but working only in the evenings, because of the extreme heat.

The 17th Infantry Brigade became complete again with the arrival from Karachi of the 156 Field Regiment, the Lanarkshire Yeomanry, who had replaced the highly respected 9th Field Regiment who were still in Madagascar and would ultimately move on to Burma. The Lanarkshire Yeomanry soon settled in well with the two Scottish and one English infantry regiments in the brigade.

The road parties set off through the desert of Mesopotamia to the First Staging Camp, once named Ur of Chaldees. It was but a mound, but once a city and the birthplace of Abraham. It was then the centre of all tracks to Egypt. But the desert had taken its toll over the centuries and so it had become necessary for each convoy commander to have a guide to show him the route through this untracked stony desert towards Baghdad. These guides left when the convoys reached the Basra–Baghdad Railway line which became the indicator of the way along the still nebulous route. Mirages were seen frequently, ranging from mountains and lakes to English Public Houses.

It was beneficial having a co-driver and mine, Belcher was a cheerful soul. The springy Dodge hopped along the track like a kangaroo and kept us both alert and aware that we were still in the convoy, and not a mislaid vehicle – always a possibility! The desert had very little vegetation, only camel thorn scrub, but the convoy had a short pause en route for enthusiasts to spend some minutes among the remains of Babylon. Along the way we met Arab convoys and passed lonely police posts, which we acknowledged with a wave of the hand, for only the desert was the enemy. A night was spent at Kwanjadwal, near a Gurkha battalion who were guarding the lines of communication and holding the peace between two violent tribes.

Baghdad, city of minarets, mosques, magic carpets and thieves, was reached without incident and all units passed through on their way north to stay for a day at Lancer camp. A visit to Baghdad showed it to be the most expensive city in the East, a visit for the day costing as much as a week in Bombay. Like Benares, it was a violent clash of splendour and poverty but unlike Benares, it had suffered from a ghastly cheap form of western modernisation. A young city, but during its twelve hundred years, it had been the seat of a civilisation, a Mongol capital, a battle-ground between Turkoman and Persian, a Turkish colonial possession, an outpost of the British Empire and the centre of a young Arab state – small wonder it has become an unfortunate mixture of strange contrasts. To us passing through it had its distractions, most of which had been placed out of bounds. Some said it was to prevent us getting VD but the more cynical claimed it was to keep the best quarters for elements of the British army and airforce units based in the area. Whatever the truth, there were posses of redcaps making sure that we in the Fifth Infantry Division did not wander into the 'Red Light' districts of the city.

After a few days on refitting our vehicles and guns we moved north to Khaniquin, which was the start of a tarmac road system and the railhead for all troops of Paiforce going north to the Iraq Frontier or into Persia (Iran). It was here that our rail parties finally detrained and proceeded for the rest of their journey by road transport. It was here too, that there was mile upon mile of Polish refugee camps, which spawned the Polish Corps that was to fight so well for the Allies in Italy – notably at Cassino.

Our road party crossed the Persian border and there was an immediate noticeable change of landscape, background and people. A distinct Kurdish flavour, Cossack hats and long frock-coats were worn by officials at the Customs post. The drive from there to the Paitak Pass was along straight poplar-lined roads reminiscent of France. The many peasants seen wore cloth caps and not the white egg-shaped felt caps – the usual head-dress seen up to the Iraq border.

The drive up the steep winding Paitak Pass was hair-raising for the Division's drivers, for we were competing for road space with African convoys taking personnel parties up to Persia and returning empty. Having carried out their task, on the return trip these African drivers drove like demons possessed, with little fear of the steep ravines that lay beyond the barrier-less roadsides. A glance over the edge showed a number of vehicles that had shot over the side with disastrous results. Moving up the Paitak towing swaying guns was in itself a harrowing business, made hazardous by speeding vehicles driven towards us by grinning mindless drivers; fortunately our convoy was intact when we cleared the pass. The Dodge I drove through the Pass was very adaptable, so driving was less hazardous for me and my co-driver than for the drivers of the more ponderous and heavier towing vehicles.

The countryside beyond the pass was of delicate pastel colours, similar to parts of dried-up India. The journey to Kermanshah, our immediate destination, crossed a series of plains and minor passes, through oases and strange villages, before reaching our garrison town. Here in a camp, at the foot of rugged tall mountains, near the well of Taqui Bustan, the whole division became reunited for the first time since the Madagascar campaign. It was 5th October 1942 and during the previous three months, the Division had crossed India twice in the heat of the summer and through the peak of the monsoon period, landed in Basra in 136°F, and had passed up into Persia across the plains of Iraq. This had been achieved with casualties, mainly from disease and heat exhaustion. In military terms, the cost was infinitesimal in that a full infantry division had arrived before the start of the winter, fully equipped and ready to play its part in keeping the supply lines open in support of the Russian forces in the Caucasus, able too to suppress civil unrest and help to keep the situation in the Persian area of the Middle Fast stable. The organisation and professionalism within the division to achieve all this had been superb.

Kermanshah

Kermanshah, about the size of Winchester, had a mixed population of Persians and Assyrians. It was the garrison headquarters of a Persian Division which was under strength. It was an indescribably filthy town with no drainage and was the centre of the Persian hide industry. The poor were wretchedly dressed, which was in complete contrast to the powdered and scented Persian officers, who wore mustard-coloured uniforms and the police, who were decked out in a sky blue musical comedy type garb. Disease was rife, accentuated by the bestial habits of the local population, who were paying for it with an outbreak of plague, in an area close to our Division's camping grounds. This was a long line of unit tents on either side of a main road, which was in a reasonably sheltered position at the foot of mountains.

The British had no friends in Kermanshah for it was that part of Persia that had been diligently wooed by the Nazis before the outbreak of war and so the Division was delighted when Marshal of the Royal Air Force, Lord Trenchard, who was the Colonel-in-Chief of the Royal Scots Fusiliers, visited us in this bleak location and inspected his Second Battalion, which was part of 17th Brigade. It seemed that the Fusiliers had many friends in high places who were willing to drop in, whatever the location.

The nearest British outpost to our camp was an oil company's pumping station at Taqui Bustan, about ten miles north of Kermanshah. The small market centre was made famous by the well, allegedly created when Moses struck the adjacent large rock and water poured into the oasis ever since. The British Colony was very hospitable towards us in the month that we were in the area. The division managed to catch up on training before moving off to Central Persia, which was to be our base for the winter. Apart from the

ON LEAVE IN BAGHDAD: PORTWAY, SAMMY BOOTH AND MYSELF

plague, winter in Kermanshah was to be avoided because of the severe cold winds that swept across the plain on which the town was sited at 5,000 feet above sea level. A tent afforded no protection, even when it was well dug in.

Our major was still suffering badly from dysentery and the cold wind sweeping across the plain of Kermanshah was causing him some distress. It became a question of whether he would be invalided back to base before the winter was out. Meanwhile, in keeping with the fashion which many in the Division had succumbed to, I obtained for him a sheep-lined yellow coat of fullish length called a *poshteen* and got a shorter version for myself. It was acceptable as a uniform in Persia and was particularly good at night, when temperatures got as low as minus 40° degrees. The locals in Kermanshah wore dirtier versions which they never seemed to remove. After training in and around Kermanshah for a month we were happy to move away for a destination strategically placed in central Persia where we could make our presence felt over a larger area.

Qum

On our way to our destination – the Holy City of Qum – two routes were taken by the Division. The northerly one, the more difficult, was over the Shah Pass, one of the highest passes in the world. This route was taken by all the Divisional Artillery and we managed to get our guns over this pass in order to show the flag at Hamadan, a town noted for being the oldest in Persia, one of the great centres of the carpet industry, and very openly anti-British. As we went through the town with swaying artillery pieces of different sizes, Persian officers and policemen solemnly turned their backs on our convoys, which made it clear that they held Teutonic allegiances.

The camp at Qum was astride a road fork a few miles west of Qum City in a sandy plain between two lines of hills. It was much lower than the mountains of Kermanshah, but nonetheless 5,000 feet above sea level. Tents were pitched in groups of three, some 200 yards apart. Under the canvas tops the tent interior was dug down to six feet plus and furnished with carpets and trappings obtained from the local bazaar. Steps were cut in the entrance side to make life easier in getting in and out of the tent. Most tents had primus stoves to heat up food, but meals were obtained from the local cookhouse. Survival was the name of the game. Accidents happened, occasioned sometimes by not taking appropriate precautions against centipedes and scorpions. These creatures also sought warmth at night and an army boot was a decent spot to be. One morning, the major's batman, hearing his master calling, put his boots on in a hurry and was stung through the arch of his foot. Judging by his sobbing, the pain was unbearable and he hobbled around for a week.

Qum was a holy city with the kings and queens of various dynasties buried there, including the daughter of the prophet Mohammed, which made this quarter out of bounds to British soldiers. Its notable feature was the gold-leafed golden dome of the main mosque which shone brightly in the sun and could be seen for many miles – making it a useful zeroing point for the Divisional Artillery's guns in an otherwise barren terrain.

The Division was now in a position in the Middle East, halfway between the Eighth Army in the Western Desert and the Russian Armies in the Caucasus. Its prime everyday task was to ensure that supplies to the Russian armies going through Persia by rail and road were not impeded by forces friendly to the Germans. The nearest Russian forces were serving in Persia in Tabriz which was north of Teheran near the Caspian Sea, an area which our staff officers were permitted to reconnoitre on occasions, but by and large our Division made no moves north of Teheran.

After a short while at Qum, disorder broke out in Teheran and the Division was instructed to send battalions to help the civil power. The Northamptons were the first battalion to go to their aid. They camped on Teheran Racecourse for a month where they shared duties with two Russian Battalions who were based in Teheran. But the Northamptons' special remit was to look after British interests and to ensure that no more British citizens were shot. The Persian authorities had refused to sanction an increase in paper money needed to accommodate the influx of troops into Persia; consequently the Fifth Division and other British units could not obtain money to pay the troops. The Northamptons were given instructions to enter the bank and forcibly remove the appropriate number of notes to meet immediate requirements. The infantry were to be aided and abetted by a unit from the Sappers to blow the safes, together with a troop of 25-pounders to show that the British Army meant business, and a squadron of armoured cars for reconnaissance purposes. Before the action took place the Persian Government relented, much to the dismay of the appointed 'bank robbers' from the 17th. This was probably the first time that the British Army had appointed official 'safe breakers'.

The Northamptons were relieved by the Seaforths, whose pipers gave great pleasure to the residents in Teheran as they marched ahead of the troops on route marches through the streets. On one occasion a troop from the Persian Army joined in at the rear of the column as they marched through the city. The Russians too – who were normally aloof – relaxed at the sound of the pipes. The Highlanders remained in Teheran until Hogmanay, which they celebrated in fine style by holding a dance in the totalisator hall of the racecourse. For this event they borrowed 120 Polish ATS girls as partners. This was a relaxing period for the troops marching into Teheran, for they were able to take a break in convivial surroundings, see a film and have refreshments before completing their march.

Meanwhile the supplies to Russia from the Allies were being ferried by lorries from Kermanshah to Tabriz on a non-stop schedule. Divisional troops detailed to work with the Persian railways, which included some from my unit, became train guards. A great deal of stores had to be moved by rail and so any train stock available was used. It was strange to see German locomotives, manned by Russian crews, guarded by British troops, hauling carriages of all nationalities and with markings such as 'Tunbridge Wells' or 'Bloemfontein'.

At this time, Teheran must have been one of the most cosmopolitan cities of the war and accordingly, bizarre situations were accepted as being normal. Here East was linked with West, and North with South, and nearly every language could be heard in the streets, which showed an international gaiety with night clubs next door to wrestling booths and massed Turkish baths. Brightly painted kiosks and urinals adorned the streets, reminiscent of France, with a background of plane trees and open drains. Behind it all rose the peaked, shapely Mount Demavend, a snow-covered cone of 18,549 feet which could be seen from Qum on clear days.

Meanwhile, life in the Qum camp, a hundred kilometres away from the capital, had settled down, with local traders appearing suddenly from the desolate terrain and plying their wares to the troops. Each morning at 6:00 as the sun started to rise and glint fiercely off the Golden Dome, a lone figure appeared over the horizon and made his way into the British *maidan*. Our dug-in tent was on the edge of the camp and so we had an early choice of his goods as he laid his wooden contraption on the ground. This contained many interesting items of which the prime eatables were packets of nougat and eggs. The eggs had crinkled shells, probably due to a paucity of grit in the hen's feed, but they tasted like eggs and so we took a daily supply for our tent to go with our canned bacon and soya sausages.

UNDER COVER IN IRAN; ON THE LEFT IS GERRY YOUNG,
LATER AWARDED THE MM IN DUNKIRK

Our major was still suffering from dysentery but was proving to be a glutton for punishment. I drove the Dodge about with him on recce. We visited all types of areas where we might site our anti-tank guns should the German Panzers break through the Caucasus. We tested various inclines to see if it was possible to drive a vehicle up and down the very rocky slopes. This type of recce was normally the job of a troop commander but the major wanted to study the terrain for himself. On one occasion we halted at the head of a cliff where no forward move was possible.

'Go back a bit, bombardier, and take it down', he instructed. I drove back along the cliff, looking hopefully for a reasonable route down. 'Take it down here, Court!' I looked downwards at what seemed to me a sheer drop, thinking his dysentery had given him a death-wish. 'Come on, Court, don't hang about!' I faced the Dodge very square on to the drop, selected the lowest gear and started praying to myself. Rocks and rubble tumbled in front of us as I held the bouncing Dodge on a straight downward path until we reached the bottom, which was in a small vale. 'We won't go back that way, bombardier...we will never get the guns down, y'know,' said the major laconically. 'No sir,' I agreed in my most matter-of-fact tone. But I was elated and surprised at what the Dodge could do!

After the long period that the Division had spent on the road, getting the troops fit was the main priority. This resulted in a period of prolonged training including route marches, arms drill, gunnery and firing camps. Sport too was given a high priority of which football, cricket, hockey and athletics held pride of place among the sporting fraternity. It seemed that the Division had in its ranks many internationals in the various sports. Apart from the football and cricket internationals already mentioned, the Cheshire regiment's padre was an English hockey international and a very aggressive centre half who took no prisoners. I played left inner for our regiment and was dumped on my backside by a shaggy-haired gentleman who was built like a bull. He was very agreeable when he dusted you off, but thought nothing of following this up by chopping your knuckles with his stick. One of their chaps sidled up to me and mentioned not to swear at him because he was their padre.

The 5th Division was the main British Force in Paiforce in the winter of 1942/43. In consequence our detachments were spread as far as Baghdad guarding the GHQ location and at the Tenth Army HQ at Sultanabad. Carrying out duties of a special nature such as removing undesirables who were acting against the best interests of the Allies also became the Division's responsibility. A case in point was the removal of an uncooperative Persian general. A special platoon from the Seaforths was sent with troops from the Division genuinely taking leave at the beautiful city of Isfahan, a place that the general often frequented. The general was taken by this special platoon, whilst taking tea at a hotel, removed to an airport and flown out of Persia. This was of course highly irregular, for we were not at war with Persia.

The winter in Qum was bitterly cold. Hands and feet were easily frozen if precautions were not taken. The sense of smell became impaired, which could be dangerous. One night we were cooking eggs in a mess tin over a stove. We had two petrol cans outside the tent – one was cleaned out and contained water, the other petrol. I was cooking and was brought a can which supposedly had water in it which I proceeded to use to cook the eggs. The shells of the eggs turned yellow and the liquid vanished surprisingly quickly. So I continued pouring the liquid onto the eggs with the same result. We then realised it was petrol but we had not noticed the smell. Fortunately, I had not spilt a drop of the liquid except into the mess tin. These were the last of the eggs and so we had no option but to peel off the yellow shells and eat the boiled eggs – fortunately without ill effects.

Meanwhile, the major's dysentery worsened and he was removed to base hospital. He was replaced temporarily by a captain who was obviously determined to see out the war. It soon became obvious that driving to the major's standards made the new incumbent nervous, and so his batman took over. I was now fit for promotion and was re-classified A1 – and promoted to sergeant.

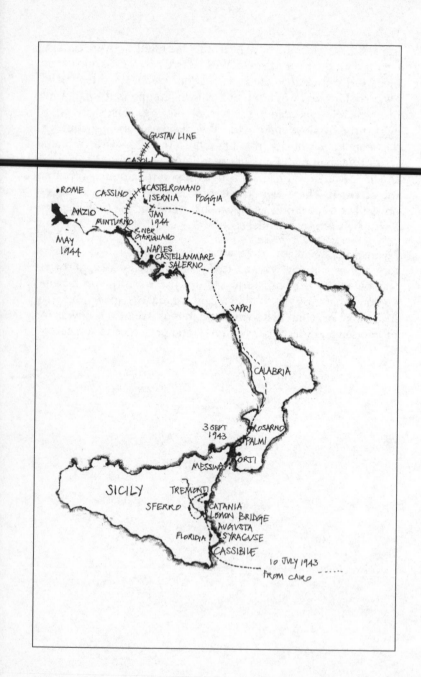

CHAPTER 7

—◦—

SICILY: AN OVERCROWDED ISLAND

In mid-January 1943, it became apparent that the Russians were winning the battles that threatened the Caucasus, and so the threat to Persia had abated. Moreover, the Eighth Army under Montgomery and Anderson's 1st Army, aided by some green American divisions, were bringing the North African campaigns to a successful conclusion. As a fighting infantry division, the Fifth was no longer required to do a policing job in Persia and had to prepare for the next move in the Allies' strategy, which was likely to be an assault landing or full-scale invasion.

Leaving Persia in early February was not the ideal time to move heavy equipment and guns – but it would be a few months before the conditions were perfect. The roads were snowbound and the Shah Pass almost impassable. It was decided to load the majority of motor cycles onto service vehicles and use only the most skilful despatch riders and the Military Police, who had proved their worth in the many miles they had shepherded 'Cook's Tours'. My worth as a driver was rated above being a sergeant so I was the co-driver with the Battery clerk on the office truck, a sluggish Bedford 15cwt with none of the hanky panky of the joyful Dodge.

From poshteens to KD

Once clear of the pass the route was non-stop to Chehar Zabab, where a typhus outbreak was raging. Onward then to the Paitak Pass which was not as formidable as the Shah Pass – but nonetheless another test of driving skills. Suddenly it became warmer at the bottom of this pass and we halted in the little village of Marta, where the layers of winter clothing, jerkins and *poshteens* were discarded. The first stage of the convoy's journey was completed at the old familiar Lancer Camping Ground in Baghdad. Few casualties were reported and a much needed day's rest was taken. Maintenance and refitting held the priority. A change too was made, to KD gear although it was still cold at night. The pay that had accumulated in the winter was quickly liquidated by the Baghdad shops and markets.

The Divisional HQ left Qum at the end of January for Cairo, to take part in the planning of 'Husky'. Their immediate task was to assist in the compiling of the loading tables, so that the assaulting brigade's vital vehicles came off the ship first. This is a tricky task, for allowances had to be made for problems arising when landing an assault division on a hostile coast – this included back-up options. Meanwhile the brigades of the division assembled in the Lancer Camping ground in Baghdad presented a stunning sight as they prepared to start stage two, which had required a regrouping, for the three brigades had different immediate destinations.

Iraq to Syria

Stage two for the Brigade convoys was the desert crossing from Iraq to Syria by way of Transjordania – a formidable wilderness that had very little highway, and even that was blotted out at times by sandstorms. The way ahead was picked out by oil barrels or the pipeline; the pumping stations en route being the British Army's staging points, they were controlled for our convoys by the inveterate Fifth Division's Provost Unit. The driving was sheer hell across sandy wastes with many stoppages, due to sand getting into carburettors. This required immediate attention from mobile fitters on motor cycles, who also had to make sure that no one was left stranded in the wilderness. The first night's stop on this desolate run was at Putbah, a fort of the *Beau Geste* type, with battlements which were being paced by Iraqi troops, who also guarded the gateway into the courtyard. The British staging post was alongside, and supplied petrol and water but not food rations, which were carried on our vehicles. The next day's run was featureless to a pumping station, identified as H4, with the pseudonym 'An Abomination of Desolation'. On the next stage to Mafraq in Jordan, things started to look up as the desert acquired features such as camel thorn and small stones developing into large boulders of lava and giving way to green grass – which many of us had not seen for months.

At Mafraq the convoys of 13th Infantry Brigade turned north-west towards Kafr Coq, Syria, and then on to the Mountain School in the Lebanon, where they would train as the mountain brigade of the Fifth Division, learning all about mules, building sangars for self-preservation in the mountains, and more importantly, polish up their climbing skills. Those of us in the 15th and 17th Brigades headed south to Kefar Yonah in the valley of the River Jordan, where the grass was studded with wild flowers. At a convoy halt, some hardened drivers, overcome by the change in the scenery, left their vehicles to pick handfuls of flowers, to decorate themselves and enjoy the perfume in the cabs of their vehicles.

At Kefar Yonah the convoy rested for the day, mainly to get rid of the desert dust, but a privileged few managed to make a quick visit to Tel Aviv and Jaffa. The next day's run was through Palestine via Gaza and Beersheba, then desert again to Asluj, on the Egyptian border. This sported one of the Middle East's favourite NAAFI clubs, where we laagered for the night. This stay was memorable for the film show, which involved an Egyptian projectionist who played the reels of a Hollywood crime drama out of order, so the murderer was revealed at the beginning of the film. The unfortunate projectionist was rewarded for his efforts by being pelted with fruit by the disappointed squaddies.

The final run for the road parties of the 15th and 17th was to the School of Combined Operations at Kabrit. The journey took us across the Sinai Desert to Ismalia, and then south along the western bank of the Suez Canal to our pleasantly sited destination – where we were reunited with the other parties from Qum. These travellers, comprising the bulk of the foot soldiers, had tedious journeys by rail, steamer and road.

As one of the main assault divisions for 'Operation Husky', the Fifth Division honed its skills on combined operations, by learning up-to-date methods and techniques at the School which included rock climbing and cliff hanging. These techniques were important for the infantry, particularly in cases when they were put ashore some distance from the objective. The methods of getting into and out of various types of landing craft, the loading and unloading of guns, carriers, and stores was practised by all the assault troops. The drivers had a lot of practice in taking their vehicles on and off these craft, so they were confident of landing their vehicles effectively under fire.

After the completion of the Brigades' training at the specialist schools, the whole Division concentrated in the area around Quatana and Jebel Mazar near Damascus in Syria. Here, under the shadow of Mount Hermon, the whole Division was able to put the final touches to training, culminating in a three-day exercise 'Topsail'. Unusually during this period of fine weather, there was an outbreak of illnesses in the camp. Cordery went down with malaria and returned to base. I was taken to the local military hospital with a very high temperature, which was diagnosed as Sandfly Fever. I was dosed liberally with Quinine which improved my condition, so was returned to my unit in two days. On return I was delighted to know that I had been posted to B Troop, the troop earmarked for the new 17-pounder anti-tank gun. My friend Cordery did not return to the unit for some months and so missed 'Operation Husky'.

17-pounder pheasants

The 17-pounder anti-tank gun had arrived in the Middle East from Woolwich under the code name 'Pheasant'. This gun would ultimately prove to be the scourge of the Panzers. The other two troops in the Battery, A and C, would continue with their more mobile 6-pounders, whereas B troop would be the heavy anti-tank gun troop with four of the new 17-pounder guns.

Surprisingly, since I was the new boy, I was given orders to take a gun team to the firing ranges near Cairo, to try out the new gun. It seemed that our recently appointed battery commander Major Shepherd, and the B troop commander Dicky Allen, had enough faith in my gunnery potential to expect a rational unbiased assessment of the new field-piece. My first sight of the Pheasant was a surprise, with its long raking barrel, tipped by a muzzle recoil unit. It gave the impression of being a difficult gun to handle, but it also suggested a reliable high-velocity weapon when propelling its 17-pound projectile. As an anti-tank gun it more than matched the outstanding triple-purpose German 88mm.

At the time, it also had the greatest penetrative power of any gun in the British Army. Its normal projectile had a velocity speed of 1000 metres per second and was able to penetrate hardened steel 180mm thick at 900 metres. The gun was cumbersome, weighing three tons, so as an anti-tank gun it lacked mobility. Before firing the Pheasant, the trail had to be lifted onto a platform with the aid of a hand spike manned by two men. It had a depressingly great height when set up for action, which made it difficult to camouflage. In short, the 'Pheasant' not only lacked mobility but in its role in the front line, it would prove difficult to hide. It had a limited free traverse on either side of centre, operated by the gun layer, but to rotate the gun further required the loader and one other to lift the handspike and move the gun around on its platform.

My gun crew, wearing gas capes for protection against dust, was the first to fire the Pheasant in sandy conditions. The first shot fired showed that the gun shield afforded only limited protection to the layer against blast. The loader, his assistant and myself, the Number One, were peppered with grit and marked with soot. We fired a few more rounds taking up other positions behind the gun, but it was obvious that serious modifications were required to the gun shield. The blast was immense and without proper earplugs, we opened our mouths to avoid serious damage to our eardrums. The armourers, present from the Royal Artillery School of Gunnery, had been making notes, so our experience and that of the other three sections from other batteries in our regiment who followed us there, would be taken up in the modifications. Three weeks later, we collected the modified guns in time for 'Husky' together with the towing vehicles – sixteen Morris Quads that turned out to be very reliable vehicles.

Syria to Suez

Towards the end of June the Division left Syria and headed for the final concentration area on the eastern bank of the Suez Canal, at a tented camp known as El Shatt. As my convoy drove through the Sinai Desert, a large army formation passed in the opposite direction headed for Palestine. In answer to the calls from our convoy as to their identity, we learned it was the 9th Battalion of the Royal Fusiliers in 56 (London) Division. I pulled my truck out of our convoy and told the despatch rider I would catch them up. I waved down one of the passing trucks and enquired if my friend Johnny Ward was with them. The driver said he was their sergeant-major and he was at the back on a motor cycle. In due course a motor cyclist came along and I stopped him, knowing by his bearing it was Johnny. He pulled up and got off the bike with a scowl which changed at once as he recognised me. It was inevitable that we could not talk for long, but it was very satisfying to know that both of us were still around and in decent condition.

Our convoy arrived at El Shatt and joined General Dempsey's xiii Corps which contained 5th and 50th Divisions plus Commando units. The combination in xiii Corps was a reunion of the 5th and 50th Divisions, who fought together as 'Frankforce' in May 1940 under the Fifth Division commander Major-General Franklin. The assault was to be led by the 15th Brigade landing on 'How Sector', and the 17th Brigade on 'George Sector', with the 13th, the mountain-trained brigade, in reserve. It was planned that the ports would be captured by the 17th. The 50th Division would land lower down the coastline and capture a plateau overlooking the vital ports. Further south still the British XXX Corps with 51st Division would land whilst the United States Seventh Army would invade the other side of the island. It would also be the first invasion that British airborne glider-borne troops would land to capture and temporarily hold certain key points for the advancing British forces.

The Eighth Army

A number of exercises were carried out on each of our landing ships to make the troops on board thoroughly familiar with the landing drill. Following each of these exercises we returned to sealed camps, which meant we were confined to the camp area. Following a major conference held by the Eighth Army Commander General Montgomery, it became obvious that the invasion was imminent, but the destination was not revealed to the troops. Montgomery visited the troops of the 5th Division, welcoming them into the Eighth Army and so it became official that we were no longer part of – or the whole of – the mythical Tenth Army.

The convoy carrying 5th Division, as part of the Eastern Taskforce, sailed from Port Said on 5th July in glorious weather. This task force contained two and a half divisions and was the landing spearhead of the British Eighth Army. The plan was for it to meet the Western Task Force sailing from Oran, Algiers, Tunis and Bizerta, carrying the US Seventh Army, at a rendezvous off the south-east coast of Sicily. However, a deception plan routed the Eastern Taskforce to a north-westerly direction, past the enemy-held Island of Crete, as if en route to attack Athens. At the last possible moment our convoy turned westward in the hope that the enemy reconnaissance aircraft, based on Crete, would draw the conclusion that we were assaulting Greece. By this time all the troops had been informed that we were invading Sicily. The first objective on landing was for the 17th Brigade to occupy the two key ports of Syracuse and Augusta, and to make them immediately available to the Royal Navy and other vital shipping.

THE 2ND NORTHAMPTONS MARCHING THROUGH SYRACUSE ON D-DAY
Photo courtesy of the Imperial War Museum, NA 4480

The other two troops in my Battery A and C with their 6-pounder anti-tank guns would be part of these initial landings, together with the other Royal Artillery assault unit – the 18th Light Anti-Aircraft Regiment with their Bofors guns. The unwieldy 17-pounders of B Troop would not be landed until 'D' Day plus 2. In the meantime, B Troop would land as back-up infantry at about 8:00 am – five hours after the front-line infantry regiments. The battle plans were laid out and discussed with us all. The main object of attacking this island was to knock Italy out of the War and ultimately get a toe-hold on the European mainland. The diversionary plan of sailing past Crete would keep us four full days at sea, with the initial landings on 'D' Day being scheduled as the 10th July. I was more concerned with a raging toothache until our MO duly obliged by removing the offending grinder as I held onto the rail of our ship. Apart from the soreness of the wound, I was in some trepidation of the imminent landing.

Into battle

The landing by 17th Brigade on George Sector surprised the enemy and got the assault off to a good start, with 2nd RSF and 6th Seaforths ashore by 0300 hours. The 2nd Northamptons landed shortly afterwards after taking Cassihile and Casa Nuove by 1000 hours, where some of the Garrison were caught in bed by the leading infantry, resulting in quite a few dying without their boots on.

Unfortunately, the airborne troops, who were mostly glider borne, and making their first assault landing of this kind, were released about midnight from their powered tugs, but in a 30mph wind. This resulted in airborne units landing in various places off target, some gliders crashing with many casualties, and others ditching in the sea with many troops drowned. Only 70 all ranks landed near enough to be effective in the area of the bridges over the railway and over the River Anapo. The object was to protect these two bridges until the advancing infantry arrived to take control. The few who reached these two objectives very sensibly removed the demolition charges placed by the enemy and gallantly hung on for a time against persistent attacks. Fortunately the 2 RSFs retook the bridges with their Bren carriers and released the few British airborne troops who were still alive. In this action, the Jocks killed most of the enemy who showed any sign of resistance. The British airborne troops had many casualties in the landing and it was estimated that over six hundred were drowned in the sea.

Most of the Italian units in the area showed the white flag as the 17th advanced into Ponte Grande, under heavy attack from the air and bitter resistance from some belligerent outposts who either still had pride in their homeland or were fascist and supported the German cause. About four miles from Syracuse, the 2nd Northamptons were confronted by about 400 Italians, supported by artillery, who were forming up to counter-attack the advancing 17th Brigade. They were persuaded to abandon such a ridiculous idea, and to release the British airborne prisoners they were holding. By evening, after a long day's skirmishing and marching, the 2 RSF and 2 Northamptons entered Syracuse, together with some Sherman tanks of the County of London Yeomanry. They were given a rapturous welcome by the civilian population, until it was realised that the 17th Brigade had not brought a great deal of food with them, at which point the attitude became less exuberant.

Although Syracuse had been severely bombed and subjected to heavy gunfire from the naval guns, the port was relatively undamaged – and was soon put into working use by other units of the division and the Royal Navy. The fall of Syracuse to 5th Division was the first of many achievements in the Italian campaign of which the Division could be proud – and it was taken at relatively small cost of life to the division. Most of the casualties were from air attacks, including our battery's A Troop commander, who had landed with the infantry and was killed during a heavy air onslaught.

Meanwhile we in B Troop had landed in George Sector. The landing craft grounded in the shallows and we waded the last twenty yards or so to reach the dry sand, and then made haste for cover as Messerschmidts machine-gunned the beaches. Until our 17-pounders landed, we were to serve as back-up infantry. The air attacks had become more intense as we moved in columns on either side of the road. It became clear that the element of surprise had gone and the Luftwaffe had stepped up their operations from the airfields on Catania Plain. Nonetheless the gunners of 18th LAA Regiment in the Division were doing a remarkable job. In one sortie, they shot down five Messerschmidt 109Gs, some of which crashed in 'Messerschmidt Valley' – an area that contained many of the wrecked enemy planes that were shot down near the beaches. Many of these planes were hedge-hopping and so in firing at them, the low trajectory of the tracer shot from the 40mm Bofors guns sometimes set alight the highly inflammable olive trees which caused casualties among friend and foe alike. By the time the division reached Catania Plain, this LAA Regiment had shot down 32 enemy aircraft. We in B Troop Anti-Tank Battery, together with the infantry in front of us, joined in with our Bren and Tommy guns and were able to note a hit here and there from tracer bullets fired from the Bren guns. But it was clear that the Bofors were the main weapon of destruction, as we watched a succession of enemy planes plough into the ground. No doubt a few German and Italian planes were brought down by the RAF, but they did not venture too low in what was a maelstrom of flying metal and burning trees caused by British anti-aircraft defence.

As we advanced, we accumulated a motley array of useful objects abandoned by the enemy, such as a mule or two, cars that were still serviceable, anything that would serve to carry equipment and supplies such as fruit and tomatoes until our own transport landed. However, we quickly learned that Italy was the home of devious mining devices – the most destructive was the 'red devil' which was generally hidden among the tomato vines. Early on, one of our sergeants lost a hand as he was picking tomatoes in a field. This led to the maxim that Army rations were the most favoured diet. Abandoned cars, motor cycles and empty houses were often mined and in some cases inquisitive individuals were blown up and killed. These devices were in addition to Telemines that were buried in or on the verges of roads, with the object of destroying transport. Additionally, anti-personnel mines were liberally sown in the ground at approaches to an enemy's defence line or site. These devices resulted in the advancing individual losing a foot – and sometimes his life.

Elsewhere, the 13th were under orders to capture Floridia, which was a key road junction. In the context of the advance by 5th Division, this road junction afforded the means to counter-attack Syracuse while it was still in enemy hands. This threat was negated when the town was taken by 2 Cameronians supported by 2 Inniskillings. They had a rare battle with Italian troops when they ran into a nest of machine guns around a well dug-in 88mm gun in a wooded area. After quelling a number of attacks and sustaining heavy casualties the Italians surrendered to the 'Skins' amidst much weeping. By this time the 5th Division had taken many prisoners who had to be moved back to base and taken into PoW compounds.

The Royal Navy landing the 15th had somehow missed 'How Sector' and landed the brigade further south. In consequence they were out of touch with the other two assault brigades in the division for two days, and were temporarily under the command of 50th Division. They were needed by 5th Division and this took a lot of marching on the division's main axis to catch up. In fact they had taken more sea water in their boots, from being landed in the wrong place, than the other infantry regiments in the division. Ultimately, they marched a hundred miles in the first three days in Sicily, before they could give their salty feet a rest. Their first task with the division was to meet up with the 17th Brigade at Priola, and then advance on Melilli, a small hillside town dominating the main road to Lentini. The 1st Green Howards met up with the 6th Seaforths to capture Melilli from the Italian garrison, who were still punch-drunk from the naval bombardment.

A 17-POUNDER ANTI-TANK GUN IN ACTION IN THE ANZIO BRIDGEHEAD
Photo courtesy of the Imperial War Museum, NA 12888

The next task for 5th Division was to capture the port of Augusta. The approach to it was through Priola, a small town surrounded by thick woods, and the route taken was along a winding narrow road with stone walls on either side. This was the setting in which the Division met the first German troops since the landing. They were from the Herman Goering Division and were holding a typically strong rearguard position. The first German blood was drawn by the carriers of the 2 Northamptons in the Priola woods when leading the 17th Brigade. The battalion, however, could not make much headway against several well placed and determined Spandau posts. The Sherman tanks supporting them were unable to give much assistance, being confined to the narrow banked road. They were to lose three of their tanks to a well sited 88mm gun before this gun was knocked out. The only way through was a full fireplan from the Divisional Artillery, who moved late at night to suitable positions between Syracuse and Priola, to make such a concentration possible. This was to be preceded by a dive-bombing programme by the RAF. The enemy, anticipating trouble that could threaten their withdrawal, evacuated their positions in the night.

Meanwhile, a platoon of 2 Northamptons had moved into Augusta and established itself in the north end of the town just as the dive-bombing started. They had to go to ground until they were able to put yellow smoke down, as an indication that friendly troops were in the town. As a side issue two Carabinieri were pestering the troops to take them prisoner as their police role was becoming untenable and they were most indignant that the troops did not want to know. The 2 RSF and 6 Seaforths then entered Augusta to stabilise the position. Meanwhile, the 2 Northamptons started to clean up the town and were kept busy mopping up the many pockets of resistance that sprang up. These harassing tactics from a few fanatical Fascists and odd German paratroopers were to continue, but after three days of fighting, the 17th had taken two major ports and captured more than 1,000 prisoners. Their own losses were not unduly high, but 2 RSF alone had lost all three of their field officers.

The advance of 15th Brigade beyond Priola had now cut off the Augusta peninsula from attack from the north-west, but there were still about 400 Italian defenders in positions on the cliffs between the two brigades and these had to be cleaned up by the 13th following behind.

Now that the port of Syracuse was open – despite intermittent air raids – the build-up of divisional personnel, vehicles, guns and equipment was proceeding well. A number of follow-up units now landed, not used in the initial assault, such as the 5 Recce Regiment, and were able to undertake their first operational role by mopping up enemy left behind south of Augusta. The 7th Cheshire (Heavy machine gun) Regiment was now available to the division and B Troop's 17-pounder anti-tank guns had landed, so we reverted to our true role of anti-tank artillerymen and moved west to our battery B echelon near Villasamundi to prepare the Quads and guns for action. As the new boy in B Troop and the spare sergeant, I was allocated to B2 in support of Willie Smith, a Territorial sergeant who I had known since the beginning of 1939. Our troop advanced with part of 17th Brigade towards Primasole Bridge – a huge iron bridge where the 50th Infantry Division was engaged in a fierce battle with German paratroopers, who had been flown in from southern Italy. In this battle our old comrades from BEF days, the Durham Light Infantry, were heavily involved.

ENGINEERS REPAIRING PRIMASOLE BRIDGE, CAPTURED BY 2 RSF
Photo courtesy of the Imperial War Museum, NA 5123

Meanwhile, 2 Northamptons in Augusta were under orders to be moved by landing craft from Augusta and land further up the coast north of Primasole Bridge and take the pressure from the battle which was holding up xlii Corps and costing many lives. However, for some reason, this apparently obvious move was called off as being too risky, but a landing force of brigade strength was available, mainly from the 17th Brigade. An element of caution and dithering seemed to have entered into the strategy, which was not present on the initial landing. Possibly such tactics were not envisaged in the original plan and so this move was rejected. Yet the American forces on the other side of the island were leapfrogging up the coast when the opportunity occurred. The Germans meanwhile were showing great mobility by flying in troops as required, including six more battalions of the Herman Goering Division, who set up positions along the Mount Etna foothills. Additional German paratroops landed to bolster their forces defending the Semeto River line, and enabled them to strengthen their hold on Primasole Bridge.

General Montgomery decided to bring in more Eighth Army troops from North Africa, including the excellent 78th Infantry Division. This had the effect of clogging up the centre of the island, which up to that point had been a smooth-running mobile operation. Moreover, the infantry battalions and tank regiments who had fought in the desert – where there was plenty of room for manoeuvre – found the narrow roads and hedgerows of Sicily difficult to contend with.

An alternative strategy was adopted by 5th Division to relieve the pressure on Primasole Bridge by moving the 13th Brigade inland to find an alternative crossing over the Simeto river, which would open the way to Catania Plain. The 2 Inniskillings sent forward a strong fighting patrol and found a bridge over the Simeto not yet blown up, which they called 'Lemon Bridge'. They were very suspicious that there were enemy tracked vehicles on the other side within the vicinity of the bridge. The leading company of the battalion sent a platoon across the river to the east of the bridge in order to come in on the rear of any potential enemy. There was in fact a small enemy post, which they dealt with and by midnight the whole battalion moved across the bridge. Almost immediately tanks were heard and what they assumed was the enemy advanced on them, shouting, 'Don't shoot, this is the Jocks!' The suspicious Irishmen let fly a few well-aimed volleys at 'where their sporrans should have been'. This started a series of battles throughout the night to hold the small bridgehead. By dawn the 'Skins' were well dug in – but any attempts to enlarge the bridgehead were fiercely resisted by the German paratroops.

Kesselring was determined to hold Catania and the north-east corner of Sicily. The increase in troops from the Italian mainland enabled him to hold dominant positions on the Mount Etna slopes, which provided magnificent observation points. His position was further strengthened by well placed strong points on the edge of Catania Plain and along the natural defensive line of the river Simeto.

The earlier advance by the British forces in the hot Sicilian summer started to slow and then came to a halt, mainly as a result of the build-up of frontline enemy forces and the stranglehold they had on Primasole Bridge. Other contributing factors to this unscheduled hold-up were the hilly terrain and the narrowness of the roads, which were often mined. After a week's fighting in these conditions, the roads had become cluttered with burning vehicles, and the trees and fields were often blazing or smoking, the result of either mortar, artillery fire, or the occasional air raid. The evidence of war was everywhere, with crashed British gliders and German fighter planes. In this hot, smoky atmosphere lay dead animals and battlefield casualties – a strange harvest in the Sicilian fields.

After ten days of fighting, the 15th Brigade put in a very hasty, and thus ill-reconnoitred, attack to expand the shallow bridgehead over the Simeto River around 'Lemon Bridge' so fiercely won by the 13th. The attack was put in with 1 Green Howards on the right and the 1st Yorks and Lancs on the left with 1 KOYLI in reserve. The infantry advance was slowed down by unforeseen ditches, adjacent to the railway line, causing the advancing infantry to lose ground on the creeping artillery barrage. Although supported by all available guns in xlii Corps and heavy machine guns from the Cheshires, the Germans had built up a very strong defensive line with Spandau posts overlooking the bridgehead area into which they poured withering fire including artillery air bursts. In the ensuing turmoil, 'B' Company of the Green Howards had moved ahead of 'A' Company and became involved in a most bitter hand-to-hand fight with a strong-point of Germans, which resulted in heavy casualties on both sides. These included 'B' Company's Commander, Captain Verity who received wounds from which he later died in captivity. He managed to order back Lieutenant Bell with a few survivors. The lieutenant later returned to rescue his Company Commander and other wounded, but he was unable to get to them because of the strength of the opposition.

On the morning of 22nd July it became quite clear that the 15th Brigade were in a tenuous situation with their battalions in exposed shallow ditches overlooked by German Spandau posts, with the Germans holding all the high ground. The Divisional Artillery gave cover so that the infantry of the 15th could move back to better positions. The 17th Brigade moved forward and took over the 15th's positions with the addition of the 1st KOYLI of 15th Brigade, so establishing a four-battalion front.

My battery, the 206 Anti-Tank Battery, moved forward as part of the 17th with the Seaforths, RSF and Northamptons. Our gun crew's 17-pounder anti-tank gun was brought into the line and we dug in on the left flank of the infantry, adjacent to one of the railway line viaducts, near the Semeto River. There was very little cover and, as predicted, the gun with its camouflage netting, although dug in, and below the crest of the slope, was visible and this would continue to be a problem with the 'Pheasant' in the days to come. It soon became evident that our presence had been spotted, first by a nosy spotter plane, which we did not engage with our Bren light machine gun, in the hope that the gun could still be mistaken for a haystack. Later, however, the German artillery fired a few ranging shots around our position.

Under fire

But it was not the German artillery that caused the first casualties in my gun team. Along with the look-out Belcher, I was placed near the gun. The rest of the gun crew with Bill Smith were in the archway of the viaduct about twenty yards away, stacking spare ammunition and supporting gear. As I moved down the slope towards the archway to communicate with them, there was a huge explosion nearby and then a scream of someone in agony. My four comrades were hurled in various directions. Boothby was mortally wounded with shrapnel in and around his liver and was obviously in great pain. Paddy McGuire was not moving and had puncture marks in his back. Bill Smith was suffering from shell shock and shouting incoherently about the German bastards, while Bleasdale was dazed but apparently unhurt. Using all the gun team's field bandages, I dressed their wounds as best I could. Boothby was already on the wane and was sobbing for his mother. We had no morphine or pain-killers and so I decided to go to the Seaforths' front line in the hope of locating the Field Ambulance unit. It took about two hours for Boothby and McGuire to be taken away on stretchers. Boothby, a First Militia boy from London in his early twenties, died that night on the operating table at the Field Ambulance unit. McGuire, a reservist from Northern Ireland, and in his late thirties, suffered serious back injuries and was invalided out of the Army.

The cause of the explosion was a mystery, because neither Belcher nor I heard the whistle of an artillery round. The possibility remained that the viaduct was booby-trapped and the moving of anything in the archway could have set off an anti-personnel mine. News of the incident got back to battery headquarters, via the infantry wireless. Later that evening, Dickie Allen came with our Quad to withdraw us from the position, which was no longer tenable, for we were down to only two fit men to handle the 17-pounder and the Bren gun.

A depleted crew

We halted for a short break on the way back to battery headquarters feeling very low, particularly about Boothby. The road was cluttered with refugees, and an Italian boy, about ten years old, came towards us holding out his hands for anything we could spare. Bill Smith picked up his Sten gun and wanted to shoot 'the little Italian bastard!'. Belcher and I disarmed him at once: delirious from shell shock, he might turn his gun on friend or foe. The gun team was thus reduced to two able men and Bleasdale – who still had to see the MO – and Hope, the Quad driver. Back at Troop HQ, I officially took over the section and was given three replacements including a lance bombardier Levett who was a Territorial and had been transferred from Battery HQ. Bleasdale was pronounced fit, and so we started to train with the replacements who were familiar with the 6-pounder anti-tank gun, but were complete strangers to the 17-pounder. Bill Smith was sent back to Base to recover and we never saw him again.

We moved back to the front with the 17th Brigade and took up a gun position near the 2 Northamptons. In this new position on Catania Plain everyone kept their head down by day as the British Field Artillery 'plastered' the German defensive positions. At night infantry patrols passed close by our position sometimes whispering among themselves – sometimes in German. It was vital that we did not give our position away, because this was tank country. The Spotters would be searching for anti-tank gun locations in the event of a planned tank attack on our infantry positions.

General Montgomery in the meantime decided to wheel XXX Corps – mainly the 51 Highland Division and the excellent 78 (Battle Axe) British Infantry Division – around the pivot of our xlii Corps position near the foothills of Etna. Our new role was to hold firmly onto the Simeto shallow bridgehead, which had been so hard won by our 13th Brigade. This position and the other 5th Division locations on Catania Plain were proving to be very costly in casualties, not only from hand to hand fighting and night patrols, for it was also one of the most notorious malarial areas in the Mediterranean. In spite of precautions, the division was suffering grievous malaria casualties as the result of this enforced stay on the plain. This might have been avoided had we made further landings up the coast and cut off Catania, which seemed possible once we had taken Syracuse with relatively minor casualties and with landing craft still available.

The three Field Artillery Regiments in the division made full use of this static period to dominate the battlefield by firing divisional concentrations, using the German observation posts as targets and also by choosing any likely enemy supply locations such as an ammunition train in Motta Santa Anastasia railway station, which blew up with such a startling effect that it could be seen and heard all over the island.

The delay by xlii Corps on the plain lasted about a week, and then on 3rd August, the 5th Division probed and then started to move on Misterbianco and Motta Santa Anastasia and 50th Division reached the outskirts of Catania. The 17th Brigade gradually overcame enemy outposts, while the Divisional Engineers cleared many minefields and removed booby-traps that were slowing the infantry's advance. They entered Misterbianco with the 2 RSF and 2 Northamptons on the evening of 6th August, to a rapturous reception. The main Catania–Adrana road was now cut. The 15th Brigade had captured Motta Santa Anastasia with 1 KOYLI and 1 Green Howards. They then moved on towards Belpasso, where after a prolonged battle on the outskirts and within the town, the 1 Green Howards, well supported by the machine gunners of the 7th Cheshires, eventually captured the town. The final entry was one of triumph

5TH DIVISION TROOPS BOARDING LANDING CRAFT
FOR THE ASSAULT ON THE ITALIAN MAINLAND
Photo courtesy of the Imperial War Museum, NA 6297

and mass hysteria as never seen before by most of the soldiers, who were overwhelmed by the handclapping and the throwing of flowers. This was as much a reflection of the joy being expressed by the Sicilians at the news of the resignation of Mussolini the week before, and their fervent wish to rid Sicily of the Germans.

TROOP CARRIERS OF 2ND WILTS (13TH BRIGADE)
MOVING THROUGH PATERNO
Photo courtesy of the Imperial War Museum, NA 5752

Germans on retreat

In this period the 5th Division Recce Regiment had done superb work in bridging a gap between xlii Corps and XXX Corps, often joining forces with the tanks of County of London Yeomanry who were still supporting 5th Division. Meanwhile, the 13th Infantry Brigade had moved up from Paterno, which had been evacuated by the Germans, who had retreated five miles following the pressure on their forward positions by the division's Recce Regiment, and the advance by British and Canadian tanks. There were now clear signs that the Germans were evacuating their positions and moving towards Messina, in order to withdraw to the mainland. Our regiment, 52 Anti-Tank and other divisional troops had pulled out from positions on various parts of Catania Plain and were assembling in Misterbianco.

The 13th Infantry Brigade – our mountain trained brigade – moved on to Belpasso, held by the 15th, and were headed towards the Etna foothills, with the purpose of capturing three vital peaks. They passed through Nicolosi which was heavily mined and booby-trapped – in some cases German corpses were being used for this purpose. The 2 Cameronians were soon established on the north end of the town and the 2 Inniskillings occupied the high ground to the south-east. For the next few days there followed some very hard and confused fighting in the lava foothills against a stubborn and relentless enemy, fighting for every possible hour of delay. This enemy appeared to be on about three sides of the divisional area in the hills. To add to the confusion, civilians arrived at the various headquarters with lurid reports of odd parties of Germans committing all kinds of atrocities.

On 8th August 2 Inniskillings set out to capture Tremonte and three prominent peaks between Pedara and Etna. The first attack on Tremonte failed. In the meantime 2 Cameronians had successfully attacked two prominent hills, Monte Arso and Monte Gervasi; on the latter they surprised from the rear some enemy who were firing on to Tremonte. The 13th then ordered 2 Cameronians to attack Tremonte from their advantageous position. On the morning of the 9th they set off to do this. The Inniskillings meanwhile launched a second attack on Tremonte which was successful; this saved 2 Cameronians a long walk and received the plaudits of the Army Commander and their Scottish comrades. The 2 Wiltshires entered Tregastani on the right and that was the last enemy stand against the 13th Brigade in Sicily.

The Brigade was then given orders to withdraw to Monte Santa Anastasia to rest and prepare for the invasion of the Italian mainland. The 51 Highland Division passed through them a day or so later to continue the chase to Messina.

The Italian mainland

The Northern advance of XXX Corps was held up at Randazzo on the eastern slopes of Etna and the enemy was actually bringing in reinforcements to slow down the German retreat. The Army Commander decided to bring back a brigade from 5th Division that was resting prior to 'Baytown' – the landing on the Italian mainland in Reggio de Calabria – in order to accelerate the conclusion of the campaign in Sicily. The 15th Brigade, being the reserve brigade, was ordered forward, and 1 Green Howards had to take the mountain village of Milo. There was very little opposition but they were on the heels of the withdrawing Germans and came under heavy shelling from the Italian mainland and sustained some casualties.

The 15 Panzer Grenadier regiment managed to cross the straits of Messina in small boats. A decision was made that it would be too costly for the RAF pilots to dive low enough to get under the enemy aircraft umbrella which was rated as effective as the well-known 'Essen Corridor'. The other attacking regiment of the 15th, the 1 KOYLI, went mountaineering up Etna in order to force the German right flank. It was hard climbing on the cindery tracks but they reached a point where the Field Artillery was able to direct significant fire onto the departing Germans. The battalions of the 15th were then withdrawn and were relieved by a brigade of the 51 Highland Division.

The Battalions of the 5th Infantry Division had created some sort of a record in marching most of the way from the assault beaches in and around Cassibile, much of this distance wearing boots which had been soaked in salt water when they landed. An example of the onerous tasks that fall onto the shoulders of the 'poor bloody infantry' – and which is rarely the lot of specialist troops! The whole of the 5th Division was now concentrated around Misterbianco and Motta Santa Anastasia and to the west, resting, bathing, eating, attending concerts by ENSA and being entertained by the division's considerable own talent. I, together with others swam out into the bay off Catania, where many of us were stung by jellyfish and beat a hasty retreat to the shore. Just before the end of August the Division moved up the coast to prepare for the second, much longer round – the assault on the Italian mainland.

In retrospect, the ultimate victory in Sicily was achieved by the infantry with great support from the artillery, engineers and naval guns. Special forces such as commando and airborne troops were used in greater numbers than in earlier campaigns and they had a limited although important role. Ultimately, it is infantry and armoured divisions who win battles and consolidate positions.

The terrain in Sicily over which the campaign was fought showed the interior to be a mountainous mass, with few good roads. Its meagre communications were hardly adequate for the quick movement of a modern army. Its small straggling towns often perched like medieval castles on the hilltops and the whole of the island was, and still is, dominated by Mount Etna, its wide base overflowing with lava and volcanic rock.

The average Sicilian lived in filth and squalor and most of the islanders were illiterate. Drinking water and normal sanitation were almost unknown and flies and mosquitoes enjoyed the resultant filth. Malaria was rife, particularly in the Catania Plain. Abundant fruit could be picked almost anywhere, but was a snare to all but the Sicilian stomach. A guide book of the time advised travellers not to visit Sicily between June and September – advice that clearly didn't influence the planners who managed to get the campaign up and running between July and late August. Fortunately, by this time the 5th Division (Cook's Tours) were used to extreme climates at ill-advised and quite unfashionable seasons.

It would have been preferable to have kept the campaign nearer the coastline rather than it being bogged down on Catania Plain. It would have been possible to use the three brigades of one division, leapfrogging up the coast with naval gun support – after all, the British Navy had complete control of the coastline from Syracuse to the Straits of Messina. Instead there was needless loss of lives on Catania Plain and around the Etna foothills. It would seem that Patton's American Seventh Army adopted the better tactics in leapfrogging up the west coast of Sicily. This was to a certain degree forced on them by Montgomery's insistence that the four main routes to Messina, mainly through the centre of the Island, were reserved for the use of the Eighth Army. Unfortunately, Montgomery had made the island over-crowded and slowed down the advance of his frontline troops, so allowing the Germans more time to prepare their defensive strategy.

Alexander, the overall commander of the campaign, never took command. As a result the two rival generals commanded two individual armies, with Patton fighting his own battle but taking a secondary role to Montgomery. Alexander had little regard for the calibre of the American troops and accordingly allowed Montgomery to set the pace and indeed communicate with Patton direct. Montgomery proposed on July 25th that, as Patton's Seventh Army was in a better position to capture Messina, they should go ahead and do so. Montgomery and the 5th Division and the newly arrived 1st Canadian Division were thinking ahead to Baytown's D day on September 1st.

At the conclusion of the campaign, the 5th Division, like the other divisions, mourned its losses, particularly that of the great England cricketer Hedley Verity. He was a well known sportsman and gentleman who chose to be a frontline infantry officer in preference to the usual route for national sportsmen, of PT instructor or visiting team representative. The Yorkshireman who had taken Bradman's wicket a number of times in the 30s was mourned by the Green Howards, the 5th Division and the British sporting public. It made the loss of his life even more painful that it occurred in a failed, ill- conceived, hasty attack which was badly reconnoitred, in an attempt to enlarge the bridgehead on the Catania Plain.

CHAPTER 8

─○─

CALABRIA, CASSINO AND ANZIO

At 04:30 on 3rd September 1943, exactly four years after the outbreak of the Second World War, the 13th and 17th Infantry Brigades of the Fifth Division landed on the beaches at Gallico Marina to the north of Reggio, while a Canadian Infantry Brigade landed further east. These landings by xiii Corps of the British Eighth Army were supported by the whole of the XXX Corps artillery and a sea-to-shore bombardment from warships *Rodney*, *Valiant*, *Nelson* and *Warspite*. In all, over 400 tons of explosive was hurled into Calabria. The barrage started at the waterline, moved inland to smother the coastal guns and then returned to the beaches to suppress any intended action by the surviving defenders.

The crossing of the Straits of Messina by the Allied landing craft was erratic, mainly due to thick smoke and dust thrown up by the intensive barrage. However, the German army, in the form of the 29th Panzer Grenadiers – the real foe – had left the area a day or so earlier, and taken to the mountainous terrain of central Calabria. The enemy on the shore were the Italian divisions, consisting of many weeping troops who were not sure whether or not they were still the enemy following Mussolini's resignation. The huge barrage had created more demolition problems on the mainland to add to the expert destruction created by the German sappers before they departed.

My troop, in the role of supporting infantry, crossed in amphibious craft. We would continue in this role until our cumbersome 17-pounder anti-tank 'Pheasants' could be brought over and unloaded. I was given the task, with about a dozen of my troop, of taking over a large mixed group of Italian prisoners who were hindering the advance of the 17th Brigade. A group of them seemed to be a cut above the rest, and were wearing an immaculate uniform, with a Tyrolean-style hat adorned by a hackle. Considering the powerful barrage, they seemed to have survived remarkably well in comparison to their contemporaries and were still showing some pride in their appearance and attitude. Their spokesman came up to me, 'Hey buddy, I'm from Brooklyn! Where you guys been? 'Tedesci', he left two days ago!'

'Well, matey,' I responded, 'as far as we are concerned, you are also the enemy. Italy is still at war with us, you know. Who are you anyway?'

'We', he said with not inconsiderable arrogance, 'are the crack Alpino regiment.' They deserved our respect since they had survived the enormous barrage and were still able to present themselves as soldiers. Our Italian 'Buddy' had been visiting relatives in Milan in 1939 when he was conscripted into the Italian army.

The first night ashore, with my dozen men I disarmed about a thousand Italian troops and took control of a wide variety of weaponry. This did not seem to dismay them, for their war was over. All night long we guarded our prisoners in an open field, while being serenaded with mandolins, guitars and vocal renderings of Italian love songs. In this eerie situation there were too few of us to take any rest, so we were quite relieved to hand over our prisoners to the Pioneer Corps in the morning. They improved the situation by erecting a temporary cage, although in the night a number of prisoners had probably managed to escape and make their way home. On reflection, Day One on the Italian mainland could have been worse.

In the meantime, our guns and quads had landed, so we were back to being anti-tank gunners and ready to support the infantry of the 17th whose role was to take over the high ground four miles inland from the coast. The 2 Northamptons led this advance towards San Stefana against very light opposition, until they came to an impassable crater in a mountain-side road with a sheer drop into a deep ravine below. This was covered by Spandau and rifle fire indicating that the rearguard of the German Panzer division was still close at hand. This expert demolition work meant that we in the 17th would have to turn around and go back to the coast road. This was the only road from the beaches that had been cleared and we would have to follow behind the 13th, who were advancing towards Scylla.

Meanwhile the 15th Infantry brigade took a pleasant boat trip and landed further up the coast to the south of Villa San Giovanni to break out towards Bagnara. The three battalions of the 15th started to advance, with the 1st Yorks and Lancs in the lead, followed by the 1st Green Howards, while 1 KOYLI did some mountaineering on the high ground of the western flank. Unfortunately, the supporting field artillery were soon out of range because they were hindered by demolition and mines. A commando unit had landed ahead of the 15th at Bagnara where they met the rearguard of the 29th Panzer Grenadier Division. After a fierce fight, they took part of the town, driving the Germans into the northern outskirts. The 1 Yorks and Lancs advanced through a long tunnel – the only route available south of the town. On emerging, they found themselves up against German rearguard forces that were between them and the commandos in the town. In order to bypass this action the other two battalions took to the high ground south of the town and reached the road from Bagnara to Euphemia. One of the Green Howard patrols contacted the enemy outside Cerimido in a strongpoint of machine guns covering all roads north, defended by Italian troops who soon gave in to the pressure of the Green Howard patrol. They were the last Italian troops to face the Division during the war. The German Panzer Grenadier units had meanwhile hastened north towards Rosarno, obviously aware that the Allies would be landing troops further up the coast.

The demolition damage around the Bagnara tunnel resulted in the infantry of the 13th being moved by landing craft twelve miles ahead of the 15th to a beach three miles south of Gioia. This was successfully done in darkness on the morning of 6th September but not without minor problems. A heavy swell took the boats away from the beach, so the infantry had to wade some distance to get ashore. In the case of the 2 Inniskillings their landing craft could not get near enough to the beach, and some of their troops were swept out to sea. Fortunately, all were saved from drowning with the help of the regimental padre.

The advance was taken on by the 2 Cameronians, who captured Rosarno after a battle along the river line. German self-propelled guns and Spandau machine guns were very active and two of the Cameronians' carriers were knocked out, with some casualties. The Divisional Engineers were at the forefront of the action, clearing mines, building bridges and making diversions in order to accelerate the advance of the Field Artillery guns and other heavy equipment which was needed to support the infantry. Some of the unmarked minefields were cluttered up with enemy dead, including Italian troops, who had obviously taken a chance in hastening to the north to rejoin the main body of enemy troops.

The Commandos and the 231 (Malta) Infantry Brigade made a landing in Porto San Venere near Pizzo. Unfortunately, the beach was occupied by German troops, and in taking the position the Malta Brigade sustained heavy casualties. In order to stabilise the position the 13th and 17th, who were some 50 miles south of Pizzo, advanced in mobile columns. Each column had a small section of frontline units, infantry, artillery, engineers, signals and heavy machine guns from the Cheshire regiment. My quad and gun was part of the 17th mobile column, which was commanded by the CO of the 2 Northamptons. The lighter 6-pounder anti-tank guns, with their shorter range, were placed near the front because they could be readied for action more quickly.

The 17-pounder which was at the back of the convoy had to be pulled onto a firing platform before it was ready for action. Every time the convoy stopped, my gun team placed the gun into an action mode and took it out again at speed in order to keep up with the convoy. This was done four times on the trip to Pizzo. Once in an action mode the 'Pheasant', with its higher velocity, could knock out any interfering tank in the Wehrmacht.

Italy surrenders

On the evening of 8th September, Rome Radio and the BBC broke the news of Italy's unconditional surrender, which had in fact occurred on 3rd September – the day of the landings in Reggio. The bulletin had not been released at the time because it might hinder the imminent landings by the Allies at Salerno. Now, at every window and balcony, white sheets appeared and the Italians gathered at every street corner and clapped their hands as the division moved north towards the Salerno area. Some of the Italian peasants mouthed disrespectful comments about Mussolini and 'Tedesci', and called us their *'Inglesi amigos'*.

A second series of mobile columns was set up by the 17th Brigade with the infantry from the 2 RSF and 2 Northamptons, which included my 'Pheasant' boosted by another from B Troop. The object was to advance rapidly and capture Nicastro, a significant town with good facilities that could ease the Division's over-stretched lines of communication. We met with little opposition and reached our objective on the evening of 9th September. My unit had its B echelon in a farm on the outskirts of Nicastro. By this time my gun team and I had either been in action or on alert since landing on 3rd September, so we needed a rest. I climbed on top of a haystack and slept a whole eighteen hours until 2 pm the following day. I awoke to the news that Mark Clark's Fifth Army had landed at Salerno. The landing included the British Corps, X Corps with the 46th and 56th Infantry Divisions, some Commandos and various other British units. Knowing that my friend Johnny Ward was a sergeant-major in the 9th Royal Fusiliers in 56 Division I felt some concern. I learned later that his battalion had been at the forefront of the landing and that Johnny had been awarded the Military Medal.

On the inland route, Cantanzara had fallen to the Canadians and so having taken Nicastro, the toe and instep of Italy were firmly gripped by the Eighth Army. Since landing around Reggio, xiii Corps had covered a hundred miles in seven days over very difficult roads and hindered all the way by minefields and severe demolition by the retreating Germans. This achievement, fronted by the infantry, was helped by using landing craft and receiving more significant support from the Navy. It clearly showed that these tactics had been under-used in the Sicilian campaign. Nonetheless, the German Army had made a clever defence of southern Italy without sacrificing their troops. As a result xiii Corps infantry were well ahead of the units with the heavy supporting weaponry such as Field Artillery – except for a few guns like our 17-pounders. It was an exhausting seven days, but it would be the easiest part of the Italian campaign for the Fifth Division. The battles yet to come in this mountainous country, where the weather and terrain were as formidable as the enemy, would prove to be some of the severest of the war.

The Salerno landings

The Salerno landings – Operation Avalanche by the American Fifth Army, ran into immediate trouble from the veteran 16th Panzer Division. The declaration of the surrender of the Italian forces, deliberately withheld until the landing of the American Fifth Army, embittered the German forces, who were further enraged at the sight of the Italian people already carrying home-made Union Jacks or Stars and Stripes. The sight of the Italian troops riding home on bicycles made it clear that the Germans were on their own. To those of us who were at Dunkirk it was reminiscent of the Belgian Army in May 1940, so we knew how they felt.

The 16th Panzer Division was being reinforced by troops brought south from Naples and Rome. The barrage they poured into the incoming landing craft sank a few before they reached the shores of Salerno. Some blew up, others exploded after hitting mines in the bay. Troops wading towards the shore were hit by endless fixed line tracer fire and a few were machine-gunned by marauding Luftwaffe fighters. Landings were made on the wrong beaches, the timetables disintegrated and the situation became chaotic. Units designated to assault key defensive points did not arrive on time. The Germans held all the high ground overlooking the bay and they used it to full advantage by pouring fire from every gun available, including their deadly 88mm triple-purpose fieldpiece.

The Allies' original attacking plan was flawed, in that the landings resulted in a seven-mile gap between the British 10th Corps and the US VI Corps. General Clark considered the re-embarkation of one of the two Corps and its relocation in the sector of the other.

The first five days were critical to the allies, for during this period the German build-up reached the strength of two corps.

The day was saved by the naval performance, which was a great improvement on that provided in the Sicilian campaign. The landing craft still afloat returned with fresh troops and supplies and landed them on the right beaches. The British 46th Infantry Division, which held the forward position, and the British 56th Infantry Division in a defensive position, withstood continuous attack and the American troops in VI Corps held their ground admirably. Ultimately this resistance was aided by the timely parachute drop of two regimental combat teams from the American 82nd Airborne Division into the beachhead – the most successful parachute drop in the war by the Allies. Finally, the superb gunnery on the part of the Allied navy, and the field artillerymen ashore, turned the tide.

The German Tenth Army Commander, realising it was the major landing, decided to withdraw and defend a line further north. Accordingly, he ordered the 26th Panzer Division, who were fighting a delaying action against the Eighth Army in southern Calabria, to disengage and move north to the Salerno front.

In the south, the British Fifth Division lines of communication were still a cause for great concern, as the B echelons were out of wireless communication with the front-line troops. On 12th September one of the patrols of the 5th Division's Recce Regiment moved up the coast to Amantea, where the roads were completely blocked by demolition. Amazingly, they discovered a train with steam up and driver standing by. In the confusion, no one had stopped this train from running, so the patrol boarded the train, despite objections from the ticket collector that they had no tickets. They lay on the floor of the train out of sight of German patrols and travelled to Cosenza, where they disembarked and captured the airfield.

The Fifth Division HQ had moved forward and become fully established in the Nicastro area. On the road to Nicastro, they were followed by newsmen and entertainers, including George

Formby and his wife Beryl, clinging desperately to a jeep as it lurched along the uneven road. They were on their way to give an impromptu concert at Fifth Division HQ. As they passed a minefield on the verge of the road with some Italian bodies lying about, the lady was heard to remark in an unmistakably Lancastrian dialect that it was a good thing she was not the fainting type.

The infantry brigades were making headway by using boats again because of the impassable roads. The 13th Brigade made a sea trip to Scalea and were followed by the 17th. Meanwhile the 15th were marching up the coast road to Belverdere and San Agate. The road to Belverdere was afterwards found to be filled with bombs timed to go off – fortunately, the advancing infantry of the 15th passed by without disturbing them.

Our B troop, for the first time in Italy, went forward as a unit in the 17th Brigade convoy en route for Scalea to rejoin our infantry battalions who had gone ahead by boat. Our four guns were towed by quads about twenty yards apart and looked splendid. The order of the march was that the gun commander's head, wearing a steel helmet, should protrude through the overhead hatch and observe the countryside and the way ahead. Cracknell, in the quad behind mine, had acquired an undertaker's top hat with silk ribbon draping, which he decided to wear. Every Italian we passed was acknowledged with the doffing of the top hat. Suddenly, unannounced, a noisy entourage travelling at speed overtook us, with Montgomery sitting in his staff car, wearing one of his selection of hats. As Monty turned around to identify the individual not in battle order, Cracknell's head vanished and reappeared wearing a steel helmet, looking the picture of a responsible sergeant. He was only just in time, as two military policemen on their bikes came roaring back to identify the culprit. After a brief and unsuccessful search, they returned disconsolate to their entourage.

The Fifth Division's Recce Regiment was forging ahead to link up with the forces of Mark Clark's 5th Army on the southern side of the Salerno bridgehead. By 12th September the Recce Regiment were one hundred miles ahead of 5 Division HQ, who were struggling to get the heavier vehicles forward in support of the

Infantry Brigades. In turn the advance patrols were almost another one hundred miles ahead of their own HQ and having difficulty in maintaining wireless communication.

The infantry reached Sapri on the coast and some of their patrols in the Vallo area contacted the rearguard of the German 1st Parachute Division who were retreating to Salerno. The 13th Brigade made a firm base at Sapri and sent out patrols from 1 Squadron of the 5th Recce Regiment under their command. On 17th September one of their patrols met a patrol of the reconnaissance troop of the American 36 Division, who were working south from the Salerno bridgehead. Complimentary messages were exchanged between the two brigade headquarters. On the same day the Canadians contacted American V Corps on their right, so that all Allied forces were in touch across the breadth of Italy. General Montgomery immediately ordered xiii Corps to move inland and take the important communications centre of Potenza.

The 3 squadron of 5 Recce Regiment, moving inland towards Sala Consalina, had a serious clash with the rearguard of 26 Panzer Division at Lagonegra. The leading troop were pinned down at a blown bridge which was covered by mortar and machine gun fire, resulting in two armoured cars being set on fire and two troopers killed. The gunner troop commander of 365 battery interceded with his 25-pounders, but the reconnaissance troops were held up by German Spandaus firing through a tunnel. Our 208 battery brought its 'Pheasant' into action and fired two 17-pounder armour-piercing shots down the tunnel, which finally silenced the machine guns. This enabled the position to be won by the 13th Brigade after a few more rounds from the 25-pounders. The 15th arrived on the outskirts of Lagonegro and the 1 Green Howards advanced to the west of the town to take the high ground. During this advance the German Panzer troops petrol-soaked the scrub on the hillside and at the appropriate time set it off with well-placed incendiary bombs – fortunately the advancing Green Howards managed to avoid the affected areas, and Montesana was captured. The main object was to take and occupy all the towns along the Potenza line and for 5 Division to link up with the American 36th. The 13th Brigade having taken Sanza, then advanced to the Auletta area where they met the American patrols. The 5th Division, with the 17th Brigade in reserve, were now on the Potenza line, having travelled over 250 miles in under twenty days.

The Eighth Army's next objective was the port of Termoli across the Foggia Plain with its valuable airfields on the Adriatic coast. First it was necessary to sort out the lines of communication of xiii Corps which were badly hampered. At this stage Montgomery decided to move the whole Eighth Army's communications across to the Adriatic sector using the much larger and the more efficient port of Tarranto. It would take ten days before an advance of any size to Foggia Plain could be supported by the new base. The British V Corps – now the right flank of the Eighth Army – were pursuing the retreating enemy up the Adriatic coast. Accordingly, the modern university town of Potenza, which towered above the pine-clad surrounding slopes, became the temporary responsibility of the 5th Division. It had been severely bombed by the Allied air forces only a few days earlier, and needed to operate a one-way traffic system which was controlled by the division's military police. One of the policemen rebuked the King of Italy for proceeding against the one-way traffic; his majesty withdrew and completed the circuit correctly.

We put on a show

The Fifth Division in reserve had time to reflect on their advance and carry out training. Our Anti-Tank Regiment's concert party was in demand and managed to put on three performances at the local opera house for the benefit of the divisional troops and other xiii Corps units. This was produced by Captain Berry, of the Regimental HQ, an amateur actor who invariably made his mark with a Bransby Williams monologue. The show was directed by my friend Ronnie Lodge with the same troupe he had used before from the four anti-tank batteries – but with a revised script reflecting the latest sketches he had received from Bud Flanagan. I was coerced into being the stage manager and general dogsbody and took part in some of the sketches. The RAF contributed too – as well they might, as they had previously put a hole in the roof and the bomb went through the stage and down into the dressing rooms. The Divisional Engineers managed to put a covering on the roof and the house was full of troops on the three nights.

Once the curtain rose, my main task was to remind the oncoming performer about the hole in the stage, and ply him with vino. Everything went remarkably well for the first two nights but on the third night, when the Lancastrian comedian stepped back in appreciation of the applause, he vanished through the hole in the stage and landed on a table in the dressing room. He decided not to respond to requests for an encore.

The Foggia Plain

At the end of September, the rain storms were more frequent and nothing like the sunny Italy we had expected. The 5th Division was now grouped under V Corps and started to move to the Foggia Plain, where it would form a firm base while the Canadians moved up into the Central Appenines and V Corps advanced over the big rivers that flowed across their front into the Adriatic. The country north of Potenza consisted of winding roads undulating through little valleys and over small mountains; as they progressed, numerous abandoned wrecked Canadian vehicles indicated the efficiency of the German engineers.

The Foggia Plain had obviously been severely bombed. The 13th Brigade concentrated in the Foggia area, whilst the 17th was in reserve near Troia for a few days. Here they were able to do some refresher training to prepare them for the vigorous winter warfare in the mountains that lay ahead. There was time for a fitness regime including sport to get the squaddies in good trim. The 15th moved through Lucera up to a line overlooking the Biferno river with Canadians on their left and the 8th Indian Division on their right. The 1st Yorks and Lancs led this advance along roads decimated by the retreating Germans as the Sappers managed to clear twelve miles of road, build five Bailey bridges and construct ten diversions. The Yorks and Lancs had a serious battle with the enemy on Pt 88, beyond Bonefro, supported by 7 Cheshires, with their heavy machine guns, 92 Field Regiment RA, and the KOYLI. The 1 Green

Howards had to cross a river in heavy rain and mist to reach Montelongo, losing the cook's lorry as the bridge was washed away. After much effort the whole battalion was across by midnight.

On 13th October, 1 Green Howards moved up to high ground overlooking Provendi. They moved up a track with a sheer drop on one side, and round a conical shaped hill, up to the little town of Morrone which was perched on the top like a fairytale castle. A fighting patrol from D Company took on an enemy post in a farm near the town, which was heavily armed with four well-placed machine guns. The sergeant of the platoon took the enemy position with a bold frontal attack, for which he was later decorated. The advance from this point was delayed by the difficult roads, the atrocious weather and by the build-up of the enemy's strength. It required an advance in strength rather than patrol work to make further significant headway. It was decided to hold the position and wait until the strategic air force had settled into the Foggia airfields before pushing forward in strength.

The 13th Brigade was brought forward to take over from the Canadians, who had advanced 80 miles in three weeks through mountainous country. The leading battalions of the brigade set off across the steep wooded slopes of the Matese mountains to occupy San Massimo and Cantalupo, and then headed for the important communications centre of Isernia. They were supported by the heavy machine guns of the 7 Cheshire Regiment and equipment for the 91 Field Regiment was brought forward – the heavy stuff being carried by Cypriot mules. The brigades of 5 Division were by now adept in using and handling mules. On occasions anti-tank guns were dismantled and carried up the mountains in sections either by the troops or with the aid of mules. These lovable, obstinate creatures were so useful that they became special targets for the enemy, and high losses were sustained during the campaign.

The rocky nature of the terrain made it impossible to dig trenches, so building sangars became an essential means of protection against shells and mortar bombs – and the biting wind. Another of the hazards in the mountains was identification from the air. Our gun positions around Bojano were bombed in error by our

American friends. We were holding some German prisoners at the time, one of whom remarked in good English, 'When British bombers fly over we duck, when German bombers fly over *you* duck, and when American bombers fly over we both duck.'

Isernia falls to the Inniskillings

There were several parties interested in capturing Isernia, for it was the last important enemy stronghold in Central Italy. It became vulnerable once the southern mountain approaches had been nibbled away by the 2 Wiltshire Regiment and the 2 Inniskillings of the 13th Brigade on the one hand and American patrols from 5 Army on the other. All three indicated their intention of capturing the town at dawn on 5th November. The 2 Inniskillings, having infiltrated among the enemy outposts late the night before, advanced and took the town, driving the enemy into the arms of the Americans. To ensure everyone knew who had captured the town they had by 0400 hours painted a very artistic representation of their regimental badge – the Castle of Enniskillen – on one of the town's most prominent walls. At 0600 the 2 Wilts arrived and two hours later the Americans, to find that Lt-Col. O'Brien Twohig had established his RHQ in the town with an immaculate 'Skin' on guard duty outside.

On the 17th Infantry front there was dogged fighting for some difficult rocky pinnacles against which enemy shelling was quite prolific. The hard ground meant building sangar-like shelters as the best means of protection. Some old soldiers said it was reminiscent of fighting on the north-west frontier of India. Nevertheless, the 2 Northamptons and 6 Seaforths took Macchiagodena and Castelpetroso with the aid of 2 RSF and 156 Field Regiment, the supporting artillery for the 17th. The going could not have been worse, or the weather more treacherous. Maintenance of the companies on these rocky outposts was almost entirely by mules, and many became casualties by shell fire, mortaring or falling from the slippery mountainside with the loads still on their backs.

Before the Division could advance towards the river Sangro, the Vandra had to be bridged by the Divisional Royal Engineers. Since landing in Italy these regiments had carried out a full and successful programme which included the development of beaches, many road diversions and lifting thousands of mines – most of this work done under fire in appalling weather conditions. The anti-tank guns of my battery, including my 17-pounder, were around the area protecting the bridge-building process, in defensive positions as a precaution against attack by German tanks – which did not materialise. Although the area was warmer than up the mountains, our position was subjected to constant mortar and artillery shelling, which splintered the rocks, making the flying debris lethal. Fortunately, our sangar provided reasonable protection and none of us were seriously wounded.

The 15th Brigade came forward to relieve the 17th after the capture of Rionero, which was a step forward before the crossing of the river Sangro. Rionero village, the surrounding area and the road down to Castel-di-Sangro were very exposed and were regularly shelled by the German artillery. Because it was impossible for vehicles and guns to move from the roads due to the rocky terrain, the whole area became known as Death Valley.

The infantry of the 13th and 17th, aided by mules and occasionally by horses as a standby, started to climb from the base point of Cerro in a serious attempt to take the dominant features overlooking the Sangro. The Cameronians, with heavy artillery support, attacked positions some six miles short of Alfedena. This town, an important communications centre on the left front of the Eighth Army advance, was just short of the Sangro, and in the shadow of Mount Greco. On 21st October, 2 RSF, supported by the Green Howards, climbed 800 feet of steep rocky cliff onto a plateau above – typical of the many tests of physical fitness imposed by the terrain. They carried a number of implements and small arms and 24 hours' rations with them as they would be out of reach of the supply chain for a while. The Green Howards took Pt 1086 and then Pt 1630 and passed into the snow line. The RSF passed through and cut the road through Montenero and then captured the high ground beyond it. Their new position dominated Alfedema and at this point their forward patrols in the hinterland beyond Montenero were the nearest Allied troops to Rome – albeit with many mountains and rivers in between.

On 2nd December the Canadians were moved to the Adriatic front of V Corps in order to add punch to the attack on Ortona. Fifth Division took over their front so that the Division was now holding thirty miles of xiii Corps' mountainous territory. The efforts by the Division were stout enough to cause the German 1st Parachute Division to maintain strong rearguard positions just north of the tragically ruined town of Castel-di-Sangro. The Division's patrols grew more and more energetic, but often unpleasant, as they came down from the icy mountain tops; they were often away for days as they probed the German positions. Patrols waded into the Sangro and on the return trip the river was sometimes swollen by the constant rain; occasionally it swept a man to his death. The 2 Northamptons were the first men of the Division – and indeed of the Eighth Army – to cross the Sangro, which they did in freezing weather. These activities kept the enemy guessing while the build-up on the Adriatic front was taking place. One of the biggest hazards to the British Infantry patrols were the 'S' mines, liberally scattered in a variety of inconvenient places. In these inhospitable conditions, there were more casualties caused by the elements than head-to-head confrontation with the enemy – although mortars and artillery fire took a constant toll.

Communications between the various units in the Division were proving to be difficult in the mountainous terrain. Divisional HQ was over twenty miles away from brigades. Battalions were nearly as far away from brigades and companies were distant from battalion HQs and often in the most inaccessible places. Gunner observation posts were also distant from gun areas. The Division's linesmen of the Royal Corps of Signals and the others involved in line maintenance duties performed heroically. The campaign stretched these and all other services in the Division to their limit.

Miles of roadways and diversions were patrolled in all weathers by the division's Provost personnel. They were the smartest body of men in the Eighth Army. Their immaculate turnout in all conditions was a morale booster to all the Division, including the unavoidably filthy infantrymen returning from action. The 'Y' route sign and the divisional lighting-up time indicator clock, which was displayed on telegraph poles en route, was an indication that the efficient Fifth Division was in the area. The New Zealand Division took the line at first that the Division was too smart to be good at fighting – until they fought at our side.

On the Adriatic sector, both Canadians and the New Zealanders were involved in very heavy fighting on the Lanciana ridge and the approaches to the impregnable Orsogna across the Moro River. The front was made worse by the German scorched-earth policy and the constant rain, which had turned the area into a morass reminiscent of Flanders in World War I. The Sangro had been successfully crossed and the town of Lanciano was now in the hands of V Corps. The natural fortress of Orsogna was proving to be a major stumbling block, despite the best efforts of the New Zealanders. The decision was taken at Eighth Army HQ that the mountain section on xiii Corps front no longer held any importance to the Germans, because their main concern was holding onto Orsogna, Arielli and Ortona – and by so doing, preventing the Eighth Army reaching Pescara and then wheeling inland along the road to Rome. The Fifth Division left the mountains in mid-December to assist in the push towards Orsogna and were replaced by limited forces from the British 78th Division, who had been in reserve.

The 17th Brigade took the lead and established themselves on the coll overlooking the Moro river, under the command of 2 New Zealand Division. On 14th December, 2 Northamptons moved across the Moro before dawn to improve their position and dig themselves well in. The rest of the battalion moved over the following night. My gun moved forward to the side of a farmhouse on the coll in a reasonable position to take on German tanks within 3,000 yards. For more than a day the Northamptons withstood heavy concentrations of artillery, Spandau and mortar fire. C

Company of the 2 Northamptons and A company 7 Cheshires moved further to a position just short of Poggiofiorita. The Germans, aware of their position, continued with their concentrations of fire and shelled a Roman road near at hand to prevent a build-up of the position. I consolidated my gun position by digging it well in and camouflaging it to fit in with contours of the farmhouse. We used our end of the large building for sleeping quarters. Our neighbour on the other side of the farm was a platoon of Gurkhas from the 8th Indian Division. The chances of us having a battle with German tanks were pretty high and we were keen to see what our 17-pounder could do. The confrontation looked likely when three companies of the Panzer Grenadiers, supported by tanks, formed up to attack the Northamptons' position. However, the Corps' artillery, firing from a mile or so back, landed their salvos right amongst them and inflicted so many casualties that they abandoned the idea.

On 17th December, A Company of the Northamptons moved into the town of Poggiofiorita and found that the enemy had withdrawn. B Company moved to the high ground west of the town where they joined up with a New Zealand company. Lieutenant Hamer, a man with some reputation, took out the Northampton fighting patrol and brought back some prisoners from 67th Panzer Grenadier Regiment. This was his hundredth patrol since Sicily and it was recognised by a bar to his MC. This and other patrols confirmed that both Arielli and Canosa were held in strength. The Ghurkas too, armed with their *kukris*, left the farmhouse each night, but patrolling a different area to our brigade; they didn't seem to bother bringing back any prisoners.

Despite the dangers, the owner of the farmhouse made occasional visits to his property from the nearby town of Lanciana. He always eyed the Ghurkas with trepidation and generally addressed me instead. One of his main concerns was his stock of vino and Marsala in the cellars. We bought some bottles from him at a cheap price in anticipation of Christmas. My smattering of Urdu and a gradual accumulation of Italian enabled me to hold a conversation of sorts with all parties in the farmhouse. The noisy group of Ghurkas, under the firm control of their havildar, played around like happy children when not under orders to fight. Mild discipline was occasionally inflicted with a clip on the ear.

The priorities changed when General Montgomery and Lt-Gen. Miles Dempsey were ordered back to the UK to take over 21 Army Group for the attack against Northern Europe – the Second Front. This, together with the appalling weather which created treacherous conditions for an attacking army, brought the Eighth Army advance to a halt. A further hindrance was a disastrous bombing raid on Ban Harbour which destroyed reserves of ammunition which would be needed for an immediate push on Rome. It was then decided that the Eighth Army should hold a tight grip around Ortogna while the big effort on Rome was to consist of a left-hook attack by the US Fifth Army. In order to do this, the relatively intact 5th Division was to be transferred to the Fifth Army to add weight to this operation.

We join the US Fifth Army

Accordingly, on 3rd January the 15th Brigade were relieved by the 2nd Parachute Brigade and they moved back to Lanciano. Montgomery and Dempsey expressed sadness that 5 Division was leaving the Eighth Army to join the US Fifth Army. In an order of the day, they stated, 'that we should all meet again'. This did not materialise for another year, when we joined 8 Corps of the Second Army in Belgium, and then took part in the final push in Germany.

The move from the east coast to the west coast of Italy excited the troops into believing that we were going to Naples en route to the UK as part of Montgomery's invasion force. But darker thoughts crossed our minds when we all assembled in the Mondragone area, having received reinforcements, badly needed by the infantry. The 5th Division moved in great secrecy, with the 'Y' disappearing from all our vehicles and unit signs, being replaced by the number '7'.

The task for 5th Division was to cross the river Garigliano on the west coastal front, with the prime objective of capturing two towns, Minturno and Tufo. To the east of them the British 56

Division was to cross and attack Castleforte and assault Monte Damiano. Several unsuccessful assaults had been made by the Fifth Army to dislodge the enemy from this area, generally referred to as the Gustav Line. A member of the Provost near the area when putting up the '7' signs declared that he didn't know who this '7' division was but they wouldn't cross the river until 5 Division arrived! In order to keep the arrival of 5 Division secret, the forefront of the Divisional sector was to be patrolled by an ad hoc force known as 'Hicks Force', who had no connection with 5th Division. The British Tenth Corps, under the command of Lt-General McCreery, consisted then of the 5th, 46th and 56th Infantry Divisions, all to be involved in the attack on the Gustav line. The nature of the assault was so complicated that the odds being openly quoted were five to one against the crossing being successfully achieved.

ROYAL ENGINEERS SET OUT TO REPAIR THE LAST TWO SECTIONS OF THE PONTOON BRIDGE KNOCKED OUT BY ENEMY FIRE
Photo courtesy of the Imperial War Museum, TR 1523

In the 5th Division area, the plan was for two brigades, the 13th and 17th, to carry out the assault of the river and the securing of a divisional bridgehead in the foothills on the northern end of the plain. The second phase was the exploitation and expanding of this bridgehead, this being the role of the 15th Brigade and the 201 Guards Brigade, who were temporarily under the command of 5th Division. The initial assault would be by two companies of 2 RSF making a sea landing north of the river and two companies of

6 Seaforth, who would arrive in assault boats near the blown Ponte Fiume on the Appian Way. The third battalion 2 Northamptons would then pass through on the high ground. The reserve companies would follow on in support of their battalions. The German 94 Infantry Division was the main enemy, well dug-in 12 feet deep and heavily armed with machine guns set on a fixed line overlooking the river.

INFANTRY CROSSING THE RIVER GARIGLIANO IN ASSAULT BOATS
Photo courtesy of the Imperial War Museum, NA 10860

The divisional engineers had serious bridging problems and made an intense study of the river from air photos and patrol reports before assembling their bridging requirements. Meanwhile, the field artillery had to plan their gun positions, dig their gun pits, and bring up their ammunition at night to avoid being in view of the enemy. All this planning and work was carried out at very short notice. Apart from two days in Naples, we had been given no respite – and in four months we had already travelled 380 miles in appalling conditions, with our logistics stretched to the limit.

The First Battle of Cassino

On the night of the 17/18th January, the First Battle of Cassino started with two brigades of the British Fifth Division making a landing without artillery support. Inevitably, things did not go exactly to plan, but in the general arena of warfare it was good enough to shock the Germans. On the extreme left of the landings the 2 RSF set off from the seashore north of Mondrogone to land on the north bank of the Garigliano between the estuary and the

Argento feature, a prominent mound which would dominate the whole front for the 17th Brigade. Their landing craft were manned by American crews who found the river currents around the estuary difficult to navigate and in consequence missed the landing lights set up by an earlier patrol. The Germans heard the noise of the boats and brought down some accurate fire. Some of the main party were unfortunately landed south of the estuary and almost attacked their own brigade HQ.

One craft was completely lost and went out to sea. A British submarine surfaced at its side and a head popped out of the conning tower and shouted, 'Who the hell are you?' 'Royal Scots Fusiliers,' came the relieved reply. 'Never heard of you!' was the response as the hatch closed with a bang and the submarine submerged.

The 6th Seaforths were ferried across the very turbulent river by a company of their brigade comrades, the Northamptons, to the landing point at Ponteflume. In the initial assault they lost a few of the boats from shelling and on landing walked into some newly laid minefields which caused many casualties.

The Germans had obviously expected that any attack across the lower Garigliano would be focused around Ponteflume; accordingly, they had the area well covered by Spandaus firing on fixed lines and mortar defensive fire and were able immediately to mount a strong counter-attack. The Seaforths were so pinned down they were unable to secure the start line for the 2 Northamptons Phase II attack by the planned time of 0400 hours. The whole of 2 Northamptons – less B Company – managed to cross the river despite heavy resistance and join the shallow bridgehead. Pockets of enemy were on the plain and tanks were able to attack the British infantry with impunity, only protected by their own portable anti-tank weapons. Some of the guns of my Regiment, 52 Anti-tank Regiment, were scheduled to be landed north of the river with the RSF and supply this defence, but they were landed on the wrong side of the river. This added to the other setbacks, and left the 17th fully exposed to tank attacks. They had so many casualties it made it difficult to hold the triangle between the Appian Way, the Garigliano and the sea.

INFANTRY CROSS THE GARIGLIANO BY WAY OF THE PONTOON BRIDGE
Photo courtesy of the Imperial War Museum, NA 10942

The 13th Infantry's crossings were also causing delays due to the sinking of a number of boats. The saving grace was the relatively successful crossing of the 2 Wilts, who had all their companies but one over the river just past midnight and had started to advance towards the foothills. The 2 Inniskillings were seriously delayed by sunken boats and some of their platoons used the 2 Wilts crossing in order to catch up. The 2 Cameronians started crossing just after and took over Epitaffio farm near to the river after a short, sharp fight – it was to be used as an initial bridgehead. At that stage all surprise had gone as the artillery barrage in support of the 56 Infantry Division's attack commenced. The 2 Wilts reached the Castelforte to Minturno lateral road by first light and crossed into the foothills soon afterwards. B Company on the right reached Pt 291 by 0800 hours, but they were counter-attacked and had to withdraw to the high ground east of Tufo.

Major Grant, of A Company Inniskillings, who landed at 0300 hours, led an attack with bayonets on a strongly held group of buildings on the right flank of the 13th Brigade at Massa Rossi. Murderous mortar fire killed him and four German prisoners he had taken. The A Company headquarters by this time consisted of two signallers and the one remaining officer, who was seriously wounded. The remainder of the company attacked the farmhouse under the outstanding leadership of L/Sgt Banton and took it over and formed a defensive position which was never retaken. There were but twenty survivors in the whole company; many were the victims of mines crossing the river. The Inniskillings' battalion HQ caught the full attack of the enemy shelling which killed the adjutant, the medical officer, some artillery and battalion signallers and a runner. The CO, Lt-Col. O'Brien Twohig and many others were wounded. However, the field artillery barrage was performing brilliantly and enabled the Inniskillings to have a foothold of 800 yards by noon.

The BBC news of the 18th contained the following extract: 'In a new attack by British troops in Italy, the crossing of the Garigliano has been made, an entry in the main defences of the Gustav Line.'

Close encounter with a Telemine

In the centre of this turmoil, my gun – the first heavy anti-tank with quad, was ferried across the river. I took off with my crew along the path of a partly cleared minefield alongside the river, the only available route which would bend away from the river to my intended gun position near the 17th Brigade. We had travelled about three quarters of a mile along this road when the swaying of the gun behind the quad caused it to touch the verges. Hitting a minor pothole, the 17-pounder left the track with a jolt and set off a Telemine which blew off the nearside wheel of the gun. I had my head out of the port hole, and fortunately the debris was blown in a different direction, but my gun crew in the back of the quad were badly shaken. There was a long pause as we examined the wrecked gun, broken eventually by a splash in the Garigliano, as our wheel returned to earth from the stratosphere – about 60 yards away.

The gun was useless without a wheel and the road had to be cleared to let other traffic through. It was a lonely spot, with no engineers available, so we started to experiment with moving the gun to the side without disturbing the minefield. I sent my bombardier back to the ferry to stop other traffic and to inform my battery HQ of what had happened. We managed to unhook the trail piece of the gun, which rested on the road, while we moved the quad away to give us some space. I sent the remainder of the crew back to the ferry as they were surplus to requirements. The driver Ted Hope and I removed parts of the gun with spanners and gently laid them on the side of the road. The long 17-pounder barrel was the last item to be moved. This, being very heavy, had to be shifted to the side inch by inch, making sure it didn't roll. We managed this successfully but sweat was pouring off us despite the cold January morning. Ted Hope climbed into his cab and slowly reversed the vehicle along the narrow strip of road, his eyes totally focused on my hand signals, as the vehicle was slowly reversed out of the minefield. The gun crew could hear the quad engine and were greatly relieved to see it reverse into the approach yard of the ferry. Twenty-four hours later, we returned with a new gun with the fond hope we would meet up with some tanks, to help our badly savaged infantry.

The 17th Brigade were held up in an exposed position in a minefield by the river mouth. Pinned down by small arms fire, it was difficult to move without setting off other mines. The brigade commander, Brigadier Dudley Ward, found it hard to contact his battalions and was fired on from a strong point position which was causing many casualties on troops entrapped in minefields. A special attack was put in by 9 Platoon, A Company, 2 Northamptons, led by Sergeant Bell. After a fierce battle, the platoon took seven German prisoners of war, a number of dead and no less than five MG34s. As a result, the many wounded Seaforths were able to be retrieved and evacuated. The end was signalled by the simple message, 'Strongpoint ours.' Sgt Bell was decorated with the DCM.

The 2 Northamptons A Company, still in a difficult position, had to be supplied by two Wellington bomber rescue boats. Meanwhile the pressure on their position was eased by the advance of the 13th Brigade. The Divisional Commander, realising that the 17th could go no further, ordered 2 Cameronians to close up to the left towards Minturno in support of 2 Wilts who were hard pressed in the battle for Tufo. It was now clear that the river had been successfully crossed, but the bridgehead was dangerously shallow. Despite serious casualties to their C and D companies, 2 Inniskillings advanced, leaning on a first-class artillery barrage to dislodge the Germans who were deeply dug in and had little time to avoid the bayonets of the Irishmen. The two companies cleared half a mile of the ridge east of Tufo, a salient which was to relieve much pressure on the rest of the Division, but still much had to be done to achieve the planned position.

On the night of 18/19th January, the 15th crossed the river under a heavy barrage from the divisional artillery. The plan was for the brigade to advance through 2 Wilts positions with 1 KOYLI on the right headed for Pt 141 and the 1 Green Howards advancing towards Minturno. The Green Howards C Company took the old Roman spa town against moderate opposition, and A Company followed and took over the north-east corner of the town. They suffered few casualties, which were mainly from mines and booby-trapped obstacles. Meanwhile 1 KOYLI had reached Pt 141 and were mopping up. In the process they beat off a small counter-attack and reported that Tufo was clear of the enemy. By nightfall on the 19th the Minturno-Tufo ridge was secure against all but a major divisional attack – and so it proved!

Breaching the Gustav Line – and the cost

The casualties sustained by the Division in getting so far were high in the front-line infantry of both the 17th and 13th Brigades. The 15th, supported by the 201 Guards, were in good fettle to take the fight to the enemy, but the planned exploitation of moving up the Ausente Valley into the Gustav line would be extremely difficult without large reinforcements.

The British 56th Infantry Division, who landed five miles further up the Garrigliano, made a successful advance, so British 10th Corps had breached the Gustav Line. The Corps Commander General McCreery was unable to exploit this bridgehead and prise open the right flank of the Gustav Line because the US Fifth Army Commander, General Mark Clark, would not release McCeery's British 46th Infantry Division nor offer American troops to take advantage of this surprise success.

The German Field Commander Kesselring was so shocked by the British assault, which gave the Allies the opportunity to exploit the vulnerability of the Ausente Valley, that he was forced to make his most crucial decision of the Italian campaign. He committed his only strategic reserve of two Panzer Grenadier divisions, who were refitting near Rome, in order to block McCreery's 10th Corps advance. This he did against the advice of his senior staff officers, who wanted to hold them in case of an amphibious landing by the Allies near Rome. Thus further British progress along the Garigliano was checked by Kesselring's hasty assembled reinforcements.

In this way the two divisions across the lower Garigliano were held in limbo. General Clark found it unthinkable that the British should gain the credit for breaking the Gustav line, even if American troops helped to carry the day. Instead he stuck to his flawed plan to attack in bits, with the key role going to the American 36th Infantry Division, whose casualties were very high since they landed at Salerno. They were given the impossible task of crossing the fast-running Rapido River at Angelo. McCreery believed that this attack had little chance of success because the 15 Panzer Grenadier Division manned positions on the west bank that enabled them to dominate the river. Clark decided to go ahead with his plan even though the British 46th Division had failed to take vital heights which would have helped the proposed assault. The attack went in on the night of 20th January and the hapless troops of the 36 Infantry Division had no artillery support and insufficient infantry to force a successful crossing of the river, exacerbated by the lack of a coordinated plan or rapport between the infantry and engineers vital in a river crossing. The result was a massacre of two of the three regiments of infantry.

This tragedy had far-reaching repercussions, which culminated in General Clark having to explain his actions before a Congressional enquiry in 1946. This debacle tainted Clark's reputation, but he was determined that American troops alone should breach the Gustav Line and ultimately only the Americans would take Rome. The breaching of the lower Garigliano by the two British Divisions was intended as a sideshow, but it had succeeded beyond all expectations. It drew from the Rome area Kesselring's reserves just before the Anzio landing of one British and one American Division which went ashore virtually unopposed just forty miles south of Rome.

Reinforcements – for both sides

The build-up of the German forces on the coastal front of the Garigliano was signified as much by increased shelling of the bridges across the Garigliano as well as taking prisoners from fresh units on the 5th Division front. The 17th Brigade, surrounded by mines and pinned down in the river-mouth area, also received greater attention from the German artillery. The British Sappers were putting all their effort into completing a Class 9 bridge, so that heavier traffic would have an easier ride across the river. This was a drawn-out affair due to shelling and the occasional bombing from the air, which caused heavy casualties among the engineers. To ease the situation the bridge area was partially covered by smoke, but fixed-line firing set before the battle commenced continued to claim casualties. The Sappers were also clearing wreckage away from a badly damaged railway bridge to the north of highway 7 to reconstruct and develop it as a road. The Class 9 bridge across the river was completed by 21st January and enabled the field artillery to move some of their 25-pounders across the river to new positions south of the lateral road. This ran along the bottom of the Minturno-Tufo ridge and put the guns in better positions.

Meanwhile the 15th Brigade were still taking the fight to the enemy. The 1st Yorks and Lancs, attacking towards the Natale feature, took fifty prisoners and this was subsequently increased to 250 for the loss of only two wounded. The 1st Green Howards attacked Tremonsuoli on their left and Pt 110 on the right. In view of the exposure of the battalion, they were assisted by 98 Self Propelled Regiment, under command of 5 Division, who laid smoke to indicate Santa Maria to air bombers. During this advance 1 Green Howards were mortared by the enemy and bombed by their own planes. They achieved their objective by noon after some heavy fighting in Tremonsuoli. Major Tanner, who led the advance, was awarded the MC. The Green Howards were left in an uncomfortable salient, a position where they had little respite from shell and bomb. The following day, 1 KOYLI moved up to straighten the front line and in so doing took some prisoners. The enemy counter-attacked in strength in the afternoon, but were repelled with heavy casualties. The enemy retreat was further harassed by Divisional artillery concentrations. In a day of fluctuating fortunes, the Division's 164 Field Ambulance were kept busy and distinguished themselves with their speed, care and attention. At this time the 13th Brigade HQ took up a forward position in a quarry on the riverside of the Tufo Ridge, a rendezvous that in due course would house many other headquarters.

The 1st Yorks and Lancs were having a hard time against the newly arrived 90 Light Division, who were trying to drive a wedge into the Divisional front, by pressing towards Minturno and then to the river. The 1st Green Howards, relieved from their positions by the 5th Coldstream Guards, were moved into a long-stop position to steady the front line against continuous attack. This was the peak of the enemy's efforts to breach the Divisional front, but he was held by the battalions of the15th Brigade supported by the Guards. It was at this stage of the battle that it was announced that one British and one American Division had landed at Anzio. These landings had been timed to coincide with the Garigliano battle which had been fought to drain away all possible enemy reserves. It was expected that the enemy in front of the Division would withdraw to meet this new threat to Rome – but it seemed to make no difference!

The 1st Green Howards C Company – by now only 33 all ranks strong – led the way to attack Pt 172 from a cemetery to the left of their objective with B Company following on the left and D Company on the right. Two German tanks held them up, but after some confused fighting D Company secured the objective and some prisoners. The battalion held on to the position under heavy shelling for nearly two days. For their fine work in this battle, the Battalion Commander, Lt-Col. Buffin was awarded the DSO and six DCMs were awarded to other ranks.

The Commander of 5th Division, Major-General Bucknall, left the division to take a new post as a Corps Commander in the Army of invasion. This meant that the three top men associated with the advance of the 5th Division in Sicily and Italy were to be at the helm of the Second Front. Fortunately the 5th Division was very strong in commanders at every level. However, the real strength of the Division was in the infantry battalions, who had been outstanding. They had already smashed up the 94th German Division, and held the 90th German Light Division and elements of the Herman Goering Division which shocked Kesselring so much that he had to use his vital reserves in order to hold on to the Gustav Line. It was a pity therefore that the 5th and 56th British Divisions were not given the necessary support to severely breach the Gustav Line. The Anglophobic attitude of the US General Mark Clark was engendered to some extent by certain British Commanders' lack of confidence in the ability of the American forces. The lack of trust between the Generals would in due course blight the correlation of the armies – and one of the key issues was Clark's abhorrence of having British and American troops fighting side by side. In consequence his policy invariably resulted in a series of individual battles taking place along a broad front with little or no cohesion. The only exception to this was Anzio, where British and American Divisions landed together under an American general. But Clark had little say in the matter here: Winston Churchill was the prime mover.

A new GOC

The new General Officer Commanding the British Fifth Division was Major-General Gregson-Ellis, who was taking over the Division with the stability of the Garigliano front uncertain. The major problem, a lack of infantry reinforcements at a time when Kesselring – who had read the situation right – was building up his forces on this front. The successful crossing of the Garigliano had not reaped the rewards that were there for the taking; moreover, holding on to the ground taken continued to cause heavy casualties in the British 5th and 56th Infantry Divisions. This meant Gregson-Ellis had to stabilise the divisional front and fight a defensive battle.

The 17th Brigade were brought into the front line, having been relieved from their enclosed position on the marshy front near the estuary, which remained surrounded by minefields right down to the river. Their main objective was to take Natale, which was surrounded by a number of high points and clear the way to capture Santa Maria. The attack went in with RSF leading to take Pt 141 on the left, supported by three tanks and an artillery barrage. Sadly, A and B Companies took the wrong line to attack their objective, leaving C Company to put in the attack, which they did with much gusto and Scottish epithets which were answered by an English-speaking German. The Battalion's Commanding officer, Lt-Col. MacInnes was mortally wounded and Major MacMichael, the C Company commander took over, but became seriously injured by mortar fire. Major Batey of 503 Battery of 156 Field Regiment then took over and arranged a DF barrage by his battery, which enabled C Company to withdraw with relatively few casualties. The 6th Seaforths were also unable to reach their objective for similar reasons. It became apparent that the German 94th Infantry Division had been heavily reinforced with the 90th Light Division together with a substantial increase in German artillery. In the circumstances, the 2nd Northamptons were held back in order that the attack could be conducted in more favourable conditions. At this time the 201 Guards Brigade were heavily attacked in the Tremonsuoli area, by an influx of enemy infantry, confirming that there had been a build-up on the 5 Divisional front of enemy reinforcements. This attack was repelled without much difficulty.

The increase in the German artillery fire put the new bridge – the Highway 7 Bailey pontoon – out of action. And during the week that followed, there were eleven serious incidents which damaged the pontoons and boats and hindered the traffic across the Garigliano. These were repaired promptly by the Divisional Engineers.

On 30th January the Corps Commander General McCreery considered it vital that the Natale feature should be taken. The Guards Brigade attacked and cleaned up various pockets of German infantry that could interfere with the taking of this difficult objective.

The main attack on Natale was to be put in by 2 Northamptons supported by the whole of X Corps artillery and the guns of two cruisers firing offshore. The lower terraced slopes of Natale with 12-foot banks, required the infantry to have porters assisting with ammunition and some extra stretcher bearers which were supplied by the Brigade's ambulance unit. Despite the slowness of the advance, C and D Companies of the 2nd Northamptons proceeded smoothly up the lower slopes and by 0600 hours on 31st January C Company had reached the highest point of the feature and D Company had cleared the eastern ridge. The whole position was consolidated for the inevitable counter-attack at dawn. It had been a most successful and well conducted operation.

The 6th Seaforths had meanwhile taken the cemetery at the side of Natale by first light and had control of the whole of the adjacent area, capturing some prisoners in the process. Shortly afterwards three tanks were sent up to strengthen the position and the battalion was able then to patrol to Santa Maria. It was a successful day for 5th Division with all its objectives being taken for less than 100 casualties. Two days of counter-attacks by both sides ensued, but 2 Northamptons held the enemy at bay.

The Corps Commander was particularly pleased with the ultimate securing of Natale. The Division was now holding a long and uncomfortably small bridgehead with no reserves to commit further and had now been in almost continuous action for nearly eight months. Far from retreating, the Germans had reinforced their defensive line. The task of the Division now was to hold on to what it had so grimly won, to recuperate as soon as possible, and to give the enemy no peace. It was hoped that the attack on Anzio would now force the pace and loosen the German hold on the Gustav Line.

The Natale position continued to be heavily shelled by the German artillery and resulted in fewer attacks on the river bridges. My 17-pounder was brought up and we dug in at the side of this feature as a part of the protection of the 17th Brigade against tank attack. Apart from using our Bren gun and Tommy guns in support of the infantry and defending against the occasional air attack, the majestic 'Pheasant' was still untested and remained camouflaged awaiting a major tank attack.

The bulk of my regiment, the 52nd Anti-Tank, was moved to the sea flank in a triple role to protect the Division against hostile landings and provide all-round defence in an unprotected area. One of our batteries set up an improvised Infantry company to help out 2 Wilts on Salvatito, where they lived in sangars and were supplied by mule trips managed by Indian porters. It was a long hike up the mountain and the only sure way to find the positions was to follow the signals cables. It took six hours to get a casualty down to the Regimental Aid Post and over an hour to reach ambulances at the foot of the hill.

On 5th February Major Houchin, second in command of 2 Northamptons, became temporary commander of 2 RSF, who had lost both their Commander and Second in Command. A further senior casualty, Lt-Col. O'Brien Twohig, (Inniskillings) who had been carrying shrapnel wounds inflicted on the initial crossing of the Garigliano, had to be referred to base hospital, which for him was a happy ending of the Garigliano front – for he met his future wife, a nursing sister who was serving in the Queen Alexandra's Royal Army Nursing Corps.

On 10th February, the bad news was that our Divisional neighbours, the British 56th Division had to leave and join the US Vi Corps on what was turning out to be 'The hell hole called Anzio'. We in the 5th Division extended our front eastwards to take over the whole of the Ausente Valley and Monte Damiano – a mountain less the summit, which was still occupied by the Germans. This made the shallow bridgehead wider and entailed thinning out our positions. This was ironic and very disheartening, because the Garigliano assault had drawn the enemy reinforcements to the Gustav Line which had facilitated a smooth landing at Anzio. The fact that we were now fighting these reserves on the Garigliano front seemed to have made the original crossing of the Garigliano of little significance – apart from taking over another of Italy's rivers and about ten miles of front at a very heavy cost in infantrymen and engineers. The Anzio landings had been given a very fair start and there seemed to be no reason why the two divisions should not have taken their specified objectives. To send the British 56th Division to Anzio – a division that had been in constant action since the Salerno landings – seemed to be a desperate measure and indicated the beachhead was in serious trouble.

There were many unidentified minefields on the Garigliano front, and casualties occurred daily when anyone moved to a front-line position. The Division's workshops invented a 'Snow Shoe' in an attempt to protect the sappers when they were probing for mines. This was reasonably successful.

On 22nd February, the 17th Brigade took over Damiano and Salvatito with 11 KRRC under command as a fourth battalion. My gun team moved up in a position at the side of the infantry. It rained for the ten days we were up there in a dug-in position. We were constantly baling water out of the gun pit and utilising gas capes and ground sheets to keep dry. It was possibly the best place to be, to receive the bad news that we too were to move to Anzio immediately to relieve the 56th Division and support an exhausted British 1st Division – the original British division to land there.

Off to Anzio

On 2nd March a Regimental Combat Team from the US 88th ('Florida Wildcats') Division arrived to take over the 5 Division's front. They first relieved the 17th Brigade in the Damiano area and an anti-tank gun team took over my position and in so doing replaced our 'Pheasant' with their 75mm gun. My gun team of five – reduced by two shell-shock casualties, sent back to recuperate in Naples – were replaced by ten very large and rather green Americans who, as I remember it, were quite shy. They were fresh from the States and taking over our position for their first action. Their Staff Sergeant and I discussed the 'Field of Fire', where the nearest infantry were located, and most importantly, the areas the Germans were firing their machine guns at night on a Fixed Line Firing Arc basis. The other considerations were the adjacent minefields and the toilet area. It was obvious they would have to dig a new gun pit, for ours was full of water from the continuous rain.

They were all very tall, and compared to us, oozing with good health. The staff sergeant eyed our gun with envy. It still looked large and impressive and dwarfed their 75mm. I remember thinking at the time, why couldn't this lot go to Anzio? The answer was obvious... although they were called the 'Florida Wildcats', there was no animal in them yet! Three months later they were given the honour of being the first Allied troops to enter Rome. And as a further insult, General Mark Clark made it clear that Rome was out of bounds to the 'Limeys' – apart from the four pipe bands of the British Fifth Infantry Division.

Meanwhile, the Americans gave us a hand to hook the 17-pounder on to our Morris quad. We wished the sergeant and his gun team good luck and made our way down to the pontoon bridge and over the river. We were needed in a hurry at Anzio and we would leave our heavy equipment behind for the anti-tank regiment of the battered British 56th Division. In return we would be taking over their guns, which were already dug-in on Anzio.

The Anzio Beachhead

The US vi Corps landed on the beaches around Anzio and Nettuna on 22nd January 1944 under the command of Major-General Lucas of the US Army. It was a fortunate landing, for not only were the enemy conspicuous by their absence, but the weather was fine. By the end of the first day a comfortable bridgehead had been secured with the port swept clear of mines and in normal use. The following day saw an expansion of the beachhead to a semi-circle of some fifteen miles to a depth of nearly eight miles. Ammunition and supplies were being built up in the harbour without any serious opposition to the landing, which did not occur until eight days later.

For the first week the front-line troops merely probed forward to establish strong defensive positions – and in so doing lost the initiative. Lucas was thinking in defensive terms and considered the successful landing was in itself the prime objective that the Allies needed. In this regard, he was reflecting some of the misgivings felt by Clark and himself following the trauma of

Salerno. Lucas therefore adopted the option of making Anzio secure against attack as his main priority, rather than following the dictates of the plan which was to seize a bridgehead and then advance across the flat Latium marshland and secure a footing in the Alban Hills overlooking Rome. Instead, the forward troops were patrolling and probing rather than going hell-bent for the Alban Hills. This lack of action infuriated Churchill who was the main architect of Operation 'Shingle'.

In the light of what followed, it became clear how crucial it was to take the Alban Hills area in that first week. Not only because of their strategic value in trapping German armies fighting in the Gustav Line, but to extend the area, thus making room for more troops and distancing the port from the enemy artillery.

Kesselring was surprised that he was given this vital breathing space. He realised that if the Allies took the Alban Hills then the whole German strategy of the Italian campaign would be jeopardised. Accordingly, he reported the landing to Hitler's headquarters and requested more troops. In due course he was able to direct the 4th Parachute Division and replacement units for the Herman Goering Division – who were north of Rome – to block the roads leading from Anzio to the Alban Hills and to Rome. The additional troops that he immediately obtained were the equivalent of nearly two divisions, which would increase to five in ten days.

The 1st Parachute Corps headquarters took command of the Anzio sector and started to hustle the miscellaneous units around the Allied positions. The stronger contingents would not come under command until 24th January and it would take a day or so before the German defensive line was stable. However, the lack of coordinated aggressive intention on the part of vi Corps on Anzio, the US 5th Army and indeed the British Eighth Army gave Kesselring – an optimist – great hope. Ironically, British 10th Corps (5th and 56 Divisions) that had given Kesselring such a headache with their breaching of the Gustav Line when crossing the Garigliano, would ultimately be called upon to help out the inept General Lucas in the defence of Anzio. Meanwhile, on the

German side, most of the trauma was being felt on the Cassino front by General Vietinghoff. He was concerned that Kesselring had taken so many units and reserve forces away for the impending Anzio battle that the Gustav Line had become vulnerable. He suggested a withdrawal as far as the Anzio line but Kesselring rejected the idea and told him to stand fast at Cassino.

At this stage the reluctant pacemaker was Lucas, but he dawdled, much to Churchill's disgust. By the fourth day, the 1st British Division had moved up to the Moletta river, a sound position from where it could anchor the left flank of the beachhead. The US 3rd Division, with various ancillary troops, took several additional bridges along the Mussolini Canal to make the right flank more secure. As a result of this the beachhead was increased in depth to nearly ten miles. A day later the 3rd Division had pushed to within three miles of Cisterna and the 1st British Division had repulsed an attack at Aprilia (called thereafter the Factory). They destroyed four German tanks and a self-propelled gun and were ready to attack Campoleone but Lucas still waited. After this, Alexander expressed his dissatisfaction at Lucas' lack of aggression to Clark. Lucas had been running things from his headquarters in Anzio and had not visited any of his front-line troops, and it was clear that Churchill wanted an attack.

Clark resented interference from London and much of his Anglophobia stemmed from having to report to Alexander, although the preponderance of the Allied troops in Italy at this time were American. In consequence, anything British in the Allied Armies was lousy in his view and his particular nemesis was the British 10th Corps commander General McCreery, who in turn despised Mark Clark. This ongoing hatred warped decision taking, yet both generals were brave, capable men. A few months later, McCreery, a positive general, was promoted to take command of the British Eighth Army, an appointment he carried out with distinction.

Eventually on 30th January a planned attack by vi Corps commenced involving three divisions, the 1st British Division, the 3rd US Division and the 1st US Armored Division supported by the 504th Parachute Regiment and the Ranger Force. It was a two-pronged ground advance with the main blow coming from the left. It had extensive naval, air and artillery support. It involved the British 1st Division driving for the Albano road to the top of the high ground, while the 1st US Armored Division swung wide around the British advance and attacked the hills from the west. On the right the 3rd US Division, with the parachute regiment and the Ranger Force under its command, would advance to Cisterna, cut Highway 7 with the possibility of driving on to Valmontone and approaching the Alban Hills from the east. Lucas insisted on keeping tight control on the two converging lines of attack to avoid giving the Germans the opportunity to split his forces down the middle in the event of his plan failing.

The attack on the right went in at dawn on 31st January with the two Rangers battalions leading, but less that half a mile from Cisterna, German fire came in from all sides as they walked into an ambush. They were armed with light machine guns and were no match for the machine guns, mortars and tanks that enveloped them in a wall of fire from troops of the Herman Goering Division. As they attempted to fight back, a convoy of German self-propelled guns and tanks arrived to join Kesselring's Anzio force and added to their problems. The Allied force was practically decimated and those still alive were taken prisoner.

The US 3rd Division advanced up country roads against stiff opposition. Their attack, which lasted three days, got their front-line troops to within a mile of Cisterna, but the build-up of the German forces was now too great and it was clear that they would have to withdraw, which they did with the assistance of heavy artillery cover fire. They suffered heavy casualties and one of their battalions was reduced from 800 to 150.

Attacking on the other side of the beachhead, 1st British Division made better progress. After three days of attack they held Campoleone and in the process had pierced Kesselring's main line of resistance. This, together with the 3rd US Division's battle for Cisterna, made it clear how close the Allies had come to breaking out from the beachhead.

Unfortunately, the tanks of the 1st US Armored Division had not been able to contribute anything towards the advance because of the cloying nature of the soil. The rough stream gullies and muddy fields bogged the tanks down, and they could not overcome the ditches. Moreover, the lack of cover made tanks in trouble an easy target. Each Italian farmhouse in this area was of heavy stone construction and became a fortification when used for anti-tank defence. In short, it was proving to be an infantryman and artilleryman's conflict, which would be the case for the next five months.

General Alexander arrived in Anzio on 1st February to consult with Clark and Lucas. He and Clark decided that they had to switch over to the defence of the beachhead very quickly, for another attack by the Allies with the forces available to them was doomed to failure now that Kesselring had managed to build up his defences. In fact it would take a full army operation to break out from Anzio, now that Kesselring had all his units in place. Meanwhile, the Allies would have to build up their defences quickly, otherwise Kesselring would break through to the Anzio harbour and in so doing annihilate the beachhead completely – with disastrous psychological results for the Allies and a bonus for Hitler. It had now become a personal duel between 'the decorator from Austria' and the 'British Bulldog.'

Accordingly arrangements were made as a matter of priority for Lucas to be reinforced with the First Special Service Force – a mixed brigade of 1800 Americans and Canadians, some of whom had arrived earlier. Two British brigades – 167 and 169 of the British 56th Infantry Division – would arrive in the first two weeks in February. It was also clear that Lucas would be replaced in due course by another American general, who apart from other considerations would be more acceptable to the British. The man chosen was the greatly admired Major-General Lucien Truscott, who was brought in as an understudy on 2nd February and officially became vi Corps Commander on 22nd February.

Truscott had served in the UK and been on landings of the French coast with the Commandos. He liked the British, understood our foibles and was familiar with British Army procedures. He alone among the American generals could have commanded a British Division or Corps but he was meant for higher things. A fearless man, he made a point of going to the various hell-holes on Anzio, believing that the commander should be seen by all the troops, whereas Lucas never left his basement.

The Germans made a number of diversionary attacks on the defences in the earlier part of February. The front line had the 1st British Division on the coastal front and the 3rd US Division defending the inland area including the Mussolini Canal. It became obvious to the Allies, with the large build-up of German forces, that an additional two divisions were needed to share the front line. The British 1st Division was particularly vulnerable to attack by the German 1st Parachute Corps, now part of von Mackensen's 14th Army. The British 1st Division was at this time holding the Vallelata Ridge, but the area under its control required more than one division. This made it easier for the Germans to practise their tactics of infiltration, thereby nullifying the affect of the supporting Allied artillery who could not be sure of the exact location of the German forces.

The German Parachute Corps put in a major offensive to pinch off the salient that the 1st Division had created in their original advance. On the night of 3rd February the German attack started with a storm of shells on the Irish Guards and the Gordons front which had to be held to allow 3rd Brigade who were at the tip of the salient to keep their supply and withdrawal route. However, there were so many gaps in the defences that the German paratroopers were able to mount a battalion attack and overcome the individual companies. British machine guns scythed down the paratroopers, but the Germans were able to push through their reserves and tear a huge gap in the British front. By morning their tanks were dominating the main road, so the 3rd Brigade became cut off.

The Divisional commander General Penney asked for reinforcements to launch an attack, and was offered the 3rd Battalion of the American 504th Airborne, which he gladly accepted. But it was an insufficient force to put in a counter-attack. The very timely landing of 168 Brigade of the British 56th Division, which Lucas wanted for his general reserve, was wrested from him to make this vital attack by the very irate General Penney. The battalion chosen for the breakthrough was the 1st London Scottish, soulmates to the Gordons. They had just arrived from the Garigliano battles and could hardly be deemed fresh troops. However, once ashore, within 24 hours they were called upon to form up behind the Gordons in sodden fields.

Brigadier James, commander of the trapped 3rd Brigade, and a cool customer, got through to his three trapped battalions and instructed them that on hearing the signal word 'Tally Ho' they were to break contact with the enemy and prepare to retreat. The Duke of Wellington's Regiment and the Sherwood Foresters would come out first; the KSLI, who were at grips with the enemy on the right flank of the salient, would form a rearguard and come out last.

General Penney was very concerned about the situation, for he stood to lose a third of his division within the next few hours. At four o'clock the attack began with the London Scottish advancing with great determination, backed by tanks. They overran the Germans but were then halted by heavy fire short of their objective; however, the British columns of the 3rd Infantry started to move in response to 'Tally Ho', bringing their wounded with them. Small groups of Germans firing from farms adjacent to the ridge managed to inflict casualties on the retreating forces. However, the British are experts in triumphal retreat, and although a relatively small operation, it had all the classic features expected from such a manoeuvre.

The darkness was lit by burning hayricks and revealed many dead bodies. Tanks were still burning, and fields smouldering. The battalions had to leave behind sorely needed equipment, tanks and anti-tank guns and a few burning lorries – but the brigade was relatively intact as a fighting unit. For good measure the last battalion to leave the area, the KSLI, had knocked out two Tiger tanks in the closing engagement, which was a large bonus. All in all it was an operation of which the 3rd Brigade and the London Scottish could be proud.

In the early days of February the British 1st Division had lost 1,600 men, and since the landings on 22 January, battalions such as the 6th Gordons, the 1st Irish guards, and the 2nd Sherwood Foresters had been decimated. New drafts landing at Anzio were hurried to the British front line but they were inexperienced and few in number. Lack of adequate reinforcements was a British problem, whereas the US Army had replacements on hand to cover their losses.

The fight for the Factory

General Penney had to defend the vital 'Factory' area, Carroceto village, and the disused railway track called the Embankment. It was fortuitous that he had 168 Brigade of 56th Division to which he allocated the defence of the Factory area. The Guards Brigade held Carroceto village and the Embankment supported by the invaluable US 3rd Battalion 504th Airborne Regiment. This was a difficult task because there were gaps in the front line which the German infantry could infiltrate. The Factory was the main prize in the coming struggle, for it was a very solid impregnable fortress, despite having been subjected to so much shelling and bombing. It was the centre point in a network of tracks and roads in an otherwise soggy landscape. For this reason the Germans were prepared to put in an immense attack to capture it so they could command a vital central position in the beachhead to launch a major attack.

The first probing attack in force was on the night of the 7/8th February to take certain key points in advance of their 'Big Push' a few days later. They broke through the most forward British unit – the 2nd North Staffs – on Buonoriposo ridge by infiltrating in force through the gaps and coming up behind the front battalions of the 1st Division. The tactics were similar to those adopted in eliminating the salient, except that Von Mackensen had more troops at his disposal that seriously outnumbered the front-line 1st Division battalions.

It seemed that nothing could stop this German advance from reaching the main road – that is, until they reached the Fossa di Carroceto, a deep *wadi* that flowed between Buonoriposa ridge and the main road. This was not easy to cross, for it was thick with brambles. Hundreds of Germans launched the attack and came running down the ridge towards the wadi where the 5th Grenadier Guards had set up their HQ with some American parachutists close at hand on the fringe of the US 45th Division's front.

The Germans were brought to a halt by a ditch hidden by the brambles and by withering fire from the Guardsmen and American parachutists. There was the sound of German tanks behind their infantry and it seemed that the position would be taken in spite of heroic conduct from officers such as Major Sidney. However, on the morning of 8th February, a mixed assortment of Allied troops still held the Fossa di Carroceta *wadi*, which prevented the German advance reaching the main road. The enemy had, however, taken Buonoriposo ridge which spelt more trouble for the future of the beachhead. The total strength of the allied force along this last ditch was 20 Grenadiers and 40 American paratroopers who stood firm against a series of German attacks.

General Penney felt isolated. The only conferences between 1st British Division and vi Corps took place in the catacombs of Nettuna and not forward at the scene of the fighting; in fact neither General Lucas nor his staff officers had visited the British front line. Penney had no idea of the intentions of the Corps Commander, nor a Corps assessment of the enemy's strategy. Moreover, he was unaware if Lucas had plans to recover any of the lost ground. It seemed that Lucas was loath to release any of the Corps reserves to hold up the British position.

Penney put in his own counter-attack in an attempt to recapture Buonoriposo ridge because it dominated the main road to Anzio and enabled an easier approach to capture Carroceto and the Factory. He did not have an abundance of troops to choose from after twelve days' continuous fighting, but he alerted 1st Battalion KSLI and 2nd Sherwood Foresters supported by A Squadron of his Recce Regiment and a squadron of the 46th Tank Regiment. The counter-attack put in by this force failed, because the Germans dominated the ridge with Spandau machine guns and artillery, so the advancing British battalions were under fire before they could launch an attack.

The Germans then did a pincer movement on the eastern sector of the 1st Division's front, and pushed back the Recce Regiment and the Royal Berkshires and ran through the London Irish of 56 Division. The battle for the Factory continued until 9th February when in the evening Von Mackensen's forces took possession. The Factory, now in German hands, could harbour their tanks and artillery equipment in a useful forward position. The Allies, on the other hand, had lost a key point in their defence system, making all areas in the diminished beachhead accessible to German weapons.

Meanwhile, after a further day's fighting by the Scots and Irish Guards, the Germans took possession of Carroceto but the Guards dug in and retained the Embankment. The British 1st Division had fought hard for a fortnight, both in attack and defensive mode, and had lost most of its officers, senior NCOs, anti-tank guns and carriers. It had shot its bolt as an assaulting unit and had lost its power to make a major counter-attack. But Major General Penney was determined to impress on Lucas that he had to do something positive by putting in a major counter-attack to recapture the Factory area which in German hands threatened the whole beachhead.

For the first time since fighting began, Lucas came to the headquarters of the Guards Brigade, bringing with him General Eagles, commander of the American 45th Infantry Division, whose task was to retake the Factory area. Penney gave his exposition of the situation in the eyes of the British 1st Division but the US vi Corps officers present were unable to give a Corps assessment of the position. It was a meeting which left the subordinate generals of the British Brigades and Artillery baffled that the Corps Commander should be so out of touch with the situation on the Anzio battlefield. Lucas sat quietly and turning to General Eagles said, 'OK, Bill, you give 'em the works.' Lucas then left the meeting and the generals remaining were left to sort out their plans. The brigadier of the British 168 Brigade was unimpressed and apparently commented that the conference was nothing like any of the American movies he had seen.

The American and British Generals remaining discussed the planned attack very amiably despite the difference in the system of command that would complicate an assault involving American infantry and British artillery. The counter-attack was put in at 6:30 am on 11th February. It was woefully weak despite massive British artillery support for the US infantrymen. Neither the efforts made, nor the heavy sacrifices inflicted, achieved any tangible results. The assault was too weak and too late. Yet Lucas was still unwilling to commit his reserves, feeling there was worse to come. His lack of positive action since the campaign started had made this conclusion inevitable.

Penney was devastated by the state of his division, knowing that Lucas was holding a complete American Infantry division and the tanks of the American 1st Armored in his reserve. Penney never understood him, and Major General Templar of the recently arrived British 56th Division remained unforgiving: 'Lucas was absolutely full of inertia ...he was the antithesis of everything a fighting soldier and general ought to be'.

The arrival of two brigades of the British 56th Infantry Division enabled the British 1st Infantry Division to be placed into reserve. The valour within the division was illustrated by the outstanding bravery of Major Sidney, who was awarded the Victoria Cross for his timely defence of the Fossa di Carroceta. He survived the war and became Lord De L'Isle and Dudley, having lived up to the traditions created by his great Elizabethan ancestor Sir Phillip Sidney.

Winston Churchill, who realised – not for the first time – that he had a dud at the helm of the assaulting vi Corps, cabled the C in C Mediterranean asking for the number of vehicles landed on Anzio in the first fourteen days. He received the reply '18,000 vehicles including 380 tanks, to supply a force of 70,000 men'. Churchill responded, 'How many of our men are driving or looking after

18,000 vehicles in this narrow space? We must have a great superiority of chauffeurs...'

The rearranging of the front line was made in the middle of February with the 56th British Division taking over the coastal section of the 1st British Division and the 45th US Division taking over the eastern section of the 1st British Division front which was now wider at the base and had become the central area of the Allied line. The battered 1st British Division, as a precaution, was placed in reserve behind the 45th US Division. The eastern area of the beachhead was held by the very competent 3rd US Division who had linked up with the Special Services Force.

The weary 167 Brigade of the 56th British Division who had landed in Anzio on 13th February was hurried forward into the *wadi* country to take up defensive positions to the west of the 157th Regiment of the 45th US Division. This competent American division was relatively fresh and had been held in the Lucas reserve. They were just settling their boundaries when in the early morning of the 16th February, the full weight of the German offensive fell on their front and the 56th British Division in the *wadis*. The Germans put in a number of unsuccessful probing attacks further east on the 3rd American Division but the German Parachute Brigade had more success in attacking through the iniquitous water courses and *wadis* held by the 56th British Division. They had troops from the Herman Goering Division in support and quickly overran the forward companies of 167 Brigade who were still reconnoitring their obnoxious front. A number of German companies reached the lateral road which ran from the flyover and was a very vulnerable part of the Allied defence line. British tanks managed to wipe out the intruders and a subsequent strong counter-attack removed the wedge the Germans had driven into the 56th British Division front, but individual battles continued in the *wadis* and this would be the case for four months until the Allied break-out at the end of May.

It soon became obvious that the main thrust was to be made along the Anzio-Albana road. The Germans came in closely packed waves with their tanks in support. They suffered terrible losses from the Allied artillery, but their sheer weight of numbers told as they inflicted heavy casualties on the US 45th Division. However, the Allied artillery were able to identify the oncoming German masses in the relatively open country, which made them easy targets. The Royal Artillery 25-pounder guns of the British 1st Division who were helping to support the 45th American Division were firing ten times the number of rounds that came from the German guns. The German infantry continually collapsed under the storm of bursting shells which shattered the morale of the vaunted Infantry Lehr unit – for which Hitler had such high hopes. Many of their officers were killed and the men finally broke after a particularly devastating concentration of Allied gunfire. The survivors turned back in confusion and hastened to the rear. Kesselring was appalled at the obvious lack of experience of 'the poor devils thrown into battle for the first time' but he was saving his seasoned Panzers for the final breakthrough.

The Germans night attacks finally drove a wedge between the flanks of 157 and 179 Regiments on the 45th Division front. They proceeded to exploit this with an early morning air attack using 35 aircraft from the supporting Luftwaffe who bombed and machine-gunned the forward positions of the 45th Division. This was followed on the ground by an attack by a powerful force of infantry and tanks launched from their new bases of the Factory and Carroceto which forced a salient in the Allied line. This was just the prelude to General von Mackensen's offensive, which was to last four days.

The battalions of the US 45 Infantry Division, holding the area on the Via Anziate, suffered heavy casualties which fragmented them into small fighting groups. One of these was with the British 1st Loyal Regiment, a North Lancashire Regiment of the British 1st Division, fighting with the US 45th Infantry division and holding a defensive sector along the lateral road by the flyover – which they called 'Wigan Street'. Three of their rifle companies were dug in along this front, with the remainder of the battalion in reserve behind the flyover.

For two days there was hand-to-hand fighting against German troops who managed to get through the Allied barrage. As the battle became more desperate, the Brigade Commander of 2nd Infantry Brigade brought forward a company of the 6th Gordons and also 'spare bodies' such as cooks, storemen and unit staff working in the docks, to plug the gaps in the Loyal's front. Elsewhere, very similar battles were taking place with pockets of the US 45th Division cut off and making efforts to get back into their divisional front line. Major-General Penney was wounded in the back at the start of this battle and the incoming general of the British 56 Division, the intrepid Major-General Templar, took over both British divisions.

The 169th Brigade of the 56th British Division landed during this battle, but their guns and equipment were still at sea because the port officer took the decision to close the harbour after the Luftwaffe dropped mines into the bay. He did this without informing General Lucas, which showed the deference in which vi Corps commander was held! A proposed counter-attack with 169 Brigade holding a key role in General Templar's 'T' Force was made without them and consequently its potency was reduced.

THE FLYOVER: THE SCENE OF HEAVY FIGHTING IN FEBRUARY, IT WAS THE FURTHEST POINT OF THE GERMAN ADVANCE TOWARDS ANZIO
Photo courtesy of the Imperial War Museum, NA 17011

On the fourth day of the German assault, the capture of the flyover became a serious possibility, one which would seriously imperil the beachhead. General Lucas, conscious of the critical nature of the battle, and aware that his main reserve formation, the US 1st Armored Division, was committed to a counter-attack under codename 'Force H' (for Harmon), phoned up Harmon to cancel the attack. Harmon refused and convinced Lucas it was essential to carry out the original plan.

The prelude to the Force H attack was the combined fire of eight British artillery regiments which was to saturate the zone of attack. Another eight American artillery battalions were to plaster assembly areas around the Factory while naval and anti-aircraft guns concentrated on the woods to the north-east. Allied aircraft joined in and the woods north-east of the Factory were pounded by 180 aircraft. Force H encountered stiff opposition as they advanced, but managed to reach the junction of the Bowling Alley and Dead End Road by mid-afternoon. The German salient was by this time a death-trap for enemy tanks and infantry and as a result more than 400 desperate Germans were taken prisoner.

The battle started to die down during the night. Minor incursions were made to recover Allied units which were trapped, particularly the 2nd Battalion of 157 Regiment who were hemmed in on the western flank of the salient. Templar, who had taken over responsibility for this front, sent the 2/7 Battalion of the Queen's Royal Regiment to relieve the trapped American unit – but the British unit met head-on an attacking German force intent on liquidating the survivors instead. The Queen's were heavily shelled and machine gunned and ended up with the beleaguered Americans, fighting a battle for survival. For a day the Germans swarmed around the caves, but were fought off. A night later, the Americans started to leave in small groups, making their way through the *wadis* to their front line. Two hundred proud but very thin battle-worn survivors out of 800 men returned to their lines. They had fought one of the most memorable infantry battles in the annals of the American Army and received the rare honour of a Presidential citation. The survivors of the 2/7 Queen's Royals returned a few days later, having suffered many casualties. The most moderate commentators found it 'a bastard of a place'.

German casualties in the four days of the battle were 5389 killed, wounded and missing. About 600 of the missing were taken prisoner. The US 45th Infantry Division recorded 400 killed, and there were many wounded and non-battle casualties, probably suffering from shell-shock. The 1st Loyals had over 200 casualties on 19th February alone. The 167 and 168 Brigade of the British 56th Division were classed as decimated by the four days of battling in the *wadis*.

It was clear that the battle-weary British 56th Infantry (London) Division deserved a much needed rest. At the beginning of March they were relieved by the other Garigliano battle stalwart of the 10th Corps, the British 5th Infantry (Yorkshire) Division, who themselves had been in constant action since landing in Sicily nine months before. As a result of this change the 'Black Cat' insignia of the London Division was replaced by the 'Y' insignia of the Yorkshire Division.

This was the defining moment on Anzio, when the German High Command realised that the beachhead had become a defensive stalemate which would nonetheless continue to cost many lives. It was more reminiscent of a World War I scenario, with friend and foe in the frontline hearing each other's conversations and corpses lying unburied. Death could come by a sniper's bullet or machine gun at the front, or mortar bomb, artillery shell fragmentation, or air-bombing attacks at the rear. There was no safe place on Anzio. Everyone was vulnerable. In spite of the scorched-earth onslaught, nature was ever present: the nightingale made itself heard in the still of spring, its notes undiminished by the havoc around.

CHAPTER 9

───────◯───────

ANZIO, STALEMATE, THE BREAKOUT
AND (ALMOST) TO ROME

In the early days of March, the 5th British Division moved to Pozzuoli, a small and ancient port north of Naples, from where they were ferried by landing craft to Anzio. Leaving behind the guns and vehicles that had been with the Division for so long was unpopular but had to be accepted. The takeover was to be made while the 56th British Division was still engaged in fierce fighting and the ground was heavy with mud, making it impossible to take out and replace guns in the face of the enemy. It was essentially a change of troops, with the weary 56th Division leaving the beachhead and the toil-worn 5th Division replacing it. As a result we were only carrying small arms and each section took over the other's heavy equipment – whatever state it was in.

The GOC of 5th Division, Major-General Gregson-Ellis, had made an early trip to visit the 56th Division Commander, General Templar, to see for himself the reported horrors of the beachhead. The sector to be taken over by the 5th Division stretched from the Flyover Bridge running west along the lateral road to the coast. This included the coast road with a hazardous junction where the two main roads met, appropriately called 'Stonk Corner'. It was frequently shelled by the German artillery, including the two railway guns 'Anzio Annie' and 'Anzio Express'. These guns had a 240mm bore and fired a high-explosive shell of 550lbs, but only every four to five minutes. They had a range of 20 miles, but when rocket-assisted the shell reached nearly 53 miles. The 5th Division sector moving south along the coast road included the port of Anzio but the adjacent town of Nettuno was in the British 1st Division sector.

The coastal sector, on the extreme left of the Divisional front, was where the river Moletta swung into the sea. In peacetime it was a haven of sandhills, so it was ideal sniper country. Being flat, it was the best place to launch a break-out attack using tanks, but it also involved crossing three minefields – one laid by the Germans, one by the British and another by the American 36th Combat Engineers who had been attached to the Allies occupying this sector since the time of landing.

La Cogna was the remains of a hamlet situated between the coastal sector and the fortress. It was the only forward position south of the lateral road and was on high ground, thus making it advantageous in observing the enemy and sighting the enemy's artillery OPs. Its reverse slope made it the ideal launch-pad for mounting a counter-attack. It was the Divisional Reserve position and had to be preserved, but it was subject to constant shelling by guns and mortars.

The Fortress was the grimmest of the Division's front-line positions. Well forward from the lateral road, it consisted of a winding *wadi* full of shell-holes, mines, splintered tree trunks and wired bushes, surrounded by banks. On one side the Germans were dug-in deep into the banks while the British had deep trenches on the other side of this lump of ground, made prominent by large bushes which divided the front and gave the feature its name. No one could stand fully erect in this area and remain alive. Here was the ever pungent smell of the dead, most of them unburied as they could not be reached. An element of decency showed where other bodies lay, marked by a wooden cross with and a light covering of earth – but this was continually churned up by shell and mortar fire. Nothing stirred by day and ammunition, food, and sometimes mail, were brought up at night. The route from the lateral road was marked by tape and coloured signal cable which showed the way between unexploded mines. Fresh incumbents were sometimes lost on the way and never met new comrades. The evidence of the enemy was often heard but rarely seen.... most notably when the roll was called. The changeover by different battalions was hazardous, but once the new battalion settled in, they made efforts to improve the dug-outs – as much to occupy their minds in this eerie place.

The Lobster's Claw, so called because of its shape, was a *wadi* south-east of the fortress. It had a more elaborate trench system than the fortress and was not dissimilar to World War I trenches in Belgium. Conditions were much the same as the fortress, but with even more evidence of death and destruction. There was a gap of about two hundred yards between the two areas, frequently swept by Spandau fire on fixed line, which made movement between the two locations a tricky business. A camouflaged communication trench named 'Mersey Tunnel' led under the lateral road linking up with a similar communication trench from the fortress, so it was possible to move between these two hellish spots underground.

There were other smaller, but nasty locations, such as Choka *Wadi*, Commando *Wadi*, The Yellow Bungalow, Sheep Pen Farm, Recce House and Lorenzo Tower, which were all part of the defensive layout at the front – and all hazardous places to be. All these dangerous areas were manned by the Divisional Infantry, with engineers, signals and anti-tank artillery in support close at hand. This was the layout at the front that the Division had to defend for the next three months.

Communication was kept simple, using well-known British locations to identify roads and tracks. This helped, because Italian place names did not fall easily from the squaddies' lips. The Divisional Commander, however, concerned with the larger picture, merely called the whole area 'A nauseating bit of country to fight in'.

General Penney had by this time returned to command the 1st British Division, having apparently recovered from his wound, so Major-General Gregson-Ellis did not have to take the responsibility of also commanding that Division. The 1st Division sector started on the eastern side of the Flyover Bridge and heading south from the lateral road, embraced a large chunk of woodland called Padiglione Woods. This sector ended in the south at Nettuno. The front line was not clearly definable between the two divisions, because the *wadis* wound their way in and out of the two sectors.

We move into the Lobster's Claw

On 7th March, the 15th Infantry took over the fortress area from 167 Brigade of 56th Division, 1 Green Howards taking the right side of the front and 1 Y & L on the left side, with 1 KOYLI in reserve. On 9th March the 17th took over the Lobster's Claw from 168 Brigade and 2 Northamptons and 6 Seaforths manned the front with 2 RSF in reserve. My troop moved up with them to man two key 17-pounder anti-tank guns adjacent to the Lobster's Claw but covering the lateral road – the obvious approach by enemy tanks for the fields around were soggy and unsuitable for tracked vehicles.

On 9th March in the early hours of the morning our two 17-pounder gun teams walked from 'Stonk Corner' up the lateral road towards the flyover bridge, led by a guide who made it clear that we were to stop when he did and to move quietly because German patrols often used the same road at night. The occasional stops were to allow Spandau bursts to complete their cycle. They were obviously firing on fixed line to some sort of pattern which our seasoned guide seemed to understand.

Our new home

The first gun we came to was behind a house on the lateral road which would also serve as the Troop HQ. Nobby Clarke and his gun team were left there together with Dicky Allen, the Troop Commander. I and my gun team proceeded further up the lateral road and then a hundred yards into a field south of the road. The sergeant on the gun greeted me like a long-lost brother: 'I didn't know when you were coming! Anyhow, this is the shit-hole position – as you'll see in the morning!'

The dugouts were not complete, for they had only been there a week and had found it difficult to move about without giving away their position. We looked at the 17-pounder in torchlight, which revealed a very wet gun-pit with a trench near at hand for the Bren gun. I took over the gun and learned that the quad was behind the house where our first gun was sited. It was obvious that it could not be left near our position, because it would prove impossible to camouflage – but it also meant that we were immobile. I signed for the gun and other paraphernalia in a torch-lit trench, and the sergeant and his bedraggled gun team hurried away. Later, it occurred to me that in the dim torchlight I had no idea what the departing sergeant looked like.

I was sure we could make the position more comfortable. We were fortunate in having a limber-gunner, Geordie Williams, who had worked in the coal mines before being called up as a Militiaman. As he had already proved, digging was second nature to him, so he was given the early morning guard duty with his unlikely mate Arthur Gross, an insurance agent. He could spend some time tidying up the gun-pit first before it became too light. I felt that we could all work on extending and improving the dugouts in the daylight without revealing too much to the enemy. Our predecessors had been hustled by the German Paratroopers' main attack into this position. There was no way we could move the gun, for it would be a major task digging out a weight of over three tons from a sodden pit, and whatever we did on the site would have to be suitably camouflaged against air observation.

In the morning it was quite a shock to see how vulnerable we were to artillery and mortar fire, so we furtively built banks to strengthen the position and camouflaged the dug soil with green sods. It was always questionable as to whether these improvements would be more revealing to air intruders but it gave us more protection against flying shrapnel.

The edge of the Padiglione Wood was in the 5th Division sector and was about half a mile south-east of our gun position. It seemed that the field between us and the wood was unoccupied, so we had this area of land to ourselves – which would have been highly rewarding were we owner occupiers in peacetime, when it would return to its true vocation of seaside resort. Just now it was rather daunting that we had it to ourselves.

On that first day, a number of German shells landed on the lateral road and some mortar bombs landed close to our position, making us think we had been spotted. A German spotter plane later came low and for a long time continued surveying the area adjacent to the flyover bridge. We were tempted to open up with our Bren gun, but resisted. We were the one heavy anti-tank gun south of the lateral road but in a commanding position for any tank attack advancing over the bridge. If there was any suspicion that our gun – which could knock out a Tiger or Panther tank with one shot – was there, every effort would be made to eliminate us. It was frustrating having this tank-killer but needing to remain doggo until a Panzer appeared in the gun-sights. This lack of mobility of the British anti-tank artillery piece continued until 1944, on the introduction of the Archer, a mobile 17-pounder issued to anti-tank regiments in British Infantry Divisions.

Meanwhile, we were no worse off than anyone else on Anzio, for Kesselring had collected all the heavier artillery pieces available from various parts of Europe and assembled them around the beachhead. Most of this heavy artillery was positioned in the Alban Hills, with the heavier railway guns, 'Anzio Annie' and 'Anzio Express' and a battery of 210mm guns firing as far back as Albano, near the Pope's summer residence. However, more destructive than these howitzers were the faster firing German 170mm guns, sited in and around the Alban Hills, with a range of over 17 miles. A battery of them could fire 600 rounds a day into the beachhead, and at ships in the bay. The longest firing Allied gun on the beachhead was the American 155mm 'Long Tom' with a range of nearly 15 miles, so the Allies were heavily outgunned.

The Germans each day poured masses of explosive into the restricted area of the beachhead from these howitzers and heavy guns, together with the rapidly firing smaller artillery pieces, including the multiple-barrel 150 metre mortar named 'Nebelwerfer'. This ominous piece was mounted on wheels, fired electrically, and was named by the Allied troops 'Moaning Minnies' or 'Screaming Meemies,' according to the pitch of the frightening sound the mortar bombs made. The Luftwaffe not only bombed the beachhead, they also occasionally showered it with propaganda leaflets. The allies' anti-aircraft guns responded nobly and shot down a few of the attacking aircraft, but it all added up to a large amount of shrapnel released over this devil's patch. Normally, the enemy was only limited by the shortage of ammunition. This was enough to kill and maim large numbers most days on Anzio.

Anzio Annie leaves a calling card

It soon became clear that the field in which our 17-pounder was sited was being used by some of the German heavier artillery for ranging purposes. On about the third day of our occupation, there was a loud screeching noise above the gun position as a howitzer round ploughed into the field about a hundred yards from our gun, throwing up massive clods of earth. We waited with bated breath for the next round from the massive gun, suspecting that our position had been pin-pointed by the spotter plane. There was great relief when the next round landed in Padiglione Woods.

Fearing the worst, Dickie Allen came across from the other gun position to see if our gun team had been swallowed up in the crater. The massive hole made it clear that either Anzio Annie or Anzio Express had left their calling card. The huge sods that had peppered our position were moved about the site to improve our defences. After this experience we managed to accept the lighter blows from the occasional 88mm shell and mortar bombs.

The propaganda war

After a week of lying doggo, two of the older members of the gun team, Hughes and Goddard, both married with children, began to feel the pressure and showed the early signs of shell-shock. Our only connection with the outside world was made each night when we collected drinking water, rations, cigarettes, and occasionally mail as well as copies of the Divisional News Sheet, the *Wadi Gazette*, and *Beachhead News*. This small array of bits and pieces was brought up by truck by a squaddie from the Quartermaster's staff. Further up the lateral road, behind the fortress and Lobster Claw, where the infantry supplies were delivered, the infantry dead were collected and taken back to headquarters for burial in the cemetery.

Propaganda aimed at splitting the Allies was distributed by frequent showers of German leaflets; also Axis Sally, the German propaganda girl, who possessed a reasonable voice, sang from a radio station in Rome, adding her 'two penn'orth' on the desperate nature of our plight and its daunting consequences. She could just about be heard on our miniature radio set, made by an enterprising amateur to fit in a matchbox. The most telling leaflet showed a bedroom in the UK with a British wife wearing a negligée, sitting on the edge of a bed unrolling her new nylons while an American sergeant is stood at the side of her untying his tie. The caption on the leaflet merely read, 'While you are away...'

15TH BRIGADE LAUNCHING 4.2-INCH MORTAR AT THE ANZIO BRIDGEHEAD
Photo courtesy of the Imperial War Museum, NA 13051

Quite a number of marriage break-ups had occurred during the two years since the British Fifth Division had left the UK. The responsibilities of marriage put a further burden on the married men in addition to the other daily horrors of the beachhead. At that time, I received a letter in unfamiliar handwriting, from an American Lieutenant, introducing himself and informing me he was engaged to be married to my sister Isobel, an ATS girl. This had no serious implications because she was single and 'fancy free' when she joined up, but any liaison between an American soldier and an English woman at this time was nauseating to the Brits on the beachhead, including me. We were quite happy having the Americans fighting at the side of us, for in a strange way Anzio created a greater degree of fellowship than any other war zone in which the Division served. Everyone on the beachhead was a target, and this in itself created a sense of camaraderie not dissimilar to that which existed between Londoners in the Blitz. Anzio was a place where time was no object and it enabled welfare officers and support services – who were very much in evidence – to deal with tragic problems on the Home Front brought to them by a suffering husband or father.

Padres too made regular visits to the most fearful spots in the Divisional sector, illustrating that everyone had a job to do and anyone could be the next casualty. Home became nearer than expected, particularly when the BBC, led by Wynford Vaughan-Thomas, broadcast the song of the nightingale relayed from the beachhead, which was beginning to sing almost everywhere around us – except the fortress.

ISSUING THE SPECIAL RUM RATION TO THE 2ND INNISKILLINGS TO MARK ST PATRICK'S DAY IN THE ANZIO BRIDGEHEAD, 17TH MARCH 1944

Photo courtesy of the Imperial War Museum, NA 13057

Fortunately, in Major-General Gregson-Ellis, the division was blessed with a commander of great imagination and humour. He invented a catapult that threw a mortar bomb a great distance and created a silent mortar and a multi-barrelled mortar. On the fun side he organised a Derby Sweepstake that gathered £7,750 in prize money, a contribution of about 7/6d per man in the Division. As part of his morale-boosting ideas, he allowed the talent within the Division to be released from their batteries or companies to perform in shows at appropriate times. The four pipe bands of the Division created a sensation in their tour of the American sector where a big demand grew for bagpipe music by 'those Limeys in skirts'.

The high morale of the Division was emphasised when the sport of Beetle Racing rapidly swept through it. Race meetings were organised about three times a week and were supported by the two British Divisions and some American troops. The race track was a huge tarpaulin with a large circle painted on it (the finishing line) and a small circle in the centre (the paddock and the starting line combined). The beetles – between six and ten of them – all marked with their owners' colours, were put in a large jam-jar just before the race started, and released at the sound of a whistle by the official starter. The winner was the first beetle to cross the outside circle line. The bookmakers were exceptionally busy, for the Anzio race-goer had very few outlets for his money. A champion black water beetle often changed hands at £20. Some were so successful that they were bought by the bookies – and promptly stamped on. The big race meetings were sometimes run at Divisional HQ, which showed the sport had approval from the top brass!

The GOC visited all parts of his division and was very popular with the troops, for he made a point of visiting all the front-line positions frequently. His main worry was the shortage of infantrymen. The few reinforcements that joined the Division were woefully inexperienced, and often became early casualties. Fortunately, Gregson-Ellis was an outstanding divisional commander who could impress his personality on his own men and his American colleagues alike.

In mid-March the 15th Infantry was manning the fortress area and the 17th the Lobster's Claw. These unsavoury locations were already resembling the Somme and Ypres in 1916 with communication trenches and barbed wire, but the addition of sophisticated mines in areas of no man's land. This section of the line was always dreaded by newcomers and it helped to maintain the reputation of the beachhead as the worst battlefront in Italy. Both brigades were keen to test the mettle of the Germans opposite their respective hell-holes. As a result the 15th captured the Sturm

Regiment's postal orderly one day with all his mail, which was a little hard on the 3rd battalion, whose mail he was carrying at the time. At about the same time, suspicious about German stretcher parties who were constantly going to and fro, four men were taken as POWs – along with their Red Cross flag they had hand grenades in their pockets. The German general in command of the 4th Paratroop Division sent messages enclosed in mortar bombs demanding the return of his men under the Geneva Convention. Gregson-Ellis promptly replied via 25-pounder to the effect that men who prowl around the front line with hand grenades were hardly genuine Red Cross men.

Diplomatic exchange of views wasn't always via explosives, however: a young German officer, who spoke perfect English, stopped an ambulance and searched it but found nothing incriminating. He said to the driver, 'I am letting you go, but tell your CO that an officer and his men from the German Parachute Division have been watching your ambulance for the last two days and have seen ammunition, supplies and personnel taken up in it. I do not wish to see this again. If I do, I shall blow the ambulance off the road and shoot the people whether they are wearing Red Cross bands or not.'

It was obvious that both sides were misusing ambulances and breaching the rules of the Geneva Convention but nonetheless they continued with an arrangement between the 5th Division and the German 4th Parachute Division that allowed safe passage twice a day for a Red Cross jeep along the lateral road to a forward First Aid Post. Despite the bitterness of the fighting, there was the odd occasion when both sides enjoyed an interlude – such as on Hitler's birthday, when the German Parachute troops, who had obviously been provided with extra schnapps, serenaded the Wiltshire's front line fifty yards away with a rendering of Lily Marlene. The German fair play attitude was generally good, and often reflected in small ways: the occasional football match played on Anzio was rarely shelled while the game was in progress, but when the final whistle was blown, an 83mm shell would often land near the centre spot, as if to say 'We were watching you!'

It was the constant squalor and apprehension as much as the fighting that eventually got the men down. To some of the infantry it was a relief to go out on patrol looking for trouble rather than staying in the dugout and being subjected to constant shelling. In an effort to get the best out of the battalion's declining numbers, the front lines were changed every seven to ten days – a dangerous but necessary manoeuvre.

On 19th March 6 Seaforth, 2 Cameronians and 9 Commando, under command of 5 Division, put in an attack to take an additional 150 yards of territory which had become vital in rationalising the Fortress area. This attack was met halfway by the Germans, who had a similar idea. This resulted in both sides suffering heavy casualties and a status quo with both parties holding on to their original territory. The Cameronians had the highest losses, with twelve killed, 49 wounded and 35 missing. The following day, the 17th was relieved by the 15th and we came out of the front line at the same time. The Division also took over an area at the front held for a very long time by the US 39th Combat Engineers, who returned with us to our B Echelon and remained under the command of the British 5th Division.

Our gun was taken over by a gun team from 207 Battery, who were not impressed by the position even when we pointed out that the facilities had been recently improved, including a swimming pool made by 'Anzio Annie' and now filled with rain water.

We moved back to our battery's B Echelon at night, never having seen it in the daytime. We rested in the clothes we had been wearing for ten days and watched the following morning as an 88mm shell removed our frying pan from the small fire. Geordie was furious: "The bastards – there go our Snorkers!" The compo sausages were not the tastiest of morsels but having existed on Compo Rations for the previous fortnight, we had been looking forward to this treat.

Looking out from our dugout, the crowded area adjacent to Gun Alley was quite colourful. Unexploded bright anti-personnel mines dangled from the few singed trees and hung from the top of the dugouts like Christmas decorations – except one dare not touch them. The whole scenario was like a devil's fairground, grossly overcrowded and with everyone doing something different, and every shell from the enemy likely to claim a victim.

I became mystified by the gurgling sound which could be heard along the whole line of our dugouts. In answer to my question, I was told it was Staff Stanton's Still. Just then Stanton himself appeared, looking more like Fagan than I remembered. 'Hallo Langley, you look grimy! I put your whisky ration in the still. The other sergeants have done the same ... it's mixed with potato peelings, dried figs and one or two other things. It's stronger than Poteen, y'know! The Yanks love it, and we get cases of Viennese sausages in exchange for some of the hooch'. He pointed out that the US troops didn't get a spirit ration, adding confidentially, 'They lose control!' It was okay by me, but I warned him my men would want their beer and cigs ration, so he'd better not get any bright ideas of exchanging those.

I made my way down to the RASC bath unit to enjoy a good scrub. Being completely nude for the first time in a week accentuated the animal-like sense that I had developed which would warn me of any missile heading in my direction. I returned to the dugout and Ronnie Lodge was there waiting to show me a script he had received from Bud Flannigan. 'I've been pulled out so I can organise a show. I was thinking of using this – it's called The Milkman.' I took the script, found it reminded me of the bright character we had as our milkman in Kennington and said, 'Yeah, I think it will do fine.'

I was keen to see my friends Gerry Young and Wally Allison in A Troop, who were manning six-pounders that were protecting Gun Alley against a possible German tank attack. I was halfway across an open area below the crest of an incline when I heard the dull plop of a mortar being fired in the distance. Instinctively I hit the deck and rolled down the slope into a pit, just as a cluster of Nebelwerfer bombs landed and exploded around my pit. I found myself lying in a disused latrine and for a while lay there wondering whether to climb out and face it, or stay down and face it. Eventually

I clambered out and wiped myself with some grass. This was witnessed by my friends in A Troop, who made it clear I was no longer welcome. So I duly went back to my dugout, took a towel and returned to the bath unit with a change of gear, to see the same attendant who was at the entrance an hour earlier. 'Christ, sergeant!' he greeted me, 'it didn't take you long to get dirty!'

Beetle mania takes over

My gun team went to the Beetle Drive at the Anzio Turf Club with plenty of money, and it was decided at the end of the racing that we would buy a winning beetle if they were auctioning them. The meeting started on a high note by the declaration that the MO had been disqualified as an owner because a medical orderly had observed him injecting his beetle with mepachrine. Whether this anti-malarial drug improved his beetle's performance was not known but the race committee were taking no chances.

We did well with our betting at this first meeting, and at the end we bought a large beetle from its owner for £20. It had apparently won a few races and Geordie placed it in a new matchbox which was marked BI – our gun number. The beetle was already heavily marked with the previous owners' colours, so we did not daub it with extra markings. Arthur Groves, an ex-insurance agent credited with brains, asked the obvious question: 'Why have we bought the beetle, Geordie? We can't race it because it's got the previous owner's colours on its back.' 'I have plans for it, Arthur, lad,' Geordie explained. 'The Sergeant and I are going to let it go and follow it and see where it goes.' Groves was still bemused. 'Why you and the sergeant?' 'Well, you see, lad, we both used to race pigeons and we understand things like pedigree!'

I was as surprised as the rest of the gun team, but followed instructions and went with Geordie the following morning to find a soft green area that was free of shell marks. Geordie released the beetle and we crawled behind it until it vanished below a strange-looking bush. We waited for a while for it to reappear and then Geordie said in a hushed tone, 'This is it!' He had come prepared and dug away at the bush, removing part of it to reveal a whole host of beetles, many of them large. 'Bloody 'ell, Sarge! We'll take the twelve largest' he said cheerfully, and placed them in a large box he had brought with him. Unfortunately, we lost the marked beetle which was to be used as our trial runner: it had obviously suffered enough from human hands and did not surface.

The trials then began. We ran the beetles on a canvas strip at the back of our dugouts in between dangling unexploded anti-personnel mines in order to gain some privacy. Having chosen the fastest six, we marked them BI to B6 and put them in marked matchboxes. Later we obtained jars which gave them more room and by putting fragments of the bush in each, we hoped to improve their wellbeing. As Geordie said, 'Y'see Sarge, we need them ta last a week – it gives us time to cash in, like!'.

The matchboxes were used to take them to and from the Anzio Turf Club and other minor courses that had sprung up. We did a round of the courses using three of the beetles at each meeting. Ultimately it paid off, for the five of us reaped a profit of about £200 each before we returned to the front. But money was no object on Anzio, it was winning that counted!

Back to the front

We returned to our gun position having left behind Hughes and Goddard, who had shell-shock and were replaced by Murphy and Bleasdale, a couple of phlegmatic characters and good friends. They had been rotating and had been in my gun team on the crossing of the Garigliano. Owing to the shortage of sergeants arising from high casualties and illness, the gun team crews had been moved around and there were only two 17-pounder guns in action positions, commanded by Nobby Clark and myself. As a result we had a choice of replacements within the troop.

Hughes was turning out to be a sad case, for reports indicated he had been visiting many brothels in Naples trying to contract VD – to save him from going back to the front line. Fate, however, caught up with him. As he entered the hospital reception tent in 'Hell's Half Acre' a shell hit the tent and killed him and other troops waiting to be admitted to the hospital.

The next ten days in early April our gun team formed part of the defensive battle. This sometimes became quite fierce, for it was imperative that we held onto the fortress and Lobster's Claw areas and that part of the lateral road. The purpose was to leave sufficient ground between this front line and the prepared positions about a quarter of a mile behind at La Cogna, which was the Divisional launching pad to break out at the appropriate time in an operation that was to be called 'Operation Wolf.' This would play its part in the vi Corp's intended advance on Rome.

In the attacks by the indomitable German 4th Parachute Division on the fortress area, a few yards of ground changed hands but our infantry's counter-attacks got most of it back. The strength of our battalions was woefully weak because of the shortage of suitable reinforcements.

Our gun position started to be showered daily by mortar shells, probably in the belief that the position was held by a platoon of reserve infantrymen. A few sporadic bursts by our Bren gun, on a line we had obtained, tended to encourage this belief and occasionally there was a response which may have given the enemy's position away to our patrolling infantry. The daily bombardment hit the banks of our built-up trenches and inflicted some minor shrapnel wounds and burns. We had to keep our heads down from continuous Spandau fire which swept the terrain, waiting for any sign of a breakthrough by the German infantry.

The lateral road, just in front of us, was a universal thoroughfare, as it was the only route available to move casualties to the clearing stations, which had been set up in the most improbable positions. In consequence we had to be careful not to fire on our own troops. The constant wet weather had caused our 17-pounder to sink even further. To move it from the pit would only be possible when 'Operation Wolf' started. The oil from the buffer cylinder – which took the pressure of the gun's huge recoil – was leaking away and this could be dangerous to the gun team if we attempted to fire the gun in its present position. Ultimately the gun would have to be winched out of the pit by the quad.

The administrative sections on the beachhead were more mobile than the frontline troops and benefited from not being in the cramped conditions of the infantry and forward anti-tank artillery. Nonetheless, they suffered many casualties in keeping the lines of communication to the front line intact. It was a great blow to our battery when a huge howitzer shell landed in the middle of our B Echelon and wiped out the Quartermaster's area, killing Quartermaster Sergeant Edwards, his assistant Bombadier Yalding, and driver Butcher. Their area was totally eliminated, leaving a huge hole with no evidence of its original function nor trace of what had been a busy staff. Such liquidation could only have been inflicted by a howitzer shell from the likes of the railway gun 'Anzio Annie'. Edwards and Butcher were senior Territorials who had survived a few battles including Dunkirk, Yalding a militiaman had been with the unit four years. In an instant there was no trace of them to remember, nor the last task they did for the Army.

Air battles over the beachhead were quite common. One spectacular dog fight over our position involved Spitfires getting amongst a superior number of FW 190s and ME109s and shooting down six of them. On 12th April our excellent 18th LAA Regiment Bofors guns shot down eight enemy planes which splashed into the sea or buried themselves into the sands of the coastal area – an event that was greeted with cheers along the Divisional front, for they had been making a particularly venomous attack on the Anzio port and the 5th Division positions by machine gunning at low level.

During March and April the port of Anzio was receiving up to 8,000 tons of supplies a day, which was unloaded and stored near the docks. This area was constantly under attack from shelling by the German artillery and Luftwaffe bombing, which included the whistling anti-personnel mines. These floated down and claimed numerous casualties among support staff. Ammunition dumps and gasoline supplies were often hit, causing massive explosions. The hospitals, recreation centres and rest camps between Anzio and Nettuno in 'Hell's Half Acre' all suffered as a result. The moral was to dig down and fast. Ultimately excavators were brought in to construct underground operating theatres and hospital accommodation.

The frequent destruction of ammunition resulted in the field artillery in the British and American Divisions being rationed. In the British 5th Division, each 25-pounder was, by the end of March, reduced to 15 rounds per gun a day from the previous 80 rounds per day. The front-line infantry were dismayed because they could no longer rely on supporting fire when they needed it. However, an accumulation of ammunition for each gun had to be built up for the breakout, which would no doubt commence with a large artillery bombardment on the enemy's front-line positions.

On returning from the front we sadly viewed the large crater which had previously been the site of our quartermaster's stores. As a booster, Staff Standen greeted us with a taste of our liquor from the distillery and an introduction to the representative from the American 36th Combat Engineers who had been supplying our battery with cases of Viennese sausages. This 'doughboy' was busy learning to play the bagpipes from the Pipe Major of the 6th Seaforths and both were supping our liquor in between notes. Alf Standen knew a number of important people on the beachhead, for it seemed that only our unit had its own distillery and consequently various people dropped by for a taste. The strength of the concoction could be gauged by the amount of enamel wearing off the universal mug which was used to take samples from the gurgling concoction. Alf was enjoying his finest hour, and it was also abundantly clear that when he returned to the East End, he would not starve!

Hit by the Moaning Minnies

Returning to base was not very lucky for me. I was walking across to watch a football match on a prepared pitch near Divisional HQ when a deluge of 'Moaning Minnies' mortar bombs caused me to run and dive into a large bomb hole with one or two other squaddies. In doing so I caught my foot in a root just below the surface and badly twisted my gammy knee, and a trickle of blood was dripping from the tip of my left ear, which had been singed by flying shrapnel. I could hardly walk and had to be helped out of the hole. The rapid swelling indicated that my much maligned knee ligaments were ruptured again. I ended up in the dreaded 'Hell's Half Acre', in a bed with a large column of sandbags at the head, and frequent applications of ice applied by the nurses to get the swelling down.

Close at hand to the hospital was a large ammunition dump and the German artillery were firing air bursts which could penetrate the flimsy roofing. I was feeling particularly vulnerable with my injured leg resting on raised pillows and for two days I lay there admiring the calmness of the Queen Alexandra's Nursing Corps staff, walking around with heads up, setting a wonderful example. In the four months of the Anzio battle, the casualties among medical personnel were 92 killed (including six female nurses), 367 wounded and 70 missing, possibly killed or captured. After two days, I was exercising the leg and was ready to go, but the sister said I would have trouble and should stay another night. I managed to persuade her that my gun team needed me – and so I parted from the hospital staff armed with crepe pressure bandages and painkillers and a strong belief that the British female was the best in the business...an opinion that has never changed!

Meanwhile, Ronnie Lodge's show was put on with some very useful talent from our 52nd Anti-Tank Regiment and proved to be quite a success. The stage area was prepared by the support units of the Division and was also used by a mobile cinema and occasional concerts by visiting ENSA troupes. This entertainment helped to relax the audience, which contained some Americans who apart from anything else wanted to be somewhere near our still. At this period on the beachhead a greater affinity was evident between the Yanks and us, mainly due to the fact that we were both in the same hole and the combined Cockney and Bronx humour would help to get us out of it. The Pipe bands from the 5th Division and other forms of entertainment from the American troops were a godsend.

The American 3rd and 45th Infantry were fairly close at hand and their troops were greatly admired by the British 1st Division and our own 5th Division. Our special mates in the American ranks were the 36th Combat Engineers. The Americans had their heroes too, and one such was an infantryman named Audie Murphy who was serving in the 3rd Infantry Division. He was forced to take a commission on the battlefield at the age of 20 and was America's most decorated soldier in World War II, having received 21 medals, including America's highest military decoration, the Congressional Medal of Honor. A high proportion of these were awarded for his bravery in the Italian campaign – a whole clutch for patrolling on Anzio. He ultimately became a cowboy hero in Hollywood films and was credited with the great quote regarding Westerns, 'The scripts were the same – only the horses were changed'.

In the British Fifth Division we had our own patrolling heroes too, such as Lt Hamer of the 2nd Northamptons, who had carried out a hundred patrols for the award of his MC and Sergeant Hughes, a remarkable sergeant in the 2nd Inniskillings already with the DCM and MM, who was making his presence felt in Northern Irish tones. However, the British did not freely dole out medals to individuals, but tended to award the commander in appreciation for the performance of his outfit. In consequence MCs were more liberally awarded to officers than MMs to other ranks. In general terms the true heroes on the British front were the infantrymen holding the *wadi* country, which was the worst piece of real estate in Italy, shared between the British 1st and 5th Infantry Divisions. In defending this small and apparently insignificant piece of land for twelve weeks, it cost the 5th Division nearly a thousand lives.

The build-up for the breakout started in mid May with the arrival on Anzio of the 34th and 36th US Infantry Divisions, both fully reinforced after their Gustav Line battles. General Mark Clark was already focused on the capture of Rome being a wholly American exercise. Some thought it was because there were more Catholics in the American Forces, but Clark had more Americans under his command than troops from other countries – and their army was in dire need of a victory. So it was decreed that no one else would share in the American moment of glory of marching into Rome and the British and other nations' forces were deemed to have played a minor role. Unfortunately for Clark, the great 'Hailing of Caesar' took second place with the news that the Allies had landed in Normandy on the Second Front. However, the four pipe bands of the 5th British Division would add colour to the occasion by performing at the Coliseum.

In the meantime, it was clear that both British Divisions badly needed a rest. The British 1st Division had been on Anzio from the outset. The 5th Division had been in constant action nearly a year, with minor rests, starting in July 1943, when they made the initial landing on Sicily and captured the two key ports of Syracuse and Augusta. They had the first battles with the fearsome Herman Goering Division, the German division that was still hindering the Allied advance on Valmontone. In this period of eleven months the British 5th Division had fought throughout the Sicilian Campaign, were the first Allied troops to land on the Italian mainland, froze in the mountains of Italy throughout the cold winter of 1943, made the initial crossings of the Sangro and Garigliano rivers, and were moved to Anzio from the Garigliano front at a critical time in early March 1944 without respite. This prolonged period of action would not be emulated by any British Division on the Second Front, who at that time had started their battles in Normandy. Ironically, the 5th Division would, after a rest, end its war joining them in the final battles of the war in Germany.

The breakout commences

At the time of the breakout, Alexander's allied forces in Italy totalled 22 divisions, the same number as the German Commander Kesselring had under his command. The Allied High Command ordered vi Corps on Anzio to prepare its plans for the 'Breakout'. The fact that the same instruction was being given to the other 16 Allied Divisions in Italy did not mean anything to the troops on Anzio, for the long stalemate made them believe their breakout would be conducted in isolation by their seven divisions plus the excellent First Special Service Force.

The 'Diadem Offensive' which covered all Allied Forces in the breakout, started on May 11th with a major assault mounted at Cassino by the Polish Corps and a crossing of the Rapido river by the British 4th Infantry Division of xlii Corps. Some 1500 guns fired several million rounds over a period of six days in support of the Poles, British, Canadians, Indians, New Zealanders, Free French and Americans. After five days of fighting the British xlii Corps had suffered nearly 4000 casualties but had driven a wedge nearly three miles deep into the German defences of the Liri Valley and had managed to bring forward one hundred tanks in support of the infantry. This, together with a strong advance by the mountain-fighting Free French troops, convinced Kesselring to pull back from the Gustav Line to the Sangro Line. This brought to an end the Cassino battle which resulted in the first part of Alexander's great offensive being started according to plan.

The breakout from Anzio started on 23rd May with the 5th British Division Artillery firing a heavy prolonged barrage along the lower Moletta river in the coastal area, as a prelude to their 17th Infantry and the 1 Green Howards of the 15th Brigade making the crossing. The Green Howards took the lead after the Divisional Engineers had cleared a minefield on the edge of the Moletta River enabling the battalion to cross. The going everywhere along the Divisional front was rough, this being *wadi* country with few tracks, and it was clear that the advancing infantry were relatively unfit from crouching in trenches for most of the winter and spring.

The main objective on the Divisional front was a location called L'Americano on the river Foce, but before reaching this small hamlet a number of machine gun obstacles had to be silenced. The advance set off mines which inflicted quite a few casualties on the Green Howards and accompanying engineers and alerted pockets of the enemy holding defensive machine gun positions. A counter-attack was beaten off mainly by the heavy machine guns of the Cheshire Regiment. As to what this small engagement achieved tactically, it is difficult to assess, for it cost the Green Howards alone six officers and 149 other ranks, but it did show how well all arms in the Division could support each other in an attacking mode after the long lay-off in a defensive situation.

These diversionary attacks by the British would enable the main attacks by four American divisions to make a significant advance towards the battered town of Cisterna and the Alban hills, although there was still considerable resistance on this front from five and a half German divisions who were containing the breakout from the beachhead – with the Herman Goering Division blocking the attacks towards Cisterna. This advance was led by the American 3rd Infantry Division and the 1st Armored Division and was aided by a massive air assault on the German front together with heavy Allied artillery support.

TAKING COVER FROM GERMAN SHELLING DURING
THE BREAKOUT (22 JANUARY TO 23 MAY 1944)
Photo courtesy of the Imperial War Museum, NA 15306

In the short term the British 1st Division moved north-eastwards into American-held territory and the 15th Infantry Brigade took over part of the British 1st Division front which included the main Albano-Anzio road in the neighbourhood of the flyover bridge. On 24th May it became possible for the main force of the 5th Division to release pressure in the fortress area and pull back 300 yards to the prepared positions before making an advance towards Ardea, held by our long-term foes, the German 4th Parachute Division.

On 25th May the advancing 85th and 88th American Divisions of 11 Corps arrived from the Garigliano front and linked up with the beachhead, which technically was 'relieved'. This was the catalyst that enabled the Allies in the coastal sector to make a general advance on Rome. On 26th May the 34th and 45th US Divisions switched away from the original axis to Valmontone – Alexander's preferred advance route – and took the line of moving towards Rome up Highway 7. In so doing the US 3rd Division, the 1st Armored, plus the Special Service Force, took three days to overcome the Herman Goering Division and capture Cisterna. This enabled the major part of the German tank army to withdraw behind it and live to fight another day.

A fundamental part of Alexander's Diadem plan was the entrapment of the German Tenth Army, by attacking in force and cutting off Highway 6 at Valmonte. This would result in the encirclement of the German Tenth Army between the Allied troops advancing from the south and the divisions breaking out from the beachhead. Clark, desperate for an American success story, chose instead to advance on Rome using only American troops.

Meanwhile on the 5th Division front the 15th Brigade with 1 Y&L in the lead made a significant advance only hindered by swiftly laid mines. The 1st KOYLI on their left was having a tougher time up against the enemy's hard core. The Green Howards, reinforced with inexperienced troops, were attacked and driven out of position. However, the advancing 1Y&L mounted a good attack against Pt 55 on the outskirts of Ardea which coincided with a similar attack by 2 Wilts of 13 Brigade on their left. The 2 Wilts then became pinned down as they attacked the two main enemy centres, and both advances were held up short of the objectives, with heavy casualties. The only reserve left to the Battalion Commander was the dismounted Carrier Platoon. This platoon was ordered to capture the north-east spur running out of Ardea, supported by a troop of 46 Regiment tanks. The platoon was led by Sergeant Rogers MM and Corporals Boyland and Cuddle with such gallantry that all objectives were taken after all the NCOs had been killed. In this action, Sergeant Rogers cut the wire surrounding the enemy's main position, advanced seventy yards across a minefield firing his Thompson submachine gun. He drew the fire on himself from seven machine guns plus mortar fire. He destroyed two of the enemy's machine guns posts and was in the process of destroying a third when he was wounded by a grenade and then killed at point blank range. For his supreme courage and self-sacrifice Sergeant Rogers was awarded a posthumous Victoria Cross.

My gun on the lateral road was winched out of its pit and after the fitters had checked it over and topped up the recoil system, I was able to move towards the Tiber in support of the 17th Brigade. The German Divisions were hastening to the north of Rome to avoid being cut off. But our inveterate foe, the 4th Parachute Division, had moved to carry out a rearguard action in the Alban Hills, to cover the retreating 10th and 14th German Armies.

Meanwhile, our 5 Recce Regt advanced swiftly to be the first Allied unit to reach the Tiber on the night of the 4th June. Our Divisional Provost could not let the occasion pass without posting a notice to later arrivals, 'Y Division welcomes you all to Rome'. Curiously, the American 88 Division (Florida Wildcats) who relieved us on the Minturno Sector of the Garigliano, passed by and were recorded as being the first of the Allied troops into Rome.

The Division had collected a large number of prisoners in the final swift advance and these were caged by our Royal Pioneer Corps. Elements of the 15th Infantry were still fighting around Pt 55. They rejoined us later when we moved south on our way to the Middle East. Our colleagues and friends of the British 1st Division moved north of Rome to go into reserve and then join the British Eighth Army after a well-earned rest.

The advancing Allies were greeted in Rome by crowds half delirious in the approved Italian manner. The Germans in the area were hastening north in any improvised transport they could get and many were in a bad way. Apart from our four Pipe Bands who were required at the Coliseum as part of the show in honour of General Clark's success, we in the British 5th Infantry Division headed in the opposite direction, away down south. Although denied entry into Rome, the British 5th Division, on the extreme left wing of the Anzio battles, had played a noble and very positive part in the ultimate victory. The price paid for this was not inconsiderable: 155

officers and 2,838 other ranks had become casualties since the Division had landed on Anzio in early March. This, added to the very heavy casualties in the successful crossing of the Garigliano, made this a very bloody first five months in 1944.

ANZIO: TWO CAPTURED GERMAN PARATROOPERS CARRYING A WOUNDED BRITISH SOLDIER
Photo courtesy of the Imperial War Museum, NA 15295

Parting of the ways

The Division parted from the 5th American Army, to be returned to the British Army. Although earmarked to rejoin the Eighth Army, we never returned and ended our fighting on a different front.

As we passed Anzio on our way back to Naples, our memories were stirred about our fallen comrades. Everything seemed quiet and peaceful for the area was about to return to its holiday setting after its interval as the 'Devil's Fairground'. After six months of concentrated hell – first on the Garigliano front, and then the beachhead – we headed back to the relative peace of the Middle East, with only the Stern Gang in Palestine to disturb us. The signs of nature were all around us, but most of all we enjoyed the sound of silence.

CHAPTER 10

THE MIDDLE EAST AND THE FINAL PUSH
IN GERMANY

Having been abroad since March 1942, on arrival at Naples the troops expected no less than a luxurious journey on the Queen Mary back to the UK. Instead, it was a short trip from Italy to Egypt, to train and re-absorb the basics that create an efficient British Army soldier. The Division was exhausted, unfit, depleted in numbers and had lost some superb NCOs and officers, mainly from the infantry battalions and engineers. It needed to recreate itself as the supremely efficient fighting force that landed in Sicily. The basic structure of the Division was intact, in that the Regimental HQ of the individual units were still sound and would continue to operate efficiently to the Divisional modus operandi, which had been successfully tried and tested in all kinds of conditions. In this regard, no other division in the British Army had been stretched more since the outbreak of war in 1939.

Of the surviving generals and some battalion and regimental commanders, the majority were moved away to new War Office appointments; in their place were a younger crop of high flyers who were expected to do great things. So the Division started to train again, absorbing the new intake. The order of the day was exercise, which had become necessary after the heavy fighting in cramped conditions. All troops were given a short leave in the Middle East, where in Palestine the Stern Gang were continuing to make themselves a nuisance. It became a Divisional responsibility to help keep them in check.

Just when morale was on the up, came the news that 2 Inniskillings was returning to Italy to join the Irish Brigade of 78th Division, who had lost the equivalent of one battalion. The 78th Division had made its mark as part of the First Army in North Africa when capturing Longstop Hill against strong German forces. Since then, it had built up a sound reputation as one of the top infantry divisions in the British Army. However, this move back to Italy of a battle-worn infantry battalion, after such a short break, highlighted the shortage of first-class infantry reinforcements in the British Army at this stage.

The whole of the Division was devastated, as were the 'Skins', who were not keen to join an all-Irish brigade. After four years fighting together, no longer would the 13th Brigade boast a Scottish, Irish and English consortium. For once the 5th Division lost its cool, resulting in a number of tramcars being turned over in Cairo. Once the dust had settled, every man in the Division had 10 shillings stopped from his pay to help settle the cost of a violent afternoon. It was also not a very welcome initiation to the Division for the incoming 6th Battalion, the Essex Regiment – the replacement for the Irish Regiment. The new Divisional Commander was a young general of 37, who was transferred from the command of the British 1st Armoured Division – Major-General R.A. Hull. Ahead of him was a magnificent career, ultimately culminating in his reaching the rank of Field Marshal; the Division's fine war record had been rewarded with a progressive leader to take us into the last phase of our war.

The Divisional Artillery went to practice camp at Harasta near Damascus, firstly to calibrate the guns and then fire our respective artillery pieces in a competitive shoot on the ranges. Our 17-pounder Pheasant, still on the secret list, proved itself in all respects – except mobility. As a result, the six-pounder was still used in anti-tank regiments and it had also become the infantry regiments' main anti-tank weapon. At this stage, the anti-tank regiments were also used as stand-in engineers and infantry – the anti-tank nature of the terrain of southern Italy had identified these other important options. Apart from military exercises, sporting activities were part of the feel-good morale booster encouraged by Divisional HQ. The pre-Sicily Division had a football team which included players Wilf Mannion of Middlesbrough and England, one of the

WILF MANNION

'famous five' players in the England forward line that bedevilled foreign opposition and Ted Sagar, an Everton and England goalkeeper. Mannion was on the verge of returning to England suffering from shell-shock, having served in 1 Green Howards since 1940. However, Sagar, a driver in the Divisional RASC, was still with the Division, along with many lesser known sportsmen in football, hockey and cricket.

The unit camps were spread over a wide area of the Middle East, stretching from the Carmel hills to various parts of Jerusalem, with Divisional HQ at Hadera. There were very pleasant bathing spots on the coast and delightful continental-style cafés near to the camps. Outings were arranged to Tel Aviv and Jerusalem, where the local population were extremely kind to our troops. In return our entertainers obliged with their efforts.

However, the favoured place to take leave was Beirut, a very lively place that had recently become the capital of the Lebanon. This port had excellent facilities and rest camps. In Syria was the more secluded Damascus which suited the less rumbustious types.

Our sergeants' mess, set up for the first time since leaving England, was in the Battery camp near Hadera. We had lost a few sergeants since leaving England through illness and war casualties and had received a new intake: Badge Bryer, a tough personality who was a PT instructor; Thompson, an experienced artillery sergeant returning to the front line; Robbie Weightman, an intelligent character and Schooly, a schoolmaster who had been promoted in

BADGE BRYER

anticipation of educating and preparing the squaddies for demobilisation after six years away from Civvy Street. Nobby Clark, my recent companion on Anzio, had been sent home with shell-shock but it was obvious that he was too old for a front-line unit.

About half of us decided to go for a short break to the YMCA in Beirut. It had become acceptable to give a large number of NCOs a short leave together in between military exercises. We were enjoying the cafés and bright lights of this town until the last night. A group of us, all spick and span, were headed towards the sea front when we were confronted by a large number of Senegalese Free French sailors who were out on the town celebrating the fall of Paris. They were cracking whips, clutching bottles of hooch and flourishing knives, blocking off the whole road and calling out 'Bastard Inglesi!'. It was a nasty moment, and in the scuffle that followed, a whip-lash cut open my left cheek as I wrested the whip away from an aggressive matelot. I heard Gerry Young beside me shout, 'Don't use it, Langley!'

I didn't, but retained the whip as we battled our way into town, in case they returned. We got rather drunk and hilarious while dressing our wounds. On returning to the YMCA we were confronted by the senior salvationist, who had apparently heard about the fracas. He viewed our bloodstains and made it clear that as sergeants we were a disgrace to the British Army and he would be reporting our conduct. I still had the whip, so he refused to let me return to my room until I handed it over. My colleagues convinced him that we had been cornered and had no option but to defend ourselves.

A report did go through to our regiment, but fortunately they realised that it was highly unlikely that we were the aggressors. The scar on my left cheek ended very close to my eye and was treated with some ointment. Sixty years later, it still shows up on a cold day.

One step forward, two steps back...

By November 1944 the Division was ready to move on, having remained doggo in one area for a longer period than at any time since leaving the UK. News came that we were to return to the Eighth Army in the Rimini area. The advance parties set off on a Canadian lake steamer and having met some appalling weather in the eastern Mediterranean, arrived as very sick squaddies. Fortunately they had time to recover in the few days spent in the transit camp at Taranto. They set off again in freezing weather for

Pescara on the Adriatic coast by rail in open cattle-trucks. At Pescara they took over vehicles from the British 4th Division who were en route to the Middle East for a well-earned rest. Meanwhile, a crisis in Greece had arisen which required a British Infantry Division, for which 5 Division, as the British Army reserve division, was earmarked.

Consequently, the bulk of the 5th Division still in the Middle East was to be directed towards Athens and the advance party had to return by road to Bari and Taranto for the guns and vehicles to be transported to Greece. The journey south was in appalling weather and exacerbated by lack of drivers for the number of vehicles to be ferried. The problem was overcome by towing some of the vehicles and using motor cyclists who could drive four-wheeled vehicles after stowing their bikes on the back of lorries. Given the slippery roads, this appealed to the Despatch Riders. On arrival at Bari and Taranto, the exhausted advance party were met with a change of plan: the War Office had decided that 4th Division was in the best position to get to Greece in a hurry – which meant that the 5th Division advance party had to hand back the vehicles to 4th Division and return to Alexandria, escorting German prisoners recently captured in Northern Italy. The journey back to the Middle East had its compensations, for the Division would spend Christmas in Palestine instead of the freezing cold of northern Italy.

The Division enjoyed a bountiful Christmas and shortly afterwards were on call to return to Italy and relieve the New Zealand Division in the Faenza area. On this occasion their trucks would be left behind, much to the disappointment of the drivers. On landing at Taranto the move to northern Italy was not immediate, for the train moved towards the Italian west coast and finally reached Salerno. Here we camped around an airfield. In due course the advance parties returned from northern Italy, making it clear that the Eighth Army was no longer our future command.

It transpired that the Division was to join a force headed 'Operation Snowflake', which involved the Canadian troops in the Italian theatre, who were joining the Canadian Army in north-west Europe to boost their advance into the Scandinavian countries.

We in the British 5th Division would be joining VIII Corps, to take part in the final push into northern Germany. This move was promulgated by General Montgomery, who had apparently asked for our Division to join 21 Army Group.

WITH OUR BELGIAN HOSTS

The weather in Salerno was bitterly cold, but it was not long before embarkation at Naples took place. Clothed in secrecy, the set-up was well tried by a number of US divisions who had already used that route when leaving Italy for France. The sea journey was very comfortable in American boats, which included our being overfed by continually joining a 'chow line' serving black coffee, waffles and bacon non-stop to Marseilles. On landing we went into a very exposed transit camp, which compared unfavourably with our accommodation in Persia. This barren location was at a place called L'Etang de Berre, to the north-west of Marseilles. We were glad to move out, albeit in draughty cattle trucks, where we tried to keep warm on the long train journey across the length of France, eventually crossing the Belgian border at Mons. We were reasonably well fed en route with American chow at the numerous comfort stops. After the boat trip, this was going from the sublime to the 'Cor Blimey!'.

Joining VIII Corps in 21 Army Group

Belgium was warm, neat, tidy and civilised in comparison to where we had been in the previous three years. The Divisional HQ was at Ghent and the rest of the division was spread around the area. Our unit was near Hasselt in north-east Belgium, which we thought appropriate, for it was near the brewing centre. The accommodation was first rate, with sergeants and officers billeted in private houses and farms. I shared a billet with Thompson, a sergeant who had joined us in the Middle East. A lovely aroma of coffee permeated throughout the farmhouse, which was owned by two brothers and a sister. All middle-aged, it seemed that none of them had married, but they were all very happy nonetheless. Neither 'Tommo' nor myself spoke Flemish and we had only a smattering of French between us, but we got by carrying out a lot of our communication by nodding and smiling. It seemed they liked us, because in the few weeks we were there we frequently had our photographs taken by one or other of them, snapping us with their old camera. Smiling was the order of the day, and got us early morning coffee and a massive farm breakfast. In the evening we enjoyed an excellent supper which we ate with the family, toasting each other with wine. All in all we enjoyed the life of Reilly.

Goodbye Pheasant, hello to the Archer

On joining 21 Army Group, the other units in the Army gave up some of their leave entitlement, enabling our 5th Division – who had been abroad for three years – immediate leave to the UK for all ranks. This leave could not be allocated straight away to our B Troop because we were changing our armaments.

Instead of the Pheasant we were getting a new advanced anti-tank weapon – the Archer, a relatively new weapon off the secret list and a standard anti-tank weapon for infantry divisions within 21 Army Group. It was a 17-pounder anti-tank gun, mounted on a Crusader tank chassis and motivated by an M10 engine. To us it was a godsend, for it made us mobile and no longer a huge sitting target. Only B Troop in our battery had these four new weapons, which meant we

BOMBARDIER LEVETT

would be in active support of the 17th Infantry. Battery A and C continued their role with six-pounders. In consequence our troop would have to accept this new weapon and train on it for two weeks before taking our leave in the UK. In particular our quad driver Belcher would have to learn to use tank tillers instead of a steering wheel. My limber gunner Lawrence would have to get used to a gun which fired from the back of the tank chassis. I, as number one, together with my lance bombardier Levett, had to hone up our map reading skills and wireless communication technique as we were most likely to be called upon to operate individually.

In short, we were to be as adaptable as a tank, but with less armour protection. The field artillery role would be thrust on us occasionally, for our new fieldpiece had a dual-purpose capability, as it could fire HE charges against enemy infantry. This was secondary to its main anti-tank role as a destroyer of armoured vehicles, tanks, and pillboxes. My new weapon, numbered B3, had the Divisional sign of 'Y' and the unit number 46. We named it 'Barricade' as representing B Troop and painted this on the front of the SP – the Self-Propelled gun. Having done all this we departed to the UK on a week's leave.

Home at last

After an absence of three years, my few days at home were quite a tearful affair. I was seeing some of the younger members of the family, who had been evacuated to the West Country in 1939, for the first time in nearly six years. My father I had seen once in 1942 before I left for India.

Now 19, my sister Phyllis had grown into a responsible young woman whom I barely recognised. Brothers Monty and David, at 16 and 14, were very streetwise and 'Courtlike'. There was an air of shyness as we got to know each other. My father was quite ill with emphysema, the legacy of mustard gas in World War I. He had lost weight but was still proud and showed masses of enthusiasm; I was quite shocked by his appearance, for he was only in his early fifties. I realised that I was needed back home as early as possible. My father, reading my thoughts, said, 'See out your demob, boy!'. My mother said very little; overcome by the family reunion, she went into the scullery and had a weep. However, the shy atmosphere was soon dispelled when Aunt Frannie bounced into the house.

Mrs Owen, her daughter Nelly and other neighbours in Methley Street who had known me since I was sixteen came along to give me the once-over. We all toddled along to the Alderman pub to toast my sister Ivy, now in the ATS and Betty, who was working and living in the West End. We remembered our other relatives, particularly those in the forces. It was then I learned that Ivy's fiancé, an American lieutenant whom I had never met, had lost part of a leg when landing on Omaha Beach. He had been flown back to the States for specialist treatment and chose to release Ivy from their engagement, preferring to return to his family after hospital treatment and convalescence. His decision was understandable, but my sister was intensely saddened and took a long time to regain her natural buoyancy. It had also been confirmed that our cousin Dennis, captured at Singapore and taken into a Japanese POW camp, had died working on an infamous railway. The bad news at home outweighed the good news and so I returned to Belgium feeling depressed.

Early in April the Division was on the move and we said goodbye to our Belgian friends. The lady of the farm dashed away a tear and it was quite natural for us all to have a final cuddle before leaving. Tommo, looking forlornly to the future, said, "Batten down the hatches, it will never be as good as that again, Langley!"

I had to agree, but getting the War over and going back home for good had become a priority. I had already ruled out taking a commission and becoming a regular officer. This matter had been raised when I was approached by the battery office. It was pointed out to me that I had been reclassified from A2 to A1 and my knee was no longer regarded as an impediment to becoming an officer. The fact that I was a War Substantiated full sergeant of 27 years of age, together with my family's military background, was something that the post-war Army was looking for in their future officers. No one doubted that there would be trouble ahead following the Armistice with Germany and Japan. The Brits' attitude, fostered by Churchill's misgivings, assumed that the Russians would pose problems and there would be large gaps in the ranks of the British Army when demobilisation started. At that time the crucial National Service mobilisation was not in the equation and would not become a fact until the National Service Act 1947, which made male British subjects between 18 and 26 liable to serve in the armed forces.

Meanwhile the War was still in progress and there were one or two rivers to cross, including the mighty Elbe – and an undoubted meeting with the Russians on one side or the other. Churchill and the British War Lords hoped that it would be as near to Berlin as possible, so that the negotiation of the four zones – American, British, French and Russian – could he negotiated as amicably as possible. We, the soldiers of the King, hoped that this last hurdle would be completed without too many casualties in our ranks.

On to Germany

We left Belgium and made our way towards Essen with our SPs loaded on tank transporters, for our ultimate destination was south of Uelzen, a long way ahead. The original configuration of Essen was difficult to identify for the roads and routes through the town could hardly be traced, so heavy had been the bombardment by the RAF. The way through the town had to be picked out between large craters and rubble from fallen buildings. Other towns en route had been badly damaged but this was the worst – only Aachen on the German, Dutch and Belgian borders, where I was based when I joined the Foreign Office's Control Commission for Germany in 1946, was as bad. In between the towns the VIII Corps' advance was evident, shown by the many unburied German bodies lying about. The units of the 5th Division joined the VIII Corps front when we reached the assembly point south of Uelzen, arriving from our different starting points between April 16th and 19th. Uelzen was surrounded and finally taken on 19th April after three days of street fighting by the very impressive 15th Scottish Division.

NEW GUNS: THE ARCHER

Our comrade divisions in VIII Corps were the 15th Scottish Division, 6th Airborne Division and 11th Armoured Division; all had been involved in the crossing of the Rhine. Our role was to take up the extreme right position of VIII Corps with the American 9th Army immediately on our right. Initially as we advanced, part of the 5th Division came under the command of the 6th British Airborne Division.

LOADING THE ARCHER

The main advance on the Elbe by VIII Corps started on 29th April with the 15th Scottish Division on our left with our 13th Infantry at their side and the 17th Infantry on the right flank. Our 15th Brigade was in reserve. We had orders to advance through 6 Airborne Division and to establish ourselves on the west bank of the Elbe between Neu Dachau and Bleckede, the latter proving to be an obstacle. This move to the river took three days through the thick Gohrde Forest, skirmishing with small parties from the German Navy and other groups of patriotic Germans which by now included both sexes fighting in mixed formations – as only the Germans knew how.

On 1st May the 13th Infantry captured BarsKamp and was astride the railway south of Bleckede. The 2nd Cameronians advanced into Bleckede against stubborn resistance, supported by tanks of the 4th Grenadier Guards. The battalion sustained fairly heavy casualties against a build-up of Germans who did not want to cross the river but ultimately gave themselves up. Apart from numerous prisoners the Cameronians captured a large dump of champagne and other wine which was divided amongst other Divisional units. Meanwhile, on the extreme right flank the 17th Infantry met strong opposition at Hohenzethen. After regrouping, their second attack was successful and they took 50 prisoners. They met several German Panzers operating individually which were dealt with mainly by the Grenadiers. The task of mopping up to the river was laborious because the opposition was hard to locate in the heavily wooded country. The 2nd RSF, in the lead, reached Neu Dachau on the river, where it was shelled by the Germans from across the river and by the Americans from the south.

Operation 'Enterprise', the Crossing of the Elbe which included the British XLI Corps, had to be altered as this corps was well behind due to the prolonged battle in taking Hamburg. The Army Commander wanted the river crossed quickly and a rapid advance on Lübeck , with the object of taking the U-boat base at Kiel. Accordingly the line-up to cross the river had to be altered and 5 Division moved up the river opposite Lauenburg where a Class 9 Bridge was in the course of construction for the Division and various other troops to cross. The Bleckede–Neu Dachau Sector we left was taken over by the 82nd US Airborne Division, part of the 9th US Army.

The initial assault of the 300-yard wide river was undertaken by the 15th Scottish and 1st Commando Brigades. The point at which they were to create a beachhead was near to Elbe–Trave Canal, an area where two vital bridges were to be taken intact to allow the two breakout divisions, our 5th Infantry Division and the 11th British Armoured Division, to make a rapid advance on Lübeck . The 6th British Airborne Division, operating with the 15th Infantry of 5 Division, would fan out to the east after crossing the river and come under command of the XVIII US Airborne Corps with the object of moving up to meet the Russian advance from the east of Prussia.

The 5th Division's artillery took up the offensive under a large-scale plan, 'Cossack', which started before the assault with the object of taking out the key defensive points. The 156th Field Regiment of the 17th, using close proximity fuses with very accurate firing, killed the whole German demolition party before they could blow one of the bridges. The field artillery performance was crucial because the planned air bombardment had to be cancelled because of the damp misty weather. The opposition had 300 guns of various calibres that were in support of the 245th German Infantry Division; below strength and not a typical first-class German Division, they were in a very strong defensive position nonetheless.

The Archer comes into its own

In this area was a vital heavily constructed mill in a low position on the far bank which had been suitably reinforced as an OP for the German Artillery and the Luftwaffe. This observation post had a clear view of a whole stretch of river but could not be easily pinpointed by the British Medium Artillery and was difficult to attack by the Allied aircraft because of the anti-aircraft defence around it. The field artillery could not make much of an impression and our waiting infantry battalions were being heavily bombarded and having a rough time before crossing the Elbe. It was decided to try out the Archer of B Troop to see if the high-velocity 17-pounder AP projectiles could overcome the problem. Our two most experienced gun teams in B Troop were B1 and B3 and so my friend Charley Bushell (B1) and myself (B3) discussed tactics before we advanced to the river bank. B1 was manned by my gun team of Anzio and B3 by my gun team on the crossing of the Garigliano.

We took our SPs forward from the edge of the wood to just above the river and immediately opened fire with armour-piercing rounds, aiming on a line halfway up the mill. After ten rounds apiece, the edifice started to crumble. Having adjusted our sights, we fired ten high-explosive rounds from each gun into the crumbling areas and soon smoke and flames started to show. Quite suddenly it became apparent from the huge flames and heavily belching smoke emitting from the mill that old chaff was burning inside. In no time the outside of the edifice was enveloped in flames, which gave our infantry something to cheer about.

By now the German Artillery had trouble ranging on us, due to the smoke and mist, and their shells were landing in the woods behind us. Before retiring from our position, we saw figures leave the burning mill and run towards a tall building about 400 yards further back. I fired two rounds of high explosives at this new target – the first was woefully short, the second ht the bottom of the building, and before a range adjustment could be made, an order was given on the wireless to cease fire and pull back. That night I and my gun team were given orders to proceed to the same area of the river the following morning and to sink any barges that could be released laden with explosive to destroy our Bailey bridges. However, in the early hours our infantry took the other bank and so this order was rescinded.

We learned about a month later, on our return to this part of the Elbe, that the ceasefire order had been given in the nick of time. The house we were firing at had been crowded with over 200 refugees, mainly women and children. There were casualties from the mill, as the fresh graves around the burnt-out relic indicated. Any remorse we felt for this action was quickly dispelled when we saw the graves of our own men – mainly Sappers – on the other side of the river.

In our eyes – and to the artillery fraternity – the Archer had moved up the pecking order. From being the Cinderella of the Divisional Artillery, the 17-pounder had in certain situations become the preferred gun. Lofty Lawrence, my limber gunner, who polished B3 on every possible occasion, was absolutely chuffed!

Over the Elbe

The crossing of the Elbe on 29th April, led by 15 Scottish Division and 1 Commando, went according to plan. The bridge over the Elbe–Trave Canal was captured with no significant structural damage. On the 30th, the 15th Scottish Division extended its bridgehead and the 6th Airborne Division with 15th Infantry of 5th Division attached, took over the extended area which involved the latter brigade capturing the railway junction at Potrau after a severe battle. The 13th Infantry went through them in the breakout, with the Royal's armoured car units on the east fringe and maintaining a link with the 6th Airborne Division on their right and thus the Americans.

The 2nd Wiltshires of the13th Infantry Brigade were in the lead on the road to Lübeck and cleared the town of Molin by midday on 1st May, after some scattered resistance. By 1300 hrs they also had a company in Ratzeburg and were three miles south of Einhaus. They continued to advance during the afternoon and by midnight had reached Grosse Gronau, five miles from Lübeck . On the way they met a steady flow of Allied prisoners who had been released by their German warders; the prisoners, many of them RAF, enjoyed their first cup of English-brewed tea for a long time, served by B Echelon of 13th Brigade.

The 11th British Armoured Division, the other breakout division on the left of the assault, crossed the Class 40 Bridge at Ardenburg and headed towards Tritton on Bad Oldesloe so as to dominate all roads leading out of Lübeck to the north and north-west. Meanwhile, 6 British Airborne Division, once clear to the east of the Elbe–Trave Canal, had proceeded fairly rapidly towards the Schwerin area to meet up with the Russians.

Both the 11th British Armoured Division from the west and the 5th British Infantry Division from the east moved rapidly towards Lübeck to conform with the Army Commander, General Dempsey's order that the quick capture of Lübeck could hasten the surrender by the Germans in Schleswig-Holstein. This area, with its important naval docks at Kiel, was a German Navy strongpoint and it was known that there were many large ships and submarines in the docks, protected by a strong force of German troops who could hold up any chance of a rapid surrender.

The tanks of the 11th British Armoured Division, with some 5th British Infantry Division on board, were first into Lübeck by a short head from the 13th Infantry foot soldiers of the 5th Infantry Division. No doubt General Dempsey was delighted that his old brigade – the 13th who he had commanded in 1940 at Dunkirk – was in at the kill.

General Sanders and the complete 245th German Infantry Division surrendered to the 5th British Division on the 3rd May. This was followed by the German XXVIII Corps surrendering at Battalion

HQ of the Cameronians. The 5th Division advanced beyond Lübeck to Travemunde and Neustadt against light opposition.

The 5th Division POW cage was soon overflowing with over 55,000 prisoners, mainly from the Mölln area. The Royals, ranging far and wide in their armoured cars, also brought in large numbers. The 11th Armoured Division had 18,000 POWs in Lübeck itself and they had liberated an Oflag and released 1,000 British and more than 6,000 Allied prisoners. The area around the Division's POW cage was like a bank holiday on Hampstead Heath, with bonfires, accordions and community singing. It seemed that everyone was celebrating the imminent ending of the war except for a few young and arrogant Nazis. My SP, as with other track vehicles, was doing a stint of patrolling around the outskirts of the cage. A smart German officer was released from it, accompanied by two of his men who were walking behind him carrying a large black metal box, which was heavily padlocked. I dismounted and walked towards him when I heard an interpreter shouting that he was the adjutant of one of the regiments in the 245 Jaegar Division and that he was holding the cash for the regimental pay roll. He wished to hand it over to a responsible English officer or NCO because it was impossible for him to pay it out to his declining regiment, many of whom had deserted and were probably heading for their homes.

I accepted the box and signed for it and took the key, in the knowledge that the defeat of Germany was likely to make the notes worthless. The conscientious German officer beamed with relief that he had completed his task and he rewarded me with a smart salute, which I returned. I passed on the box to our Regimental HQ. Little did either the German officer or I know that he had passed his money to the future Chief Cashier of London Transport.

The 11th Armoured Division moved out of Lübeck and advanced towards the Kiel Canal and the Danish frontier. The British 5th Division moved east to join with the British 6th Airborne Division, who had already met up with the Russians at Wismar on the Baltic coast. These actions represented the effective break-up of Vlll Corps, because from that point on we would be operating as individual divisions.

We in the 17th Brigade on the extreme right of the British Army, were headed towards the Wittenberg area to join up with the American 9th Army, so that the Allies maintained an unbroken front. The flow of refugees towards us, mingled with German troops, made it difficult for them to surrender but it was clear that the Russians were close behind. As we passed houses, Union Jacks and the Stars and Stripes were being hastily withdrawn from the windows and replaced by the Soviet hammer and sickle. News of Hitler's suicide on 30th April was now generally accepted by the population, as was the occupation of Berlin by the Russians.

Germany surrenders at last

The latest news on 4th May was that a German delegation had been received by Montgomery at his headquarters on Luneberg Heath. All German forces in Holland, Dunkirk, north-west Germany, Schleswig-Holstein, Denmark, Heligoland and the Frisian Islands had surrendered unconditionally. This news made it clear that all German resistance had ceased and the logical acceptance of 'the state of play' was that people living on the Berlin side of the Elbe would be controlled by the Russians. The exact border lines of the four zones would be settled later but every expectation was that when the borders were agreed, more land would be ceded to the Russians. This was a situation that Winston Churchill had tried to avoid in 1944, by making a swift capture of Italy a priority and enabling an advance by the Allies into Austria before the Russians reached there.

Our first sight of the advancing Russian Army was a surprise to us, and a considerable shock to the local people. Not marching troops, but a mass of soldiers spread-eagled across the road, with rifles slung across their shoulders. Here and there were a few Cossack types on horseback and shepherding goats, pigs, chickens and cattle they had procured on the way. In the rear came their camp followers, mainly women who were driving the animals along. Wives or, more likely, part of a mobile brothel; but no doubt many were hoping to cross the Elbe into one of the Allied zones. Soviet officials appeared and directed this throng to an area just outside the village which would serve as a temporary front line and avoid unnecessary confrontation – in which our artillery held sway.

We made the first move away and headed south to join up with the US 9th Army. They would move further south later to the US zone around Frankfurt. In due course we would move back across the Elbe and occupy a front line around the Hartz mountains with various headquarters at Brunswick and Hanover. Ultimately, the overall governing control of the British Zone would be transferred to the Control Commission for Germany.

Our general move towards Magdeburg was directed towards a small town called Penig and in particular to a concentration camp named Ebensee, where we would relieve elements of the 82nd Airborne Division who were required to move rapidly to the new American zone in the south. This area contained small factories and a Luftwaffe emergency battle station, with grounded planes such as Messerschmidts and Heinkels. Demobilised and not airworthy, their guns were still loaded with belts of live ammunition. Close to the planes were stocks of high-octane fuel in rather insecure bunkers.

A grim task

At the side of the aerodrome was my unit's destination, a concentration camp of the most obscene kind, holding thousands of prisoners mainly of Russian and Jewish origins. It was predominantly male but there were a large number of women inmates too. It had been used by the Germans as a dumping ground as the armies swept towards each other, with the emphasis on driving Jewish inmates into the future Russian Zone. It contained many unburied bodies.

It was a warm day in early May when we entered this camp. Skeletal figures in long striped shapeless garments revealed the denigration of the human species in its most hideous form. They were tottering about, occasionally colliding with each other. The Americans were guarding the entrances, for the inmates were incapable of taking care of themselves and the majority needed medical attention. Some had managed to get onto the airfield and had been drinking the aircraft fuel; they were now blundering around as if blind. More active ones had managed to climb into the fighters and had fired the machine guns, causing casualties. Here and there couples were entwined together on the grass verges of the road having sex – apparently oblivious to our convoy passing close by. The Americans had liberated the camp a few days previously and had removed the German guards, which probably resulted in the free intercourse between men and women which was now out of hand. The Americans had rightly concentrated on feeding the inmates, improving sanitation and keeping the survivors alive. Later it became apparent to us that a number were dying daily from hunger, disease and self-inflicted wounds.

I was given the task of feeding over 3,000 male inmates of eastern European origin, a cross-section of which were probably long-standing prisoners of war. Some were seriously incapacitated, probably from war injuries. Their nationalities ranged from Latvians to mid-European nationalities such as Poles, with a predominance coming from various Russian states, and a number were Jews.

A lieutenant from the US 82nd Airborne Division met me in a strictly unhygienic cookhouse, where the chow was dished out at 13.00 hours each day. He advised me: 'Open the doors at one o'clock and then stand clear, Maurice, otherwise they'll run right over you.' I responded, 'Don't you get them in a queue, so that the injured get a fair chance?' 'Look pal, we only hit on this place four days ago, on our way through to the south. We took all the Krauts prisoner and were told that the Red Cross and our nursing staff or someone would take it on. Maybe it's too soon for them to take it over? Yesterday they said you guys were coming, so bad luck, pal... it's your problem! The only thing I have to hand over to you is a requisition book, for you to order three horses a day, their rations.' I was shocked. 'Don't they get any vegetables? There were loads of potatoes in the fields as we came along.' I was obviously straining his patience. 'Look, Maurice, we haven't had a chance to sort it out. All I can say is good luck, pal!' 'Well, thanks, Al. One last question – who does the cooking?' 'We got six guys who we picked out. They're quite clean. But whatever you do Maurice, make sure you get plenty of salt. They made a hell of a noise on the first day because there was no salt in the stew. Well, so long, Maurice!' With that, he was off.

I was allocated twelve men, including part of my own gun team. Some I exchanged for hard cases who would be more suitable for the task. I selected the ex-miner Geordie Williams, and Brennan, who was from a Liverpool docker's family. Both had experienced life in the raw and would bend the rules if the occasion demanded it.

The British way, queues and all

On our first day Levett and I watched and took notes in order to identify where we could make improvements. The lame and infirm were bundled on one side as the rush started; in particular, a huge Russian swept through the untidy throng, shoving aside the unfortunates in his way. It was a general habit by the inmates, as they entered the feeding area, to spit on the wall which became covered in dripping saliva as the mealtime progressed. At the end of this first day I reported my observations to a captain in the Service Corps who was monitoring the camp procedures. He was very understanding and took on board the urgent need for vegetables and for the walls to be scrubbed. Before mealtime on the second day we had plenty of potatoes and forty very reluctant German ladies from a local town of Penig peeling them. They were shocked by the camp and made it clear that they didn't like the task of helping to feed 'animals'.

A team of men from the Pioneer Corps also scrubbed the walls of the kitchen along with other tasks including removing the dead bodies. In best British manner, we established a number of queues to cater for the seriously disabled, partially lame, and the fit, divided between old and young. Just as the seriously disabled were moving forward first into the cookhouse, there was a loud roar as the huge Russian ploughed his way through the queue, brushing aside the fit and the lame until he reached the front. He was confronted by Brennan, who was a six-footer and had instructions to stop him. The Russian looking down on Brennan, uttered a few threatening noises as he attempted to move to the front. Brennan kneed him in the groin and hit him on the head with his Sten gun butt as he was falling. This was greeted by cat-calls and hoots of approval as the queue moved forward around the recumbent figure, who was occasionally spat on by the seriously disadvantaged who had been the main victims of his bullying. He was dragged to one side and laid out as a lesson to anyone who felt disposed to disobey the unwritten laws of British queuing.

I came from the cookhouse on hearing the cheering and hooting and observed the prostrate figure with Brennan standing by, busily examining his Sten gun, by now showing signs of maltreatment. Brennan loaded the carbine and fired a short burst away from the camp and turning with a grin said, 'It's awright, Sarge!' I went back to the cookhouse in the knowledge that Brennan's tactics, although unorthodox had the desired effect. Thereafter, Brennan's movement up and down the dinner queue was greeted by the inmates with respect.

On the third day we posted a notice in the various Eastern European languages to stop spitting in the cookhouse area, with the added threat that any culprit would be taken out of the dinner queue. By this time we had included green vegetables to the meat and potatoes, making the meals more attractive.

To assuage the nauseating nature of the task and stimulate British humour, we had a menu printed each day showing the contents of the day's stew as such British Racehorse Classic winners as Reynoldstown, Midday Sun and Bahram. We drew the line at Golden Miller – it would have been sacrilege to tarnish his memory in such dire circumstances, albeit in fun!

Each day Bleasdale and Murphy made a trip through the huts in my section to find any dire cases too weak to get to the cookhouse. They also took cases suffering from alcoholic poisoning to a separate unit supervised by military medical staff. They moved food to seriously bedridden cases and took large food containers to the Alcoholic Poison Unit. One special case I remember was a very sick old Jewish gentleman, whose son would not leave his side. He could not keep food down. Bleasdale had the bright idea of trying him on British Compo Rations, which were not greatly favoured by the troops. We carried a few cases for emergencies in our SP. The canned Machonichie stew and canned rice pudding put the old man back on his feet and on the road to recovery. This gave Bleasdale great satisfaction and the opportunity to explain to the disbelieving squaddies the vitamins they had been missing.

Around the middle of May the Red Cross and medical specialists took over the camp from the troops of the 5th Division. The inmates were being prepared to return to their countries after receiving appropriate medical treatment. During our time there the Pioneers had cleaned up the camp, filled in unhygienic latrines, sanitised the sleeping accommodation, and removed all unhealthy objects, which included decaying bodies.

Our regiment was given notice to move out and head for Magdeburg and prepare to move on to our base in the Hartz mountains. The distance was not far so we managed to load everything on our SPs and support vehicles, before handing over the kitchen to better trained specialist staff. As we left, there were quite a few friendly waves and shouts from the incumbents. The loudest roar, accompanied by a wave of the fist, came from the huge Russian, who made a point of pulling an ugly face at Brennan as he waved – much to Brennan's delight.

CHAPTER 11

○

GERMANY IS DIVIDED AND WE PART COMPANY

The meeting up of the British Fifth Infantry Division and the Russians established a temporary front line, albeit a ragged one. Nonetheless , it was generally accepted that until the Zone areas were finalised, convoys of the Western Allies would not infringe upon the Soviet front line.

After leaving the Ebensee concentration camp, we moved into a camping area near the Elbe and carried out maintenance for a day. The following day we crossed the river and headed towards Braunlage in the Hartz mountains – our new regimental HQ.

Ultimately our 206 Battery would move to St Andreasberg in the OberHartz. This town would be our base until the majority of us were demobbed, and we would share the town with a Polish detachment who would act in the capacity of a German-speaking frontier police force. It was evident that we would be supplying the military force at the frontier posts, with a mobile role in the OberHartz rounding up the SS on our side of the mountain. Close at hand to our base stood the massive 3,730 feet of Mount Brocken, but it would be on the Russian side of the border.

On the road to the Hartz we passed through Elbingerode, which was in farmland that seemed devoid of life. There was ample evidence of a tank battle having been fought, for here and there were blackened relics of once proud fighting machines, attended by small wooden crosses. This was tank country without adequate cover. The road was pitted by holes where Telemines had exploded, causing a jerky movement when the SP's tracks hit the craters, making it a bumpy ride as the tracked vehicle climbed upwards.

Ahead could be seen the tree-line of the Hartz, the only mountains in the north German plains. The formidably rounded outline of the Brocken summit rose above it all, a brooding sight that inspired some of the Grimm brothers' fairytales and remained the source of much superstition. This was the first test of the SP on mountain roads, for northern Germany is relatively flat. The higher pitch of the diesel engines caused game birds such as pheasant and partridge to scuttle away into the undergrowth. There were other pleasant distractions as the banks on the roadside became lightly populated with beech woods. The darker slopes above promised a more profuse forestry of pines and conifers. In between the forestry were expanses of peat bogs with tracks in between, leading to long disused copper and silver mine shafts.

The forests suddenly gave way to a large clearing in which nestled the town of Braunlage, overshadowed by one of the Hartz summits, the vast forested Wurmberg, which towered above the town. We followed the ubiquitous regimental signs which routed the way to the HQ. The townspeople showed some interest and children walked forward unafraid, calling out 'Englander!' We acknowledged with 'Yahwol!' and, for good measure, the thumbs-up that could not be linked with any other race. We stopped at HQ for a brief meal and collected various impedimenta to take to our new home. The probability was that we would be cut off from HQ during the winter, so we would have to be totally self-reliant, with the Polish detachment obtaining their rations from our unit.

The few miles to St Andreasberg were uphill all the way, with the SP drivers grimly moving the tillers to counteract the slide of the tracks caused by fallen fir branches and cones that littered the road. We all wondered how on earth we would handle the SPs when the snow came.

St Andreasberg

At last the road straightened out as we reached the top and soon we passed a sanatorium for various chest complaints. Ahead stood a large ski-jump which dominated the small town of St Andreasberg, which seemed to be on the apex of a hill. Refugees carrying their bags were tramping along towards a large building which proved to be the Burgermeister's office.

The townspeople wore plain clothes. The skirts of the womenfolk were long and many wore short socks and clogs. A girl went by in bare feet herding a flock of goats. A young, handsome blonde youth gazed moodily across, standing very erect on one leg; his bearing showed he was proud to have sacrificed the other for the Fatherland. It seemed that as yet no other male companions had returned from the war. The town was full of guest houses and small hotels, a reminder that in happier times it was a tourist attraction. Now it was coming to terms with its new role as a frontier town.

Unit signs had been placed at the front of buildings that had been requisitioned, either as offices or billets. These battered regimental boards sat uneasily in front of tidy timber-framed apartments, but there were no plans to replace them with new signs at this stage of the war. St Andreasberg was not only coming to terms with the occupation, but for the first time with the war. Ironically, the new frontier had brought the war closer than before. The tidy German mind would adapt to the situation that had brought foreign fighting machines to their own doorstep – a liberty the Wehrmacht had never taken.

The SPs were left in an area identified as a vehicle park. I climbed down gingerly from B3 feeling stiff, as the slim wiry figure of Sergeant-Major Jackson approached. I had not seen him since Belgium – sergeant-majors generally look after the unit requirements at base and rarely come to the front line. Anzio was the exception. Jackson, a Geordie, was a regular army reservist, called up at the outbreak of war. He had the rare ability of being able to lay out the relative facts in a few, terse words – it seemed to be a gift possessed by all decent sergeant-majors. The untidy situation in St Andreasberg would make him the most important man in our battery.

'Langley, good to see you.... rough on the Elbe, was it?' 'The guns were an eye-opener – put Anti-Tank back on the map!' He patted my shoulder, 'Come on, lad, I'll show you our mess – you'll like it! It's owned by Frau Kelmar, who is staying in residence and will do the cooking for the sergeants.' We were met at the door by a slim woman of about forty, who came forward as if greeting a guest. She was a very tidy person, and her reddish blonde hair was parted in the centre, enhancing her light blue eyes and fair freckled complexion. 'This is Hannah, my daughter!' she added, as a fair-haired child came skipping up and stood shyly by her side. 'You are most welcome Sergeant – er?' 'Court', I supplied rather shyly. 'We in the town are very happy we are this side of the border,' she added firmly. I gave a little jump as a cuckoo popped out of a clock on the wall behind me – this broke the silence and made us all laugh.

This was the first sergeants' mess we had had since Palestine and would undoubtedly be the best, judging by the first meal of game pie. Monty Sansom was appointed the Mess Sergeant to oversee our bar – and had the first task of appointing a barman from the ORs.

Jackson put us in the picture regarding our links with the Polish unit, and the likely positions of the frontier once the Russians erected their fence. The line would not only divide the Hartz community but also divide East Germany from West Germany. Various armies were still on the move and had to be clear of each other's zones before the border posts could be settled – and that had to be agreed by the respective Control Commissions and be in accordance with the terms of the Potsdam Agreement. In the meantime, temporary controls would be introduced on the roads into the St Andreasberg area. These would consist of a noticeboard spelling out in the various languages the rules for entering the British Zone.

Each control point in the OberHartz would be manned by a guard with a Polish interpreter in attendance. Any dubious persons would be taken under guard to the Poles' main centre in St Andreasberg. Our main role was apprehending SS troops (usually identified by their blood group tattooed on the soft flesh under the arm or behind the knees, or by scars in these areas). Some refugees avoiding the Russian frontier posts to get into the British zone could cause problems by approaching St Andreasberg along footpaths through the mountains and forests.

It was accepted that the Poles had more experience in identifying likely SS or hardened Nazis. Already they had introduced daily patrols in the streets of St Andreasberg and were helped by paid German informers. Likely suspects were taken to a special room for interrogation. This was a clearance process and tough measures were taken to get at the truth. After interrogation the detainees were moved quickly and Nazis from East Germany were returned to the Russians and senior SS removed to the Polish HQ in Brunsweig for further interrogation.

The Poles had set up their main HQ in a large house in the centre of the town where all newcomers into the town were quizzed. The Burgermeister could not register refugees until they produced a clearance chit from the Polish unit. In the months ahead our main problem would be coping with a town overladen with refugees and the requirement to feed them – particularly in the winter when St Andreasberg was cut off by snow.

As far as we Brits were concerned, there was the added menace of SS carrying arms and hiding out in the silver and copper mines during the winter. These hideouts would enable them to reconnoitre the area and even make ammunition for their guns. In the early spring thaw they could leave the OberHartz and be absorbed into an overburdened British Zone.

After a discussion on the main security points Jackson stated that he had met the Burgermeister, and promised the battery's support with the administration and in feeding the refugees. It would probably mean organising shooting parties in the autumn for game. Our basic task was to help a crowded frontier town to void unnecessary casualties.

Jackson and Monty Sansom had met the Poles and made arrangements for the sergeants – who would become the prime movers in the administration – to visit the Polish unit at a social get-together at their headquarters. The evidence showed them to be a hard lot, who hated the Germans. At the outbreak of war some of them were in the notorious Warsaw POW cage, which was placed in a vulnerable position in the town centre. It was here they lost friends and relatives who were killed or seriously wounded in the RAF bombing, although it enabled prisoners to escape.

Some of this detachment had escaped in this way and made their way through Allied friendly territory, eventually getting to the UK. Included in the unit were a number of women and a teenage boy Stepan, whose parents had been killed in Warsaw and he had been adopted by a senior officer. They joined the Polish Army in England and became part of the Allied Forces. Some had fought at Casino as part of the Eighth Army, so they understood the British Army structures and procedures. Our problem would be accepting their harsh treatment of the Germans during interrogation.

STEPAN

We party with the Poles

A few days later we received an invitation to attend a buffet at the Polish HQ in celebration of a saint's day. Since arriving at this new base, maintenance of guns and equipment had been first priority, but Jackson made it clear that this was a good opportunity to discard our dungarees and overalls and wear our best uniform for the first time in months. Accordingly, ten of us from the sergeants' mess arrived at the Polish HQ on the appointed evening, feeling curious rather than hopeful about the evening ahead. We were the senior British representatives available – Major Shepherd was at Brunswick attending a seminar for COs who would be acting as military governors until the Control Commission made official Foreign Office appointments. The Adjutant was busy preparing the paperwork for the British General Election. It was the sergeants who would be involved with the basic duties on the new frontiers

– so we were a fairly representative bunch.

On our arrival, the door was opened by a heavily moustached Polish officer. We were offered a glass of schnapps from a gentleman with a generous array of gold teeth. Sansom and Allison, the two musicians from our mess, wandered over to the piano in a corner of the room. 'Play you?' asked Gold Teeth of Allison. 'No, but him play good!' responded Allison, gesturing towards Sansom. The Poles gathered around in anticipation, for they had no pianist in their group. Sansom gave a short rendering of classical stuff and some boogie woogie, while Allison went back to the sergeants' mess to get his piano accordion, which had recently been sent up from base.

Meanwhile, the remainder of the Polish contingent emerged from the upstairs rooms, including half a dozen women who were part of the unit. Allison returned with his piano accordion and the party took off... The buffet, which included very tasty raw Polish bacon on toast, went down well and soon everyone was very happy, particularly Lena, a buxom Polish girl who was not short of admirers, both male and female.

SGT-MAJOR JACKSON AND MAJOR JACKSON IN THE MIDDLE ROW;
GERRY YOUNG LOOKS STURDY AT THE RIGHT

The wine and music was a toxic mixture and soon Monty became aware of Lena's admiring gaze and sang two numbers by Cole Porter in his rich tenor voice. This was too much for Lena, who uttered a strange guttural sound as she stood up and with glistening eyes walked seductively towards the piano. Monty was an actor of many years' experience and started to play it up by stretching his fingers in artistic fashion, and encouraging 'Gold Teeth' to wipe the piano keys with a cloth. 'Could do with a clean, old chap, probably last used in a brothel,' he said smoothly.

Lena leaned over and stroked Monty's hair. 'I love your music. You play and sing beautiful! I want you verra much, Englishman!' and so saying, she took a vicelike grip on his jacket, ready to take him to her room. The Polish Captain was starting to look worried and stepped in. 'Stanislaus will not be pleased with you, Lena.' 'Ah', said Monty. 'We must not upset Stanislaus,' just as Stanislaus, who apparently respected the Queensbury rules, appeared with two pairs of boxing gloves. 'Monty must not damage his hands!' interposed Allison. 'Badge Bryer takes care of his fights,' he added, pointing out our large PT instructor. Bryer, who was quite drunk, looked belligerently around for the offended Pole. Fortunately, Stanislaus did not want to know. And Lena flounced out of the room, highly offended that the offer of her body to the Welshman had been rejected without a fight. In spite of some sticky moments, from then on we were all good friends.

Home leave

A ten-day leave was on the agenda for B Troop because we had missed a few days' leave in Belgium doing extra training on the new Archers. It was expected that we would report back before the new frontier posts were built. The other troops would get a week only, but all of us were expected to vote in the British General Election before we left Germany. The vote was being held in a sealed document and opened somewhere on election day.

Bushell and I were the first sergeants in our battery to take leave in the UK. His home was in Wiltshire and I arranged to meet him for a day at my sister Isobel's ATS camp near Wilton.

I arrived home and was greeted by the three evacuees, who were back at Methley Street for good. My father was incapacitated, having just returned from hospital. He had obviously coerced the doctors to send him home to be with a family he had been separated from for six years. Brother David was an asthmatic, but was able to start school at Alleyn's College in Dulwich, having passed his matriculation examination. Monty had passed his school certificate exams and had got an office boy job at the *Daily Mirror*. Phyllis continued her studies and had passed various shorthand and typing exams which would ultimately lead to her joining the *London Evening News*.

My mother was much happier with the younger family home, but both of us were worried about my father's health. I went to the local hospital in Kennington to see the specialist. He didn't think it would be beneficial for my father to return to hospital and advised that he would be better off at home under the supervision of our family doctor. Although father was suffering from emphysema, his hobby of racing pigeons and studying pedigrees was still a passion. Having regard to the acid nature of the pigeon's droppings, it was not the ideal hobby for someone with a chest complaint. On the plus side, it got him out of bed each day and his planning and breeding expertise enabled his hobby to make a profit from the sale of eggs and squeakers, and the loft continued to win races.

The sight of his frail figure in the armchair each day, wearing an old cardigan that the pigeons recognised, brought tears to my eyes, for he was only 55 years of age. For the first time in my life, I cuddled him each morning and he patted my arm in return. This apart, the house was a happy place with Aunt Fran bringing in some goodies each day once she had closed her florist's shop at the Oval.

Johnny Ward came up from Colchester barracks while I was home, bringing his new bride – the RSM's daughter. He was a company sergeant-major in the Royal Fusiliers and had decided to continue in the Regular Army. He was wearing his MM decoration, awarded for bravery at Salerno. He had managed to overcome the wounds that put him in hospital during the Italian campaign. My father had treated him as a son ever since he had knocked on the door in the mid-thirties – with a horse and cart outside – collecting old clothes and other unwanted items. He treated my father with great respect and felt duty bound to show off his new wife to the man who was his adoptive father.

I took my trip to Wilton, leaving early from Kennington to arrive at Salisbury station about midday. I had arranged to meet Charlie there, and have a pint in a pub to allay my friend's fears. The tough Bushell always seemed very ill at ease when in the company of women. I suppose this shyness applied to all of us, no doubt due to being in men's company for the best part of six years.

We arrived at the ATS camp in time for afternoon tea. I was concerned how my sister would look after losing her fiancé following his serious wounds on Omaha beaches with the US 4th Infantry Division. Ivy met us with her friend Carol, a bright girl from Bristol, who was very cheerful. It seemed to me that Carol was the ideal friend for my sister at the time. Ivy was 24, seemed more mature, and looked quite stunning. Charlie was very bashful and flushed up a bright red and only spoke when prompted. Ivy was in a buoyant, giggling mood, determined to enjoy herself. Carol kept things going by telling us what life was like in the camp. The time passed too quickly for me, but possibly too slowly for Charlie, although he said later how much he had enjoyed the afternoon.

Before leaving Kennington I spent a morning in the City, which showed a few gaps between the buildings in areas that had been cleared of debris. At Stephenson, Harwood and Tatham, Mr Bond was pleased to see me. He took me in to see Anthony Lousada, the partner who had served in the Ministry of Economic Warfare for four years and had just returned to the firm after a year in the War Cabinet Office. He said he had followed my war in the 5th Infantry Division and was very impressed with my war record. Since I had left in 1939 a number of clerks had taken my job and much as he would like to take me back, the position that I held in 1939 at the age of twenty was out of character with my present age of 28. He said he would still consider me for a position if I wanted it, at a maximum of £5 per week – but I was getting more than that as a sergeant. We parted on very good terms, with the firm paying me three months' bonus of £60 to be paid at the beginning of February 1946 when I started my demob leave. In the meantime, the firm would continue to pay my mother the wartime allowance. I thought this arrangement was very fair because I had only been with the firm for two years before the war. My family position was such that money rather than future career was the impelling factor. Obviously I would have to move on and start again.

On the way back, I dropped in to White Drummond to see Mr Hudson. The offices at 9 Cloak Lane were relatively intact, although there were missing buildings further down Cannon Street. Hudson was eating his lunch, the inevitable sandwich and an apple that I remembered so well when I was the lift boy. It didn't seem that much had changed in the intervening nine years, despite the Blitz. I had a pint in a Cannon Street pub with Percy Cope, before returning to Germany and what was left of the war in the Hartz mountains.

The last stint

On my return to St Andreasburg I was sad to hear that my friend Ronnie Lodge had been posted to an Army Entertainment Unit, where his talents as an artist and director were in great demand. He was due for demob the same time as me, and I never saw him again. This was the start of the parting of the ways, which made me realise that soon I would lose other friends who had been my comrades for more than six years.

I was surprised that our new frontier control post was nearly completed, and that my gun team were to be the first occupants when it was finished. Many of the other sergeants were due to take leave and could not be considered for the task. As the first guard commander it was also necessary to establish and record a routine to be updated in the light of experience. Jackson and I decided that the first step was to take a Jeep trip around the terrain to assess the vulnerability of the approaches into the British Zone. The 'dodgy' areas noticed on this patrol would be noted in a brief report – a copy of which would be on file in the guardroom. The British Frontier Post was located about two miles out of town, on a hillock at the side of the road to give a clear view of the Russian Post, which was about half a mile further along.

The Russian Post comprised a cabin and a large outhouse with a heavy barrier across the road to control vehicles. Adjoining the supports of the barrier were tall wire fences guarding the open ground on either side of the road for a great distance. This temporary fence would ultimately be replaced by an official dividing line across Germany, which would establish the borders between East and West Germany.

POLISH OFFICERS

In time, this borderline would be over 800 kilometres long, with watchtowers, strongholds and searchlights in between.

However, for now the temporary fence was adequate to divide the residents of the Hartz community between the two Germanys. This had caused grief and despair to families who had become divided – although there had been sufficient time to move the elderly from the East German side to their kith and kin in West Germany before the temporary fence was completed. The movement of families during this interim period tended to be from East Germany to West; I was not aware of any families in the Hartz moving to the new East Germany.

The Royal Engineers had made rapid progress on our cabin, which was placed in a strategic position once the Russian post and fence had been legally established. The road was already blocked off by uplifting gates which controlled the flow of vehicles. There was frequent liaison by telephone with the Russian post by the Polish unit who were permanently on duty in the partly completed cabin. A British armed guard would booster the control post once the cabin was ready – which would contain a dozen bunks for the guard.

Most of the battery were looking forward to being demobbed, although a few of the Scottish and Lancashire intakes of 1941 decided to extend their service for a year or two. Our government – particularly Churchill – was concerned about the Russian situation: the division of Germany meant that the Allies had to keep a substantial number of troops in Germany for at least a decade.

The greatest priority at this time was to educate the troops in current affairs so they could fit more easily into Civvy Street. The Royal Army Educational Corps was already in being, but the number of troops being demobbed from November 1945 onwards would be immense. Accordingly, classes had been started in St Andreasberg and a new 'Schooly' sergeant who joined the battery at Stockport in 1941 became an agreeable intake into our sergeants' mess. His first tasks were helping on British General Election matters and taking classes on the changes that had occurred in Britain since war started. He particularly focused on rationing, apart from brushing up on educational subjects to make the squaddies more suitable applicants for employment, after five or more years in the Army. The Territorials who were mobilised before War started had been serving six and a half years and were top of the demob list but an age priority was taken into account. There were about 20 Territorials left in the battery – over half were lost in the first year of the War, mostly at Dunkirk. I, having served throughout the war, from the age of twenty to twenty-eight was scheduled for demobilisation at the end of January 1946.

Meanwhile, the General Election was the hot number, particularly with trade unionists in the battery. They were openly canvassing for Labour on the ticket that Churchill was the man associated with their Army troubles – particularly now that Hitler was dead and could no longer be blamed. The educational element in the Forces, who were traditionally leftish, did not disagree with this point of view. Many of us, including me, who needed to get back home, could not have cared less about the General Election result.

Once our frontier post was completed, I and my gun team took over and posted a permanent armed guard outside the door to show the Russian Post we were now in business. In threatening support, our SP B3 was alongside the cabin. The Poles vetted occupants in cars and on foot coming into and going out of the new West Germany. We provided the heavy back-up and included a Jeep to move potential troublemakers to the Poles' HQ in town.

Life – and death – at the Russian Post

One of my first tasks was to hand over to the Russians two of their soldiers, who had been taken by the Red Caps in a Brunswick café and were reported as being drunk. How they got there was a mystery which did not bother us very much, except they had to be handed back. It was considered a delicate affair and so arrangements were made to firstly meet the Russians at their Post and explain the situation.

Accordingly an appointment was made to meet a Russian intelligence officer to arrange the transfer. Our battery adjutant, a Russian-speaking Pole and I were driven down to the Russian post by one of my guard. We waited outside for a minute or so before the door was opened. A very tall, thin officer emerged immaculately dressed with a cigarette holder in his mouth, clutching a glass of wine. He removed the holder from his mouth and allowed the smoke to waft away revealing very good teeth – he was nothing like any Russian we had met in the recent campaign, and seemed to have stepped from a 1930s film. He waved an arm airily and said, 'Come in, gentleman, it gives me a good opportunity to practise my English.'

We were somewhat bemused as we followed him into the cabin. 'You speak very good English,' the adjutant said diplomatically. 'Ah yes!' the Russian agreed. 'But not good enough to always understand your wonderful Mr Shakespeare!'

He led the way to a table covered with bottles. The Russians in the room stood up and bowed to us and we acknowledged by nodding our heads. They were an entirely different type of Russian to the scruffy front-line troops we had met on the road to Magdeburg. 'What can I offer you, major? It is major, is it not?' 'No, I am a captain. Perhaps a glass of white wine would be fine. Thank you.' As he turned to me, I nodded and he handed me a glass of wine before replacing the bottle on the table. The Pole stood ill at ease, obviously feeling surplus to requirements. The Russian jerked his head towards him, and the Adjutant nodded. The Russian gave the Pole a glass of wine in the most offhand way. The Pole immediately raised his glass and gave a toast: 'The great Russian and British Armies!' The Russian gave no acknowledgement, but the Adjutant gave a spontaneous response of 'Your very good health, gentlemen!' The Russian raised his glass and said, 'Yes, I drink to that. I think I should introduce myself. I am Colonel Gregorio Litvinov, an intelligence officer, of the 1st Belorussian Front – Marshal Zhukov. I am only here for a short time, from my headquarters in Magdeburg.' 'Oh?' responded the Adjutant. 'Does your visit here affect us, the British?' 'Oh no, but the Brocken area of the Hartz will form an important part of our defence system in North Germany.' 'It's a pity they have divided the Hartz and separated families,' remarked the Adjutant. 'Pity, what you mean pity, after what they did to my country?' said Litvinov angrily. 'Pity is a word we do not understand. Take it from me, gentlemen, we shall he here for a very long time.' He pointed out of the window. 'That fence will be replaced very soon by a steel wall with towers in between going right across Germany and our side will be the new country, East Germany.'

The uneasy silence was broken by the Adjutant reminding us of our task in returning the two Russian soldiers. Litvinov was helping himself to a glass of schnapps and looking askance at the others, who declined another drink. The colonel paused for a while, and then turned to the other Russians, who shrugged their shoulders. 'We know nothing of these defaulters. Just shoot them,' he said.

The Adjutant was shocked, 'We don't shoot the soldiers of our Allies.' Litvinov said angrily, 'We are busy dealing with other important things and these, these defaulters – they make trouble between us.' He then spoke in Russian to the frontier post commander, before turning to the Adjutant, 'I tell you Captain, bring them to your post tomorrow at 12 o'clock and we take them from you.'

As we were leaving, Litvinov came outside the cabin with us. 'Tell me,' he said to me, 'that is a very long barrel you have on your tank, sergeant?' 'It is an anti-tank gun, Colonel. The projectiles have the highest velocity of any known gun in the world today ... higher than its American and Japanese equivalents and also the outstanding German 88mm triple-purpose gun. In saying that, Colonel, I do not know very much about your Russian anti-tank guns.' Litvinov smiled. 'Well, good day gentlemen, I will meet you again some time, Captain?' 'Yes, I am sure we will,' said the Adjutant pleasantly. As the jeep sped towards our frontier post, he added, 'That, sergeant, is one awful White Russian turd. Tomorrow morning I will arrange for those two poor bastards to reach you by mid-day!'

The next day a Bedford 15cwt truck pulled up outside the frontier post before midday and I took over the two Russian prisoners, who looked anxiously about them as they were ushered to a cabin bench. My gun team, obviously shocked by their youth, made themselves busy doing odd jobs. I nodded to the Pole who phoned the Russians. Shortly afterwards we heard the sound of an engine starting up at the Russian post. 'By God, they don't look any older than the Polish boy,' said Levett in a hushed voice. 'Poor wee sods!' said Brennan, as the bewildered prisoners were taken outside. 'Are we going to present arms, Sarge, when they're handed over?' asked Bleasdale. 'Not effing likely!' I responded bitterly.

We formed up with our rifles at the slope, with the Pole in attendance. I had a small table at the side of the guard, with the document used for the transfer of prisoners. The Russian truck stopped and their guard piled out and stood opposite our guard. The prisoners were then handed over. I said to the Pole, 'I want the escort commander to sign the form...tell him!' The Russian shrugged and then signed, but refused to take his copy. Once the prisoners were loaded onto the vehicle, we broke ranks and hastened into the cabin, not wishing to see them departing. At about one o'clock I heard a volley of shots from an area near the Russian post. The sentry outside came to the door and said in a shocked voice, 'I think they've shot them!'. I endorsed my report accordingly.

We completed our week's duty on the frontier post without any further physical contact with the Russians. The daily telephone communication continued. If the Pole had any confirmation of the Russian prisoners' fate, he made no mention of it. We did not ask him, for we did not want the matter discussed and we were afraid of the answer.

I went back to the sergeants' mess and had a good stiff drinking session, with my friends Cracknell and Wally Allison – and there the matter ended. We realised then that we and the new West German population were on one side, and the Russians and the new East Germany were on the other.

Life in the Hartz

In mid-July the results of the British General Election became known, showing a large victory for the Labour Party. In Britain this result was unexpected, but the Forces did not particularly care for the Conservative slogan, 'Send him back to finish the job'. As far as they were concerned, the job was finished and a new chapter was starting in their lives.

In St Andreasberg, the summer months were beautiful and we began preparing for the winter, which included learning to ski. Summer classes started, with us being taught the technicalities by a German skiing instructor. He used grassy slopes, which enabled our skis to move. But when the snow came, we would move a lot faster and hit the deck a lot harder. From being masters of our terrain in summer, we would become complete idiots as five-year-olds hurtled by us in winter. Army boots were not the best footwear for getting around and we found that gym slippers were the best option but while the summer lasted, we enjoyed the Hartz.

Bob Cracknell had broken the ice and soon other squaddies were escorting German girls, both from the Hartz area and intakes from 'East Germany'. It seemed that the demise of Churchill had loosened the wartime commitment and we no longer felt guilty when fraternising with the Germans. The squaddies' attitude was rather malleable, for we had convinced ourselves that the Hartz ladies were a different sort of German to the warlike breed in the Rhineland. The sergeants' mess held dances and the only females available in the OberHartz were German – apart form the Polish ladies, who were spoken for. It was too soon for the Poles to fraternise with the Germans, and it would hinder their particular task in the Hartz of rooting out committed Nazis. Our indefinable role had turned into holding the line against what had become the opposition – the Russians. And so the Hartz people in St Andreasburg were on our side, and in our corner.

At the behest of his adopted guardian Mietek, I started to teach the young Pole Stepan how to swim. I don't remember any of the Polish adults ever swimming in the St Andreasberg pool, possibly because it was used by the townspeople.

About this time, our patrols rounded up some SS living in one of the silver mines. They had small-arms, and were busy making ammunition to fit these rifles. Their main object was to shoot the wildlife and store the carcases for the winter. They were on the right side of the Hartz and had no desire to start a minor war with the British. However, there was always the chance they would retaliate if cornered – particularly if there was a chance they could be returned to the Russians. They were escorted to the Polish HQ in Brunsweig, but we were not told their ultimate fate.

In the autumn, when the town started to fill up with refugees and food started to be a problem, the Burgermeister organised shooting parties with skilled beaters – but only the Brits were allowed guns. I had early experience of game shooting while still a boy in India and was a competent marksman. After the first shoot, the sergeant-major and I had the job of weeding out a few of the Brits who were poor shots – they were more competent with a Sten gun. The German woodsmen and keepers cringed at the sight of wounded animals roaming around the mountains in agony. In one case a German attendant grabbed the Brit's gun and finished off a stag that had been hit before it could vanish into the undergrowth. He then bowed to the 'marksman' as he handed back the rifle.

The winter came early and the most mobile creatures in St Andreasberg were children on skates. We found it difficult walking down the main street, but were more at home playing football on a nearby field. We practised our ski jumping without too many casualties and began to adapt to the icy conditions in the town. A 30 cwt vehicle with chains on the tyres took troops on furlough to Goslar for an evening out, once a week. It was a precarious trip down the mountain on icy roads. On one of these trips the driver became ill in Goslar and I was the only one in the party who was qualified to drive the truck. And so at midnight, with the truck loaded, including the sick driver in the back, I climbed into the driving seat and started to fiddle with the gear lever, clutch, while holding grimly to the steering wheel. I realised I was rather rusty and probably should have refused to drive, but the noise in the back and the call in the back, 'It's cold enough, Sarge, to freeze the goolies of a brass monkey' gave me the necessary impetus to cautiously drive the truck back up the mountain.

THE MYSTERIES OF SKIING

Major Shepherd was the first in the battery to be demobbed, some time in November. He was about forty years of age and was returning to his stockbroking business. He was quite popular, so the battery lined the streets to wave goodbye as the Jeep left the town packed with his gear in the back. It was the start of a feeling of nostalgia, by some of us who had been with the unit from the outbreak of war.

Christmas was a wild period with most of the sergeants 'under the weather' but not seriously drunk. The mistress of the house was concerned about her lovely furniture and made it clear to us which guests were not welcome. I did my spell as orderly sergeant and visited our outposts down in the valleys by Jeep. Sammy Booth, a sergeant friend, had been on patrol and was back with his unit and having a party in the house of a German family, gathering information about well known local fascists. He was well settled and had no desire to return to the sergeants' mess until after Christmas. I went to another location where the guard was immaculate and strictly in accordance with Army regulations, and had no doubt that Sammy would surface with the most useful information, having had a good time in the process.

I returned to St Andreasberg to learn that the German informer on duty outside the Polish offices had been killed by a rifle bullet. This had occurred shortly after a local man had been arrested in the street by the Poles. The odds were very high that a Brit in the battery had done it – probably a new-found friend of a German family. It would depend on what type of bullet had killed the informer; the only rifle legitimately in use was the British Lee Enfield, and none had been reported missing. This incident sobered up the sergeants and officers of the battery, who were responsible for the authority in the town. Cracknell, with his ever widening group of German friends, was unable to get any information, so it was left to the Poles to find the culprit.

By New Year's Eve the incident, although still unsolved, had been thrust into the background in favour of celebration. In any case most of us were demob happy, waiting to be given the date for our demobilisation number. Nonetheless, there was a feeling of nostalgia and uncertainty about parting with our mates and leaving the 5th Division – which had been our 'home' for just over six years, in over twenty different countries where we travelled under the pseudonym 'Globetrotters' – and occasionally 'Cook's Tours'. Our last New Year in the Army was an occasion for celebration, so we had a massive party in the sergeants' mess, with Frau Kelmar's best furniture stored away and really undesirables banned.

At midnight, three of us who were well oiled and encouraged by the female company, carried a metal bed to the ski jump, and took off on a bright moonlit night. We parted company from this skiing apparatus, one sergeant broke a leg, Sammy Booth injured his elbow, and I was fortunate and landed on my face. I suffered a cut lip, but in the bright moonlight I was shocked as I watched a pool of blood gradually forming in the snow, and by a loss of feeling in my face. The metal bed had hurtled in the air ahead of us and was impaled upright in the ice, looking like a forbidding emblem of remembrance. In the circumstances we were quite lucky.

THE SKI JUMP: NOT TO BE RECOMMENDED

At last the great day came for demobilisation group 25 to travel to Brussels and to become officially discharged from the Army – but placed in reserve for a time. I said goodbye to a few Army friends I was leaving behind, and felt sad parting company from Ingrid, our interpreter, who gave me a friendly kiss and a photograph of herself.

Our group arrived at Brussels wondering what to do with ourselves. Once we got our billet and stored our kit, we went out the night before our general release and got drunk on Belgian beer. Like a fool, I got mixed up in a scuffle and took a swipe at a military policeman who was apparently helping us along. I missed him and my right hand went through a shop window, seriously severing some tendons and nerves. I lost the feeling of some of the nerves, which did not come back until I was in my sixties, but more importantly this was not the state I wanted to be in when greeting my very ill father.

The following day, very pallid from loss of blood, I signed my release documents with my left hand in front of a very amiable group of staff who made no mention of the night before. Several mates gave me a hand with my luggage until I got a taxi from Waterloo Station. Eventually I got out at Methley Street, Kennington, looking like a man who had fought to the last. I felt suitably guilty when my father cuddled me from his bed and said, 'What have you done with your arm, boy?'

CHAPTER 12

ENDINGS AND BEGINNINGS

I arrived home to a subdued household, for my father was by now bedridden with emphysema. I saw the specialist at the hospital in Kennington, and he recommended Father should stay at home, particularly now I was on hand and the family were there to keep him company. The local doctor examined my right hand and after the first week, he removed the stitches. I was greatly relieved that I could once again use both hands, but still felt a fool for being so irresponsible. Jack Heavens arrived most days on his motor cycle to take care of the pigeon loft.

I had invited my friend Wally Allison, who had a later demob number, to stay at Methley Street, en route to his home in Kirkaldy. My mother thought it would be a morale booster for me and would not hear of this arrangement being cancelled. The main objective in the two-day visit was to see our former CO, Major Shepherd, a stockbroker, at his office in Throgmorton Street. He had invited us all to do so in a spirit of great bonhomie in St Andreasberg before he was demobbed – but I don't think he expected us to take up the invitation.

Wally had visited Methley Street before and was quite at ease. Being a ladies' man, he enjoyed the company of my sister Pip and the other ladies of the family who dropped in. Since his earlier visits he had become seriously involved with a German girl called Maria. I had doubts about her, for she was more flighty than Cracknell's Edith and he had only seen her at parties. Like many of us who had been in the Army for over six years, Wally had no intention of returning to his pre-war job, which was in the fabrics trade. He was a talented lad, whose heart was in music, but he also had golfing ability and had played and caddied at St Andrews, which was fairly near his home. It seemed inconceivable that he would return to factory work for a living. In quieter moments in the Army, Wally practised on his accordion and wrote songs – one of these, *Is there a man in the moon above, dear?*, was taken up by Jimmy Shand. Wally imagined his future being in music and dressed and presented himself dapperly – when the Army allowed it!

We found Shepherd's office, and made quite a striking pair in our uniforms with medal ribbons and stripes. The girl in Reception looked up and eyed Allison with a certain amount of interest ... whatever Shepherd thought of the visit, one of his staff seemed to approve. She knocked on Shepherd's door and following some mumbling, we heard Shepherd say, 'Who did you say is out there?' I felt it was up to me to tell a white lie. 'You see, sir, we were visiting my old firm Stephenson, Harwood and Tatham... we were so near in Old Broad Street we thought we would look in.' 'You've left Stephensons, then?' 'Yes. You see, four other people filled my post during the War. Now I'm six years older, I'm no longer suitable for it. Anyway, I need a lot more money, because my father is seriously ill and I'm the oldest in the family. I've applied to the Foreign Office for a job in CCG. In the meantime I'm taking a correspondence course in accountancy.' 'Good for you!' responded Shepherd. He seemed to be warming towards us when he realised we were not looking for a job. and offered us tea. The pile of papers on the desk made it obvious we would not be staying long. The secretary brushed against Allison as she placed his tea on the table. Wally looked up with a smile and she spilled Shepherd's tea over his papers. We left shortly after. 'Very nice to see you both...' Shepherd said gallantly as we left.

Wally left the following morning and I never saw or heard from him again. My mother had meanwhile unpacked my trunk, and at an appropriate moment she produced the photograph of the German interpreter. 'Who's this, then?' 'Oh, that's the German interpreter I was friendly with... met her on most occasions in the swimming pool. Nice girl!'

No doubt in the knowledge that both Cracknell and Wally Allison had become seriously involved with Germans, she could not resist asking, 'Is it serious, Maurice?' 'No, mother ... I am returning to somewhere in Germany for the money. It reminds me – assuming

I get a post out there, I shall open a joint account with you at Barclay's in Kennington, so you can withdraw money when you need it.' 'Well, you are a good boy! I will only draw on it if I am short,' she responded, adding 'you won't need this photo, then?' 'No, mother,' I said with a laugh. 'Just tear it up!' Mother seemed relieved and gave me a kiss. My father then called out, 'Ethel! Why don't you take the boy out to get him his demob suit? His uniform is the only thing that fits him!'

I noticed that 'the boy' seemed to be my new title when my parents were speaking of me. I was still thinking and addressing my father as 'Father' but as my brothers and sisters were calling him 'Daddy' I decided to call him 'Dad' which seemed to please him. My mother, I called 'Mother' until her death.

The demob suit was to be purchased on a gratuitous chit, awarded to servicemen as part of the signing-off package. We set off for the Fifty Shilling Tailors at the Elephant and Castle. My mother loved this outing, mainly because she liked handling new cloth. After a good half an hour of fiddling with new fabrics, the pattern for my suit was chosen from a roll of rather thick cloth which was primarily a dark greyish blue with a faint red line. It served me for the next three years, and was ideal for the treacherous winter approaching in 1946.

In due course Cracknell brought his new wife to Methley Street. The charming Edith won Mother's approval. I realised then what an important role my mother had played in other people's lives during the War – particularly my Territorial friends – so that they felt inclined to share their happier times with her. My mother was a great cook and during these days of rationing she made the most of what we were entitled to – bolstered, I have to admit, with a good supply of fish from unknown sources. One of her great dishes was soused herrings. This source of food enabled the family to entertain occasionally, so we were never short of company. In the last weeks of his life this gave my father great pleasure.

Cracknell had a similar experience to me, for it was not sensible to go back to his job in insurance. His first step into Civvy Street was to search for an occupation commensurate with his age. As a temporary move he joined London Transport as a driver, because they were paying good money and he had a wife to support. Their stay in England lasted only a year then they returned to the Hartz mountains, where Edith's parents had a comfortable standard of living. I never heard of them again, but I had no doubt that Bob would take German citizenship, for he adored his wife.

At about the same time, I saw Connie Martin, our googlie bowler from Trafalgar Sports club days. He had left the Navy and was also driving a bus. Before he drove off I asked him how his googlie was going. He leaned out of the cab to reply: 'Maury, I haven't played cricket for years. I have a wife and a kid now. Maybe I'll play for the garage team some time.'

As I watched the bus move away, it occurred to me that however serious the question of resettlement, it was small cheese in comparison to the miracle of surviving the previous six years. In that time most of the friends I admired had served in some pretty nasty places – at least as survivors they were being given the chance to start again.

Plans for the pigeons

During February I spent a lot of time with my Dad as I was determined to carry out his plans for the 1946 Pigeon Season. This would entail racing the pigeons on the North Road with the Peckham Pigeon Club. We would race under the name 'Court and Son,' so we had much to talk about. The main issues were feeding, training, and pairing the birds. The likely winners in the loft were identified, and Dad's ideas on pairing the pigeons. Cocks and hens had been separated in the winter months and were paired again to enrich certain pedigrees. A number of odd cocks were to be raced under the 'Widowhood' system which we hoped would give the necessary impetus for them to hasten back to the loft. Such birds were perfectly happy looking at themselves in a mirror which we put in their nest box. In some cases it seemed to work, as they hurried back to see the creature they had left behind.

The previous year my Dad had received a commendation from the RAF, stating that one of his squeakers of the Barker strain – reared for The National Pigeon Service – had returned to its RAF loft badly shot up. The bird had been on board a bomber that had been shot down and had ditched in the channel. The pigeon's return had instigated a search that had resulted in the bomber crew being saved. He was elated that his loft had become part of the war effort. The ring number of this brave bird showed in his records that there were other Barkers of the same strain in the loft, probably with the same gutsy potential.

Whilst he was ill during the War, Dad had taught himself shorthand as a means of stimulating his mind, and assisting in the evacuees' education when they returned from the West Country. In order to teach Monty this art (as well as bolstering certain other aspects of his education), Dad locked him in his bedroom each day. Phyllis, who had a greater inclination to learn, attained a great speed as a typist and was already very fast at shorthand. She had started work at *The London Evening News* as a junior in 1943 and by 1946 she had advanced in the Sports department. Monty by this time had advanced from office boy at *The Daily Mirror* to be, at the age of seventeen, the sole reporter on a local paper, *The Fulham and Hammersmith Advertiser.*

My youngest brother David had a very intelligent mind and was still at school at Alleyn's School in Dulwich, as the result of obtaining a good matriculation result. He was, however, fretting to get a job, particularly as he had an aptitude for making money. This was a strong trait in my mother's family. Later, when I moved to Germany, he started running a book on horse racing, covering the Ravensden and Methley Streets area. He had an aged runner called Mick and between them they were quite successful. Inevitably, they were caught by the police. At the age of 15, David was too young to be prosecuted and so Mick ended up in court. David had enough money to pay the fine but his source of income dried up.

Farewell to Father

Towards the end of February, Dad's condition deteriorated. I now spent much of each day in his bedroom. One of the last things he said to me as I held his hand was, 'It's up to you now, boy!'

He died mid-morning on 1st March. Mother stepped to the bed and kissed his brow and walked out to tell those of the family who were in the house before retiring to a bedroom to be alone. Isobel Ivy, returned from the ATS and Betty, who had left the wartime factory at Staines and had become an actress, returned from Scarborough where she was appearing with a repertory company.

It was my mother's wish that Father should be buried, and so we bought a plot in the Honor Oak Cemetery at Brenchley Gardens. Dad is buried at the highest point of the cemetery, close to three large elms; an appropriate resting place for a nature-loving man. He was ultimately joined there by my mother in January 1983.

MY MOTHER, IN THE EARLY 1950S

Court and Son enter the race

I now started training the pigeons with brother Monty's help. We were quite clear from my father's precise instructions which birds we would be flying in the 'Old Bird Programme'. The first step was to send the racers by rail to stations en route to the racing points on the North Road. The longer distance races from the north started at Selby in Yorkshire with race points up to Thurso in Scotland. It was possible at this time to put pigeons in a pannier labelled 'To the Station Master' at the destination station, asking him to release your pigeons at a stated time and to return your basket to the station of origin. The railways carried out these functions as a matter of course all over the country. Our job in training was to identify a station about forty miles out of London, on the route to our loft to give them a racing hop and reduce their excess weight. Jack Heavens took our panniers to a local station on the pillion of his motorbike and picked up the empties when they were returned. This was to be the last season of 'Court and Son' and the loft, pigeons and other equipment were to be sold after giving our breeding stock to Jack Heavens. The money from these sales would be given to Mother.

We had not met the members of the Peckham club and so we attended the AGM which was held before the Racing Season started in a pub near Peckham High Street. The Chairman made glowing reference to our Dad in acknowledging our attendance at the meeting. Much was made of the vast increase in traffic since the war started and the effect it would have on racing in London. The standing joke at that time was the high number of pigeon fanciers being run over – every time a bird's shadow flashed across the road, they instinctively looked up. We made some good friends, particularly two short happy characters who raced as the 'Moore Brothers'. As greenhorns, we were overburdened with advice. We managed very well, winning one race from Northallerton and being placed in two others and we held our own on betting in the club's pools system. The Old Bird Racing ended in June and so we were no longer competitors, but retained an interest by attending at the pub on the Young Bird Race nights.

I join the Control Commission for Germany

In July, I was called up for an interview at a branch of the Foreign Office in Knightsbridge to assess my suitability for a post in the Control Commission for Germany. It was quite a formal interview, considering my rather meagre background. However, my army reference made a great play on my administrative ability, and although I was not a specialist I was a decent all-rounder, so I was appointed a supervisor of postal services and administration. I went into another room where I was measured for my CCG uniform, signed various papers and from that day I was on the payroll – I had become part of the establishment of CCG North Rhine-Westphalia. My reporting date at the HQ in Dusseldorf was expected to be the end of August but ultimately it proved to be the end of September. The great thing was I was on the payroll and the intervening period gave me a chance to make strides on my accountancy correspondence course so that I was at least at ease with a balance sheet and a profit and loss account before I reported for duty.

At the end of July I was called back to pick up my uniform. On the way I passed through Charing Cross Station where a stentorian voice on the loudspeaker greeted me, 'Good morning Langley!'

It was my Army friend, the station foreman, Jerry Young. I raised the briefcase I was carrying, and the commuters on the crowded platform realised that there was a genuine 1940s style personality among them. The uniform of serge fitted very well. It was black with flashes in the shape of a shield at the top of the blouse sleeves, with the lettering 'CCG' in red. My first thoughts were that I looked like a Salvationist, but I soon got used to it and in the awful winter of 1946, it was a welcome garment indeed.

I parted from my mother, whose life in the past few years had been a constant saga of goodbyes. Monty too was about to start two years' National Service. My journey to Germany was through the port of Cuxhaven and then on to Dusseldorf, where I was given my orders to report to Aachen. My post was supervisor of the internal British postal services for 227 CCG, based in Aachen, but also included outstations at Julich, Monschau and Duren. There was an element of security involved in the job and I would also have other supervisory responsibilities mainly connected with sport.

A new Volkswagen collected me from my overnight billet in Dusseldorf and the German driver loaded my baggage and said in reasonable English that we would be delivering some items on board to the General office when we arrived. I nodded approval at the smooth running of the car. The driver explained that the British car units in CCG were being stocked with new cars from the new Volkswagen factory that was in production in the British Zone.

We came to Julich, one of the CCG Aachen outposts. I had never seen a totally flattened town before. There was no one in the streets and it appeared to be deserted. The Dutch and Belgian borders were close and a major job of 227 CCG was guarding the new frontier posts to stop illegal goods being moved over the borders. Apparently the Burgermeister of Julich had refused to surrender to the advancing American First Army. Rather than fight for it, the American general had got the US Air Force to flatten it.

When we came to the outskirts of Aachen (Aix-la-Chapelle) I was shocked by the sight of the battered city, which had also suffered at the hands of the American First Army. It had been an unnecessary assault on this beautiful city, which could easily have been bypassed once the main defensive position of the nearby Siegfried Line had been overcome. Its misfortune lay in being the first major German city to fall to the Allies, so it was taken following a four-day battle that achieved little tactically.

WITH THE CCG: (LEFT TO RIGHT) SANDY UNWIN,
MR AND MRS LANGLANDS-DUNCAN

Most of the residents were living in their basements, a feature of the German houses. At first sight it was a surprise to see people popping up from the ground, like marmots emerging from their burrows, but pausing to make sure there was nothing nasty about. In truth there was still loose rubble everywhere, and you had to be careful where you walked, for the ground in places was unstable. This city, and the nearby town of Julich, had become part of the responsibility of 227 unit of the Control Commission for Germany. Both had taken such a hammering that it would take years to restore them to their former stature.

New beginnings

I reported to the Rathaus, which was also the HQ of 227 CCG. I wandered up the steps to the British Section of this large handsome building, which was remarkably untouched and still functioning as the Aachen Town Hall. I went to the British Commandant's office to report to Brigadier Pownall. The only person there was a girl up a ladder, getting down a file from a rack in the very high ceiling.

'Yes?' she queried, as she reached the floor. 'My name is Court and my instructions are to report to Brigadier Pownall.' 'Oh, of course, you're the new administrative supervisor. You were expected earlier in the week – it's Saturday, you know, and the offices are officially closed.' I gazed at the dark-haired, blue eyed, slim girl, who looked immaculate in her CCG uniform. 'The boat was delayed and the journey wasn't too clever,' I explained, adding lamely, 'I had forgotten it was Saturday.' 'Well, go to Kaiser Wilhelm Strasse, the men's mess. You can't miss it – it's one of the few buildings standing in that road.' 'My Volkswagen is downstairs with my kit – maybe the driver knows the way?' 'Have you come here direct from Dusseldorf, then?' 'Yes, my orders from London were to report there. I didn't know I was coming to Aachen.' She smiled. 'Oh, I am sorry. If he's one of the regular drivers he will know the way to your mess.' Reassured, I added, 'Oh, by the way, we've brought some mail.' 'Right! I'll come down with you, but come here on Monday about ten to see the Brigadier.'

This was my first meeting with Audrey Greenough, an ex-WAAF from Widnes, Lancashire. Little did I realise then that I had been looking into the blue eyes of my future wife ... but that is another story!

A Tribute to The British Fifth Infantry
(Yorkshire) Division –
The Globetrotters (Y)

Tis with feelings mixed, that we summarise our tours.
We've met good blokes, we've met bad blokes,
Scallywags and whores.
Rubbed shoulders with the best of them,
Seen in hell the worst.
We've been happy, we've been sad
We've been praised and we've been cursed!
We've seen the Indian monsoon, the blazing Basra sun,
The chilly cold of Kermanshah, and a desert on the run –
and other freakish elements that do not heed the gun.

We've been in bloody battles in Italy and France,
We've seen our nation struggling,
with what seemed half a chance.
But the right has lived within us, our fellowship has rid us,
of the odds, that others may enhance.
Some of us are left behind, many who are gone,
these will never see another rising sun.
For god's sake let us cherish the friendship and ideals
That storm, fire and hatred wrought, and breath of danger seals.
And may we in our later life worthily portray
The spirit born of comradeship with our fellows along the way.

MLC, October 1945

POSTSCRIPT

———◦———

WHAT BECAME OF THE BARRACK RATS?

My father, Maurice Garnett (George) Court (Sahib), a sergeant-major in the Royal Artillery, ended his operational army career when he left India in December 1933. He was released from the Army in March 1934 and was placed on Reserve. My mother, Ethel Elizabeth, née Langley (Memsahib), married him in Lambeth, London, in January 1918. They had six children, known during our years in India as 'Barrack Rats'.

We children all benefited in later life, from our parents' serious attitude towards our education. This responsibility towards us and being brought up in a Raj cantonment environment encouraged us to act independently. This probably accounts for our individualism and relative success in entirely different occupations. My father's Soldiers' Service and Army Pay Book (AB 64 Vi) lists us as follows:

Names of (Court) Children	Date of Birth
Maurice Langley	24 - 9 - 18
Isobel Ivy	21 - 3 - 21 (Died 1996)
Ethel Mary (called Betty)	30 - 3 - 23
Phyllis Joyce (Pip)	14 - 3 - 26
Montague George Albert	6 -12 - 28
David Victor	6 - 6 - 31 (Died 1997)

Six children was relatively large for a British family in the Raj at that time, and the name 'Court' became a familiar one in the schools where we were educated. Possibly someone out there may have asked, 'I wonder what happened to Sergeant-Major Court's six kids?', to them – and anyone else who might wonder whether we lived up to our parents' expectations – I submit our relative CVs:

Maurice Langley Court (Langley)

Internal auditor within British Transport Commission, then Assistant Accountant BRS (Meat Haulage); senior internal auditor on the Underground System. In 1968 appointed Chief Cashier (later Cash Projects Manager) of London Transport Executive. Retired as an officer in 1983. Had joint control of the Decimalisation Conversion in 1971 for the largest coin handlers in the UK. At that time London Transport Executive was handling 90 per cent of the coin circulating in the Greater London area. Involved in the main programme of converting 53,000 wages for staff paid weekly in cash to bank credit transfer – which was a major step in improving security within London Transport.

Isobel Ivy Court (Ivy)

Isobel had a changeable career and worked for a time in the Money Market. The possible high point in her life occurred in the Second World War, whilst serving in the ATS. She modelled for the Games recruitment poster which Churchill had withdrawn, because he considered it too sexy. It's just possible that, had he known she was the daughter of a sergeant-major, he would have changed his mind. After the war she married an aviator, George Fellows, who won the Cinque Ports air race in the late thirties. He was a ferry pilot in Air Transport Auxiliary throughout the Second World War and took part in the Berlin Airlift.

Ethel Mary Court (Betty)

Ethel, known as Elizabeth Gamberoni, worked in a factory on munitions during the Second World War. In 1945 she started a career as an actress with a repertory company in Yorkshire. She speaks French, Russian and Italian fluently and has interpreted for the Foreign Office – notably at Margaret Thatcher's British Festival in Kiev. She has translated and adapted some of Chekhov's short stories to English plays and directed them at fringe theatres.

Phyllis Joyce Court (Pip)

Phyllis originally worked in journalism and became known as Phyllis Bowman. She adopted Catholicism and became co-founder of The Society for the Protection of Unborn Children and since founder of The Right to Life. She has fought assiduously for the anti-abortion lobby and made many representations to parliament. She was awarded the Order of St. Gregory the Great by the Pope in 1997.

Montague George Albert Court (Monty)

A well-known Fleet Street journalist, after National Service including a spell attached to the 1st Battalion The Loyal Regiment in Mogadishu, Somalia, Monty worked on a variety of provincial newspapers before moving to London as a reporter/feature writer. He became News editor of the *Daily Mail* and later of the *Sunday Mirror*. His lifelong love affair with horseracing led to him becoming the editor of racing's greatest newspaper, *The Sporting Life*; breaking all records, he became the most successful editor in the paper's 160-year history.

David Victor Court (Lulee)

David worked in the communications industry and became a well-known figure in London advertising circles before taking part in the launching of a group of magazines in East and West Africa. He then moved to public relations and worked for the American construction firm Bechtel. He served eleven years in Saudi Arabia with this firm.

———————————○———————————

The segregation of India in 1946 brought to an end the Troopers leaving Southampton Waters reinforcing the British Forces in India in the long-standing maintenance of the Raj – of which my family had been a part. My outlook has been shaped by the influences of the Raj, but protected in those early days by the loving care of my parents – to whom I and my brothers and sisters owe a large debt.

Appendix

Corps and Regiments that served with 5th Division 1939 – 1945

In Full	Abbreviation

THE ROYAL REGIMENT OF ARTILLERY — RA

9th Field Regiment (until May 1942)
91st Field Regiment
92nd Field Regiment
156th Field Regiment (from 1943)
52nd Anti-Tank Regiment
18th Light Anti-Aircraft Regiment (from 1943)

THE CORPS OF ROYAL ENGINEERS — RE

38th Field Company
245th Field Company
252nd Field Company
254th Field Park Company

THE ROYAL CORPS OF SIGNALS — R SIGS

13TH INFANTRY BRIGADE

2nd Battalion The Cameronians (Scottish Rifles) — 2 Cameronians
2nd Battalion The Royal Inniskilling Fusiliers (1939 – 1944) — 2 INNISKS
2nd Battalion The Wiltshire Regiment — 2 Wilts
6th Battalion The Essex Regiment (from 1944) — 6 Essex

15TH INFANTRY BRIGADE (YORKSHIRE BRIGADE)

1st Battalion Green Howards
1st Battalion Kings Own Yorkshire Light Infantry — 1 KOYLI
1st Battalion York and Lancaster Regiment — 1 Y and L

17TH INFANTRY BRIGADE
2nd Battalion Royal Scots Fusiliers	2 RSF
2nd Battalion The Northamptonshire Regiment	2 Northants
2nd Battalion The Seaforth Highlanders	2 Seaforth

HEAVY MACHINE GUN BATTALION
7th Battalion The Cheshire Regiment	7 Cheshire

RECONNAISSANCE
5th Battalion The Reconnaissance Corps (from 1943)	5 RECCE

SUPPORTING UNITS IN 5TH INFANTRY DIVISION
Royal Army Chaplains Department	RA CH D
Royal Army Service Corps	RASC
Royal Army Medical Corps	RAMC
Royal Army Ordnance Corps	RAOC
Corps of Royal Electrical and Mechanical Engineers	REME
Corps of Royal Military Police	RMP
Royal Army Pay Corps	RAPC
Royal Army Educational Corps	RAEC
Royal Army Dental Corps	RADC
Royal Pioneer Corps	RPC
Intelligence Corps	INT Corps
Army Physical Training Corps	APTC
Army Catering Corps	ACC
Queen Alexandra's Royal Army Nursing Corps	QARANC

Military Index

General Index

Alban Hills 169, 171, 189, 206, 208
Alexander, General Sir Harold 96, 134, 170, 172
Allison, Wally 196, 238, 239, 248, 254, 255
Anapo, River 118
Archer anti-tank gun 79, 189, 216, 219, 220, 222, 223
Aure, River 45
Belcher, Fred 91, 92, 98, 100, 126, 127, 216
Biferno, River 145
Billotte, General 55
Brooke, Lt-General 62
Bryer, Badge 212, 239
Bushell, Charlie 117, 125, 126
Churchill, Winston S. 44, 89, 163, 169, 170, 178, 219, 226, 244, 248, 267
Clark, Lt-General Mark 140, 159, 160, 163, 168, 170, 172, 203, 204, 207
Cojeul, River 57–9
Cracknell, Bob 41, 95, 96, 142, 248, 251, 255, 256
Dempsey, Lt-General Sir Miles 63, 152, 224
Eagles, Major-General 177
Ebensee Concentration Camp 227, 232
Elbe, River 219, 220–224, 226–7, 232, 234
Euphrates, River 96
Foce, River 205
Franklin, Major-General 57, 59, 62, 116
Garigliano, River 152, 154–7, 160–4, 166–7, 169, 174, 183, 198, 204, 206, 208, 209, 222
Gort, Field Marshall Lord 3, 56, 59, 61
Gregson-Ellis, Major-General 163, 184, 186, 192–4
Gustav Line 153, 159, 160, 163, 165, 166, 169, 170, 203, 205
Harmon, Major-General 182
Hitler, Adolf 4, 44, 74–5, 96, 172, 180, 244
Hull, Major-General 211
Jordan, River 112, 113
Jumna, River 97, 98